Handbook of Secondary Marketing

**Edited by
Jess Lederman**

Mortgage Lending Handbook Series

MORTGAGE BANKERS ASSOCIATION OF AMERICA
Washington, DC 20005

Copyright © 1997 Mortgage Bankers Association of America

All rights reserved. No part of this book may be reproduced or used in any form or by any means, electronic or mechanical, including photocopying, recording or by any other information storage and retrieval system, without written permission from the publisher.

Real Estate Finance Press
Mortgage Bankers Association of America
1125 15th Street, NW
Washington, DC 20005

Paul S. Reid, CMB, President

Warren Lasko, Executive Vice President
Joyce E. Kappeler, Sr. Staff Vice President, Education

ISBN 1-57599-013-X

First Printing, March 1997

Disclaimer

This publication is designed to present, as simply and as accurately as possible, an authoritative overview of the fundatmentals of secondary marketing. It should be noted that the information presented is not all inclusive. Regulations and overall processes may change because of changes within the industry. This publication should not be used as a substitute for referring to the applicable rules and regulations and is sold with the understanding that the publisher is not engaged in rendering legal or other personalized professional service. If legal or other expert assistance is required, the services of a competent professional should be sought.

Table of Contents

About the Editor   xv

About the Authors   xvii

Preface   xxv

Introduction   xxvii

Pipeline Hedging and Fallout Risk   1

   Hedging Objectives   2
   Mortgages   5
   Profit & Loss From Pipeline Hedging Activities   7
      Pricing Subsidies   8
      Trading Gain/Loss   9
      Net Interest Income   10
      Convergence   11
   Pipeline Behavior and Fallout   12
      Option Analogy   12
      Fallout Measurement   13
      Pricing Fallout   16
      Path Dependency   19
   Hedging Strategies   22
      Long Position Management   23
      Hedging Instruments   25

The Optional Nature of Mortgage Rate Locks: Implications for Pipeline Risk Management   29

    A New Environment   30
        Technology and the Consolidation of an Industry 31
        Servicing Technology and Efficiency   31
        SFAS 122   32
        Commercial Banks and Opportunity   32
    Competition and the New Realities of Origination   33
        Economics and the Value of Servicing   33
        Market Share and Concentration   34
    Loan Production Programs and the Quest for Market Share   35
        Narrow Margins and Little Tolerance for Risk   35
        In Pursuit of Refinance Business   36
        Proliferation of Lock Options   39
        Production Programs — Options Sold Short   39
        Measuring the Cost of Originator Options   41
        Option Delta   45
        The Likelihood that a Loan Will Close   47
        Measuring Option Risk in a Pipeline Context   52
        Delta as a Hedge Ratio   52
        Mechanics of Delta Hedging   54
    Example A: 55
    Example B: 56
    Example C: 57
        Rebalancing the Option-Inclusive Delta Hedge   59
        Replicating an Option with Traditional Delta Hedging   60
        A Delta Hedging Caveat   62
    Observations of a Wall Street Dealer   62

Improve Data to Ensure Effective Hedging	63
Identify the Risk	63
Hedge the Risk	64
Administrative Methods for Hedging	66

Real-World Secondary Marketing Strategies 67

Marketing Policy and Objective	68
Cooperstown's Hedge Strategy	70
Pipeline Coverage: Mandatory/Optional Mix	70
Mandatory Forward Coverage	71
Options	72
Purchase of Options versus the Delta Hedge	75
Fallout Analysis	76
Cooperstown's Delivery Strategy	77
Fannie Mae/Freddie Mac Master Commitments	78
Servicing Retained versus Released	79
Fixed-Rate Conforming Loans	79
Jumbo Loans	80
Conclusion	81

An Analysis of Popular Hedging Strategies 83

An Overview of Popular Hedging Strategies	84
Implications of Hedging	84
Cross Hedging	86
Delta Hedging	87
Volatile Markets	88
Mandatory Forwards and Options	89
Options	90
Measuring the Impact of Volatility	91

vi Table of Contents

Test-Driving Hedging Strategies	92
Nondeliverable Cross-Hedging Strategies	92
Case 1: Tanking Market	94
Case 2: Rallying Market	97
Case 3: Flat Market	99
Conclusion	100
Case 1: Tanking Market	102
Case 2: Rallying Market	105
Case 3: Flat Market	106
Summary	108
Appendix — Chapter 4	**111**

Pricing Profitability Analysis
How Much Are You Really Making?   115

Pricing for Profits	115
Quantifying Quandaries	118
The Profitability Equation	119
Interpreting the Numbers	120
How to Use Profitability Analysis to Set Prices	126
Value of Servicing	128

Analyzing Interest-Rate Trends   133

A Historical Overview	134
The 1980s	135
The 1990s	136
The Inflation Factor	136
Cyclical Considerations	138
Product Considerations	138
The ARM Factor	139

Buydowns	140
Fixed-Rate Mortgages Return	141
Summary	141
Technical Analysis	143
Trading Ranges	144
Relative Strength Index	146
The 20-Day Moving Average	147
Recap	148
The Head & Shoulders Pattern	148
The Yield Curve	149
Calendar Buys	151
Mortgage Prices	152
Gaps	153
Technical Conclusions	153
Implications for Pipeline Hedging	154
Fundamental Analysis	154
The Unemployment Factor	154
Federal Reserve Policy	156
Predicting Reactions	157
Combining Technical and Fundamental Analysis	158

EDI: Applications for Lenders in the Secondary Market   **159**

The Four Methods of Communications	159
Direct Dial	160
E-mail	160
Value Added Networks	161
The Internet	162
File Formats and MBA's X.12 Initiative	162

Automated Underwriting and Its Impact on
Communications 163
Communication with Third Party Originators 164
    Improving Communication and Enhancing Service
    Levels 165
    Rate Distribution 165
Eliminating the Paper Loan Package 172
Communications with Vendors 173
    Appraisals 174
    Credit Reporting Companies 175
    Flood Services 176
    Private Mortgage Insurance Companies 176
    Loan Servicers 177
    Closing Documents Providers 177
    Title Companies and Settlement Service Providers 177
    Fannie Mae and Freddie Mac 177
    HUD 178

Working with a Wall Street Dealer: Advanced Tools for Pipeline and Servicing Portfolio Risk Management   179

Mortgage-Backed Securities 179
Treasury Securities 181
    ARM Hedging and Treasuries 182
Basic Strategies for Trading Volatility 184
    Straddles 184
    Strangles 185
    Fence Trades 186
Servicing Hedging and Wall Street Dealer Products 187
    Servicing: Another Mortgagor Option 188

OTC Mortgage Options	188
Treasury Market and Option-Inclusive Delta Hedging	189
Treasury Floors and Swaptions	189
Mortgage Derivatives and Swaps	191
Bullish Fixed/Floating Swaps	191
Mortgage Price Spread Hedge	192
Concluding Thoughts: A Complementary Relationship	192

Managing Mortgage Optionality: An Innovative Approach to Protecting Pipelines with Futures and Options — 195

The Nature of the Risk	196
Locating the Intuition	197
Basis Risk Considered	199
A More Fruitful Line of Inquiry	200
Defining an Intuition	202
Relating Bonds and Options	204
Reviewing Prior Approaches	204
Pipeline Hedging in a New Key	206
Designing the Hedge	211
Evaluating the Hedge	213
Two Caveats	215
Turning the Process Around	216

State-of-the-Art Systems for Risk Management — 219

Current State of the Industry	221
Loan Tracking	221
Position Analysis	221

Position Reporting	222
Hedge Position Management	223
Trading Analytics	224
Mark-to-Market	224
Pricing/Profitability	225
Loan Tracking	225
Position Analysis	227
Position Reporting	235
Hedge Position Management	244
Global and Delta Hedging	245
Global hedging advantages and disadvantages	246
Delta hedging advantages and disadvantages	247
Trading Analytics	256
Mark-to-Market	258
Pricing	260
Conclusion	261

Fannie Mae: Programs for Mortgage Bankers   263

Fannie Mae: The Company	263
Fannie Mae's Products	264
Mortgage Sales or Securitization	264
Cash Sales Program	266
MBS Swap Program	268
Fannie Mae's Affordable Housing Initiatives	271
Fannie Mae's Technology Initiatives	273
How To Do Business With Fannie Mae	274

Freddie Mac: Programs For Mortgage Bankers   277

Eligible Mortgages	279

5- and 7-Year Balloon/Reset Mortgages	279
ARMs	280
Cash Programs	280
Gold Cash®	281
RNY Cash	281
ARM Cash	281
Considerations in Cash Sales	282
Contract Requirements	282
Purchase Contracts and Commitments	282
Delivery Periods	284
Pricing	284
Sales Transaction	285
Swap Programs	285
Guarantor and MultiLender	287
Considerations When Swapping	288
Whole Loan versus Participation Interests	288
Minimum Swap Amounts and Servicing Spreads	288
Purchase Contracts and Master Commitments	289
Pooling Mortgages	289
Buy Ups and Buy Downs	290
Remittance Cycle	291
Swap Transaction	292
After a PC is Issued	293
Lending to Underserved Borrowers: A Profitable and Expanding Business	295
Expanding Markets	295
Affordable Lending	296
Fair Lending	299
Community Development Lending	300
Expanding Markets: Going Forward	301
A Freddie Mac Expanding Markets Case Study: Meeting a Community's Housing Needs	303

    Location   303
    Participants   303
    The Need   304
    The Solution   305
    Background   305
    The Advantages of MRBs   306
Loan Prospector   307
    How Loan Prospector Works   308
    Loan Prospector's Risk Classification Definitions   309
    Electronic Access to Third-Party Service Providers   310
    Key Loan Prospector Advantages   311
    Advantages for Loan Production and Delivery   312
GoldWorks: The Mortgage Industry's Electronic Marketplace   312
    A Single-Link   312
The Relationship with Advantis   313
    Electronic Commerce   313
    GoldWorks and the Mortgage Industry   315
Conclusion: Meeting Lender Needs   315

The Role of Conduits in the Nonconforming Mortgage Market   **317**

The Nonconforming Mortgage Market   318
The Benefits of Conduits   321
Early Conduits   322
Second Generation Conduits   323
New Credit Enhancements Evolve   324
    Pool Insurance   325
    Subordination   326
    Letter of Credit   326

Corporate Guarantees	327
Surety Bonds	327
The Middle Years — A Transition	327
The 1990s — Expansion, Consolidation, Differentiation	329
Product Differentiation	332
The Home Equity Sector	332
The "B and C" Mortgage Sector	333
The "Expanded Feature" Mortgage Sector	338
Product Sources	339
Evaluating a Conduit	340

Selling Nonstandard Whole Loan Packages 343

Background	343
Product Descriptions	345
Pricing and Delivery	347
Market Dynamics and Future Outlook	353

The Secondary Market For Mortgage Servicing Rights 357

Historical Overview	357
Valuation	363
Valuation Methodology	365
Components of Income	366
Service Fee	366
P&I Interest Float and Interest Earnings on Escrow	366
Ancillary and Other Income	367
Components of Expense	369
Servicing Costs	370
Foreclosure Costs	371

Amortization	372
Other Costs	373
Computing the Net Present Value	373
Discount Rate	373
Prepayments	374
Valuation of ARM-Servicing Portfolios	375
Multifamily Servicing Valuation	378
OAS Analysis	379
Price Sensitivity	380
The Market in 1996	384
The Impact of FASB Statement 122 on Hedging	384
Future Outlook	386

About the Editor

JESS LEDERMAN

Jess Lederman is one of the pioneers of the private mortgage-backed securities market, and the editor and coauthor of over 30 books on the financial markets. Currently, he directs the secondary marketing activities for Ohio Savings Bank and serves on the Board of Directors of the Jackson Hole Community Housing Trust. Among his many accomplishments, Lederman co-founded two of the nation's largest private sector counterparts to Fannie Mae and Freddie Mac, and was the principal architect of several innovative securities. He was formerly chairman of The Asset Backed Capital Group, an investment banking and money management firm, and earlier held the positions of executive vice president for Bear Stearns Mortgage Capital Corporation and associate director of Bear Stearns, & Co., Inc. Before joining Bear Stearns, Lederman was vice president of sales and marketing for Sears Mortgage Securities Corporation, and also served as director of pricing and research for The PMI Group of Companies.

Lederman received his B.A. from Columbia College in New York, where he graduated summa cum laude and Phi Beta Kappa. He earned his M.B.A. from the Columbia University Graduate School of Business.

About the Authors

DAVID ANDRUKONIS

Mr. Andrukonis is senior vice president and general manager of the Seller Division of Freddie Mac, which includes sales, pricing, transaction processing, and product development. Previously, he served as senior vice president of Freddie Mac's Competitive Advantage Program, and earlier held the positions of vice president of mortgage finance and manager of product development and pricing. Mr. Andrukonis holds an MBA in finance and a BS in economics from Virginia Polytechnic Institute.

SIRRI S. AYAYDIN

Mr. Ayaydin is a principal and co-founder of the Quantitative Risk Management Group. Previously, he was vice president and director of options research for GNP Financial, where he did innovative work in portfolio insurance, dynamic options replication, MBS valuation, and hedging. Mr. Ayaydin has been published in numerous industry books and journals. He earned a BS in operations research and computer engineering, summa cum laude, from the University of Michigan, and holds an MBA in finance and econometrics from the University of Chicago.

DAVID BEADLE

Mr. Beadle is the owner of a decade-old licensed residential mortgage lending company in Massachusetts and president of BestRates, Inc., a mortgage consulting firm. He received his master's degree in journalism from the University of California at Berkeley, writes regularly for various trade publications, and posts daily commentaries updating mortgage market developments on his free World Wide Web site.

SCOTT COOLEY

Mr. Cooley is president of Contour Software, Inc., a Campbell, California-based provider of mortgage loan software systems for the financial industry. Previously, he worked for several mortgage companies, developing software for the mortgage loan industry. Mr. Cooley has written numerous articles for industry publications and has been a frequent keynote speaker at industry seminars nationwide. Mr. Cooley graduated from San Jose State University where he majored in business with a double concentration in management and marketing and minored in computer science.

FRANK DEMARAIS

Mr. Demarais is vice president for product development with Fannie Mae. He is responsible for researching, designing and implementing mortgage product and program enhancements for Fannie Mae's single family mortgage programs. Prior to joining Fannie Mae, Mr. Demarais had been senior vice president for Metro Mortgage Acceptance, a Washington-area retail mortgage banking firm, and had worked at Freddie Mac as a MBS senior trader.

DOUGLAS D. FOSTER

Mr. Foster is senior vice president for secondary marketing at Alliance Mortgage Company in Jacksonville, Florida, where he oversees interest-rate and credit-risk management as well as marketing operations. Previously, he served as product manager for secondary marketing systems at MortgageFlex Systems, Inc., and earlier held secondary marketing positions with BancFlorida, North Carolina Federal Savings and Loan Association, and First Federal Savings and Loan Association of Largo, Florida. Mr. Foster has written numerous articles for industry publications and authors a regular column for *Secondary Marketing Executive*. He holds a BA in psychology from the University of Michigan and an MBA in finance from Florida State University.

STEPHEN S. HARRIS

Mr. Harris is a vice president and the manager of the mortgage banking group of Goldman, Sachs & Co., where he has been employed since 1987. Previously, he held positions with Weyerhauser Mortgage Company and ICA Mortgage Company. Mr. Harris has published numerous articles in industry journals and speaks regularly at mortgage banking industry functions. He is a graduate of the University of Maryland, with degrees in both finance and economics.

STEPHEN Z. HOFF

Mr. Hoff is president and chief executive officer of Hamilton, Carter, Smith & Co. His responsibilities include managing and directing the firm's activities in the marketing of servicing portfolios, the sale of mortgage finance assets and operations. He also has responsibility for Brokers Commitment Corporation and

Builders Funding Corporation subsidiary operations and activities. Mr. Hoff's career began with his work on Wall Street as a foreign-exchange dealer and trader. Subsequently, he held positions as senior investment officer for J.I. Kislak and managing director of Reserve Financial Management Corporation. He is a featured speaker and panel member for the Mortgage Banker's Association, national and state level Mortgage Banker's Associations, Fannie Mae, Freddie Mac and various regional level agencies. Mr. Hoff earned his MBA from the University of Maryland.

MADELINE JOHNSON-OLER

Ms. Johnson-Oler is a consultant with Mortgage Dynamics, Inc., providing technical and strategic advice in secondary marketing. Her responsibilities include operations assistance, due diligence reviews, operations reviews of secondary marketing departments, and other functions. Previously, she was assistant director and vice president of secondary marketing for a major mortgage banking company. Ms. Johnson-Oler has an MBA in international business, banking, and finance from George Washington University.

JOHN P. MCMURRAY

Mr. McMurray is executive vice president of risk management and secondary marketing for Crestar Mortgage Corporation, headquartered in Richmond, Virginia. Previously, he was senior vice president of capital markets at BancPLUS Mortgage Corp., where he was responsible for risk management, secondary marketing, and underwriting. Earlier, he had held positions in finance and management information systems. Prior to joining BancPLUS, Mr. McMurray was a financial analyst with Datapoint Corporation. He has published numerous articles in industry publications. Mr. McMurray holds a BS in business and economics from Trinity University and an MBA from the University of Texas. He is a Certified Public Accountant and a Chartered Financial Analyst.

DONALD R. PALUMBO

Mr. Palumbo is a senior consultant with Mortgage Dynamics, Inc., where he manages the firm's software development and implementation. Previously, he performed valuations of servicing assets and whole loans as well as financial analysis studies. His background includes over seven years experience in secondary marketing overseeing selling, pricing, securitization, and modeling mortgage transactions. Mr. Palumbo also has spent several years creating and developing software applications for related industries.

BRUCE J. PARADIS

Mr. Paradis is president of Residential Funding Corporation (RFC) in Minneapolis, Minnesota. He has held several different positions with RFC since its formation, including vice president for marketing. Previously, Mr. Paradis had been an account executive with Mortgage Guaranty Insurance Corporation, and had worked for First Federal Savings & Loan of Mankato, Minnesota. He received his BA in economics from Mankato State University.

CHARLES A. RICHARD III

Mr. Richard is a founding principal, director of marketing, and head of the Client Services Group for the Quantitative Risk

Management Group. Previously, he had been director of institutional products marketing for GNP Financial and had represented the futures department of Goldman, Sachs & Company in Madrid, Spain. Mr. Richard has published many articles in industry books and journals and is a frequent speaker at mortgage conferences. He earned his BA in economics from Central Connecticut State University and is currently working on an MBA in finance and marketing at the University of Chicago.

STEPHEN R. RIGSBEE

Mr. Rigsbee is a principal and cofounder of the Quantitative Risk Management Group. Previously, he was senior vice president and director of research for GNP Financial, where he developed one of the first option-based pricing and hedging models for MBS. Mr. Rigsbee has published extensively in industry books and journals. He earned his BA in history and economics, summa cum laude, from Duke University and earned both an MBA in finance and econometrics and an MA in economics from the University of Chicago.

KEITH SCHAP

Mr. Schap is a manager in the Market and Product Development department of the Chicago Board of Trade. After 20 years of teaching, he left academe to become a technical writer, ultimately specializing in topics related to the derivatives markets and risk management. Among his books are *Hedging Financial Instruments* (with Jeff McKinzie), *Commodity Marketing: A Lender's and Producer's Guide to Better Risk Management*, and *Derivatives: State & Local Government Investment Guide Series*. Mr. Schap earned his BA from North Central College in

Naperville, Illinois, and both an MA and a Ph.D. from Indiana University.

MARK TURNER

Mr. Turner is the head of mortgage finance and the mortgage-backed security portfolio manager at the Federal Home Loan Bank of Chicago. His primary responsibility is to quantify and hedge the option, prepayment, spread, duration and volatility risks inherent in the bank's mortgage holdings. Mr. Turner is also a key member of the bank's asset-liability committee and is involved in the bank's overall strategic asset-liability management decisions. He has a diverse background in banking and finance, with previous experience in a federal savings bank, a national credit union, and a family investment consulting practice. Mr. Turner earned his BS in economics from the University of Illinois at Urbana-Champaign.

Preface

The secondary mortgage market is an immense and rapidly growing segment of the capital and global markets. It is also constantly changing — with lenders continually challenged by a myriad of new instruments and complex techniques to hedge risks and optimize returns.

The *Handbook of Secondary Marketing* has been developed to provide an in-depth look at the many segments of the residential secondary mortgage market. This handbook offers the reader an extensive discussion and analysis of this profound and often misunderstood sector of the mortgage banking industry.

The *Handbook of Secondary Marketing* is a notable addition to our "Mortgage Lending Handbook Series," and hopefully a complement to your bookshelf.

Warren Lasko
Executive Vice President
Mortgage Bankers Association of America

Introduction

Secondary marketing managers face a critical and profoundly challenging task. Structural changes in the mortgage banking industry have resulted in intense competition and razor-thin margins, while interest rate volatility is as dramatic as ever. This combination makes it extremely difficult to price competitively, hedge risk, and maintain acceptable levels of profitability.

Fortunately, the art and science of secondary marketing have advanced considerably in recent years, and mortgage bankers can now avail themselves of valuable new strategies and analytical concepts. *The Handbook of Secondary Marketing* is the most comprehensive compendium of state-of-the-art strategic thinking on a broad range of topics in the secondary market. *Part One: Strategies, Tactics, and Analytical Techniques* covers the fundamentals of secondary marketing. It explains the pipeline, discusses and contrasts alternative hedging strategies, analyzes pricing and interest rate trends and explains the role of electronic data interchange. *Part Two: Advanced Concepts in Secondary Marketing* explores a number of sophisticated tools and techniques, including products offered by Wall Street dealers, methods for using exchange-traded futures and options, and the latest risk management technology. *Part Three: Sectors of the Secondary Market* covers programs offered by Fannie Mae, Freddie Mac, and private conduits and discusses the sale of nonstandard whole loan packages and the trading and valuation of mortgage servicing rights.

I would like to thank the sixteen chapter authors, all of whom took time from their hectic schedules to produce this important book. I would also like to thank the staff of the Mortgage Bankers Association of America (MBA), without whom this book would not have been possible.

Jess Lederman

1

Pipeline Hedging and Fallout Risk

John P. McMurray, Executive Vice President
Crestar Mortgage Corporation

Under present industry practice, most lenders allow mortgage applicants to "lock." Locking establishes a firm rate and discount at which the applicant will close if the application is approved. The *discount* is a charge the lender collects from the borrower (or a third party such as a home seller) in exchange for offering a lower interest rate. To calculate discount from price, subtract the price from 100 (for example, a price of 98 implies a discount of 2). Discounts can be negative — *premium pricing* — where the lender absorbs certain closing costs on behalf of the borrower in exchange for the borrower accepting a higher interest rate.

By locking the application, the lender exposes itself to *interest rate risk*. If rates rise between the time the applicant locks and the loan is ready for sale, the loan will be worth less. If the loan is unhedged in a rising rate situation, the lender will incur a loss on the sale of the loan. In addition to interest rate risk, lenders face *fallout risk*. Fallout occurs when a locked application fails to close. If a lender hedges a locked application by selling forward on a mandatory basis and the application fails to close in a falling rate environment, the lender will incur a loss.

The purpose of pipeline hedging is to mitigate the interest rate and fallout risk during the period of time between when a loan locks in and the time that it either falls out or is finally sold. Before a lender can successfully hedge its pipeline, it must:

- Determine its hedging objectives.
- Understand mortgages.
- Understand how profits and losses arise from pipelines.
- Understand pipeline behavior and fallout.
- Understand basic pipeline hedging strategies.

Hedging Objectives

As in portfolio management, the first step in pipeline management is to set objectives. Hedging the pipeline against interest rate and fallout risk is an appropriate objective for mortgage lenders since their business is making mortgage loans. In the mortgage industry, however, the term "hedging" is often used to describe activities which are not hedging. Before delving into the specifics of pipeline hedging, some general comments regarding hedging are in order. A simple graph illustrates the difference between speculation and hedging. Figure 1-1 shows three lines. The first line, which slopes up and to the right, represents a long-asset position with an initial purchase price of 100. If the market price increases above 100, the long position is profitable. At market prices below 100, the position is unprofitable. The second line, which slopes downward to the right, represents a short-sale position with an initial sales price of 100. A short position is the exact opposite of a long position. If the market price increases above 100, the position is unprofitable. At market prices below 100, the short position is profitable. The third, horizontal, line is a combination of the long and short positions. For any market price, gains in the long position offset losses in the short position and vice versa. It would be speculative to hold either a naked long or naked short position by itself. A long position could be fully hedged by simultaneously entering into a short position. A fully hedged position entails no market risk.

As Figure 1-1 illustrates, speculative and fully hedged positions differ in their risk and reward profiles. A speculative position can be profitable or unprofitable depending upon post-transaction market price movements. A fully hedged position is protected from adverse price changes, but it also gives up the benefit from positive market price movements. Pipeline hedging strategy choices are similar to Figure 1-1: One can be long, short, or fully hedged. Being fully hedged protects one from

FIGURE 1-1
Long and Short Asset Positions

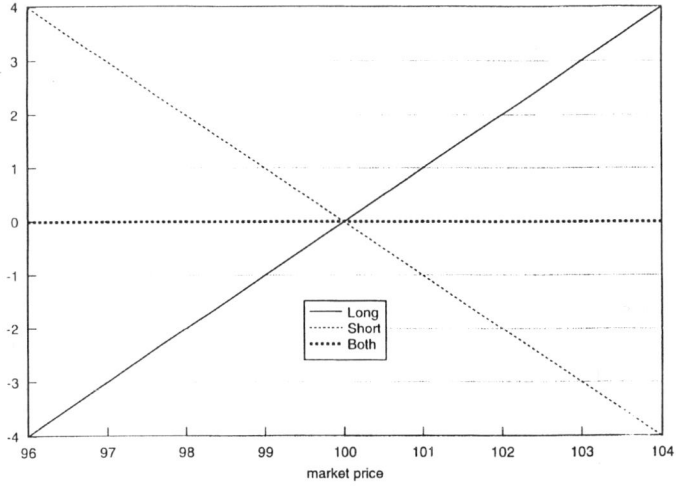

adverse market moves but also precludes one from benefiting from positive market movements.

An ideal pipeline hedge preserves asset value over a wide range of market fluctuations. Unfortunately, many mortgage lenders use the term "hedging" to describe speculative or semi-speculative activities. One of the more popular sessions at the Mortgage Bankers Association (MBA) National Secondary Conference is titled "Here's the Market — What Would You Do?" The MBA is merely accommodating the approach used by many lenders. Instead of carefully evaluating their pipelines and constructing an appropriate hedge, these lenders try to predict the future market conditions. If rates are expected to decline, sales are postponed to create a long pipeline position. For those lenders who lack the ability to foresee future interest rates, a better approach is to construct a hedge that protects the pipeline over a range of rate movements. In other words, "Here's Your Pipeline — What Would You Do?"

While a few mortgage lenders practice overt pipeline speculation, others claim to pursue fully hedged pipeline strategies when they actually engage in disguised speculation. The disguise can be intentional or inadvertent. Intentionally disguised speculation usually results from a lender's desire to follow a speculative strategy while placating bank or investor requirements to be fully hedged. Inadequate pipeline systems and/or incomplete knowledge of mortgages and pipeline behavior create much of the inadvertently disguised speculation. Lenders who believe they are fully hedged end up long or short as a consequence of shortcomings in their systems or knowledge. Inconsistent objectives also cause disguised speculation. For example, competitive factors often force lenders to price lock-ins below the secondary market price. Nevertheless, these same lenders wish to be fully hedged and overcome the shortfall priced into the initial lock. Pursuing a fully hedged strategy precludes the lender from recovering any of the initial pricing loss. Although the loss might be reclaimed through speculation, a speculative strategy involves the risk of making the loss even larger.

Pipeline management strategies span a wide spectrum of risk — from outright speculation to fully hedged. Lenders should understand the risks associated with a speculative strategy and the opportunity costs associated with a fully hedged strategy. Though each lender decides at which point on the risk spectrum it intends to operate, all lenders require a pipeline system capable of accurately assessing interest rate and fallout risk. In short, successful pipeline hedging requires knowledge of pipeline behavior and a reasonable hedging objective.

Mortgages

Mortgages and mortgage securities rank among the more complex fixed-income instruments. While mortgages are *callable* by a prepaying borrower (in other words, borrowers can pay off their mortgage from the mortgage holder at any time for a price), the exercise of this embedded option is sometimes based on unpredictable and seemingly irrational factors. Figure 1-2 compares the price changes for a 10-year Treasury note (the T-note is shown as the dotted line) with a Fannie Mae 30-year fixed-rate pass-through security (the solid line). The comparison covers upward and downward interest rate moves of two hundred basis points. Like the T-note, the 30 year fixed-rate mortgage possesses a significant amount of interest rate risk. The mortgage's call feature makes its price-rate relationship less attractive than that of the T-note.

Different mortgage instruments respond differently to the same rate movements. Figure 1-3 compares the price changes that occur for a Fannie Mae 30-year fixed-rate pass-through (solid line) and a Freddie Mac 5-year balloon pass-through (dotted line). Notice that the 5-year balloon has less price sensitivity than the 30-year fixed

FIGURE 1-2

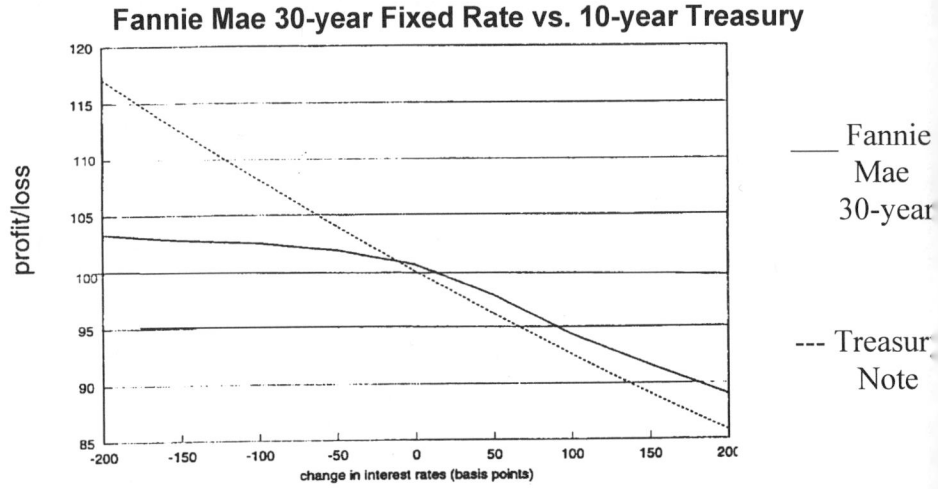

FIGURE 1-3

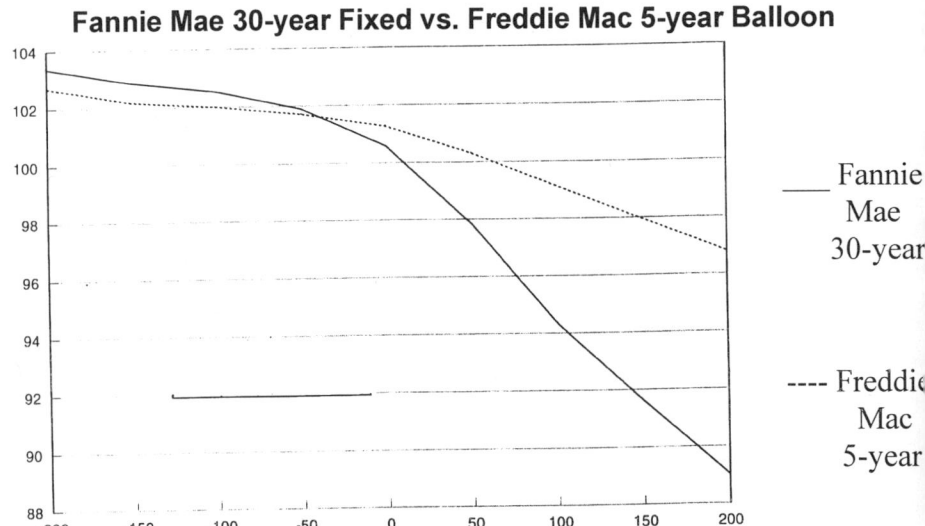

Pipeline Hedging and Fallout Risk 7

rate. The 5-year pass-through is particularly less vulnerable to upward rate movements because of its balloon feature. One of the nation's largest mortgage origination companies incurred pipeline hedging losses when it hedged its balloon pipeline with short forward sales of 30-year fixed-rate mortgage securities at a one-to-one ratio during a period of falling rates. The 30-year securities appreciated more in price than the balloons and a loss resulted. Had it been a rising rate environment, this hedge would probably have generated a gain. Duration and convexity measurements are one of the easiest and most convenient, though not the best available, methods to evaluate an instrument's price-rate relationship.

A significant amount of interest rate risk accompanies most mortgage instruments. As a result, mortgage pipelines contain a correspondingly significant interest rate exposure. In spite of the complexity of mortgages, successful pipeline interest rate risk management requires a familiarity with how each mortgage instrument responds to changes in the interest rate environment. The interest rate environment encompasses not only the absolute level and direction of interest rates but the slope of the yield curve and volatility of rates. More lenders should integrate existing fixed-income valuation technology for modeling mortgage price behavior into their pipeline systems and hedge construction.

Profit & Loss From Pipeline Hedging Activities

The mortgage origination process creates two assets — a loan and servicing rights. In the classic model of mortgage banking, the lender sells the loan to an institutional investor or capital market intermediary (for example, a securities dealer) as part of an mortgage-backed security (MBS) or as a whole loan.

There are two common variations on this theme:

8 Handbook of Secondary Marketing

1. The lender might sell the loan servicing rights to another lender. The second lender would then retain the servicing rights and sell the loan.

2. A portfolio lender might decide to retain both the loan and the servicing rights.

Pricing Subsidies

The pricing environment in the primary market has changed considerably over the past decade. (The *primary market* is where loans are originated. Lenders are the suppliers of mortgage loans to borrowers, who "consume" mortgage credit to finance investments in residential housing.) Mortgage loans were once priced to "break even" against the capital-markets price. This pricing approach — an example of which is shown in Table 1-1 —

TABLE 1-1
Calculation of Break-even Pricing

Settlement Month	Settlement Date	02/06/96 Forward Prices (32nds)	02/06/96 Forward Prices (decimals)
February	02/20/96	99-02	99.06250
March	03/19/96	98-30	98.93750
April	04/18/96	98-27	98.84375
May	05/20/96	98-24	98.75000

- Assume 60 day lock period plus 8 days shipping = 68 days
- 68 days from 02/08/96 = 04/16/96
- Break-even price is between March and April

Break even price

$$= \text{March price} = \text{interpolation factor (March price} - \text{April price)}$$
$$= 98.9375 - .9333 \, (98.9375 - 98.84375) = 98.85$$

$$\text{interpolation factor} = \frac{04/16/96 - 03/19/96}{04/18/96 - 03/19/96}$$

$$= \frac{\text{today} + 68 \text{ days} - \text{March settle date}}{\text{April settle date} - \text{March settle date}}$$

excluded any consideration of the value of the loan's servicing rights. Servicing rights, which could be retained or sold, were considered the revenue against the lender's loan origination costs, which often exceeded the loan origination fee charged by the lender, as well as the lender's profit.

Increasing competition has rendered the break-even pricing approach obsolete. In the current primary market pricing environment, lenders usually subsidize the price with some of the servicing value in most markets and for most mortgage products. There are remote markets where the price can actually be marked up (a negative subsidy) instead of subsidized. This phenomenon can be found in some non-metropolitan areas in the continental United States, as well as in Hawaii, Guam and Puerto Rico. In addition to the isolated markets, there are certain products where the price can be marked up and still be competitive in the primary market. In many markets, Federal Housing Administration (FHA) 203(k) loans exhibit this characteristic.

Pricing subsidies and markups should be excluded in the calculation of hedging results. Subsidies and markups are additional costs or revenues related to a particular product in a particular market. Unfortunately, many lenders distort their hedging and loan origination results by mixing pricing subsidies with their hedging results. By doing so, these lenders restrict their ability to evaluate the efficacy of either their hedging or loan origination activities.

Trading Gain/Loss
A properly calculated trading gain/loss begins with the assumption that the loans are priced to break even relative to the capital markets price excluding servicing value. Pricing subsidies and markups are accounted for separately.

Trading gains and losses include several elements:
- Gain/loss on the sale of the loan

- Gain/loss on any cross hedges
- Gain/loss on any options activity

A gain or loss will result in the sale of the loan as an MBS or whole loan. If the loan is sold servicing released, the servicing value should be removed before calculating the gain or loss. A gain or loss also results from the use of any cross hedges. Lenders commonly employ cross hedges as intermediate hedging vehicles while accumulating the necessary minimum volume of various loan products and coupons. Some lenders utilize options as part of their hedging activities. The gain/loss on cross hedges and option activity for a specific loan should be included with the gain/loss on the final sale of the loan to calculate a trading gain or loss.

Net Interest Income

A mortgage generates interest income from the day it closes. Loans leave the pipeline and become part of inventory at the point of closing (loan inventory is sometimes referred to as "warehouse"). Loans leave inventory when they are delivered to and paid for by the investor. Like locked loans in the pipeline, warehouse loans have interest rate risk. The term hedging usually refers to hedging the interest rate risk in the pipeline and warehouse.

Because of the time delay that occurs between the time the loan closes and the time it is delivered by the lender to the investor, the lender receives interest income. Much of this income is offset by interest expense associated with the financing facility the lender uses to finance the loan inventory. Financing costs vary considerably from lender to lender, with bank-owned mortgage lenders often enjoying the most favorable terms (these terms are often favorable in both rate and operational flexibility). Factors other than financing arrangement that affect net interest income include the term structure of interest rates (that is, the slope of the yield curve) and product mix. Steep yield-curve environments generate higher net interest income because most mortgage loans are tied to longer maturities and most financing facilities are tied to shorter maturities. In contrast, net interest income can be negative in times where the yield curve is inverted. Product mix is also a factor; a high proportion of adjustable rate mortgages (ARMs) will generally lower net interest income.

Convergence

As the Ginnie Mae prices in Table 1-1 illustrated, delivery date influences loan and MBS pricing. The price of loans or MBS sold for future delivery is usually less than the price for immediate delivery. (Note: This may not be true in an inverted yield curve environment.) These forward prices for future delivery "converge" on the spot price for immediate delivery as the amount of time between the spot and forward delivery dates decreases. The difference between the *spot price* (immediate delivery) and the *forward price* (future delivery) is called convergence cost. Like net interest income, rate-term structure drives convergence cost. Steep yield curve situations render higher convergence costs. Convergence cost exists in the locked pipeline as well as in the warehouse.

Convergence cost affects pricing for various lock periods. The break-even price for longer locks is less attractive than for shorter locks because of higher convergence cost. Lenders benefit from applicants closing before the lock expiration date. If an applicant locks for 60 days and closes after 30, he or she has paid for 60 days of convergence cost but has used only 30. The lender in this example can earn an extra 30 days of net interest income or recover 30 days of convergence cost by selling the loan 30 days sooner at a better price.

Industry practice varies from lender to lender with respect to warehouse-related convergence cost. Loans pay interest from the moment they close. Therefore, net interest income offsets the convergence cost associated with the warehouse holding period. Most lenders, however, include a minimum warehouse holding period in the calculation of a break-even price. The break-even pricing example previously shown assumes an eight day period of warehouse convergence cost.

Pipeline Behavior and Fallout

Not all applications become loans. Some applications are declined in the underwriting process. Other applications abort for reasons unrelated to the mortgage transaction. Even once an application is approved, the applicant can choose to close or not to close. A lock that does not close is *fallout*.

Fallout complicates the pipeline hedging process considerably. The lender does not know with certainty how many or which loans a locked pipeline will yield until after each lock closes or falls out. Fallout projections that are too high frequently occur in a rising interest rate environment. If the fallout projection is too high, the lender will end up with more loans than anticipated and an underhedged position. Rising rates, combined with an unhedged position, generate trading losses. In contrast, if the fallout projection is too low, an overhedged position will occur from too few locks becoming loans. An overhedged position in a period of declining rates creates trading losses. In spite of the enormous hedging consequences of fallout, many lenders take a careless approach to measuring, projecting, and managing fallout.

Option Analogy

A mortgage loan applicant has the ability to close or not close the lock granted by the lender. For this reason, locks are often compared to put options where the applicant holds the option. *Put options* are the right to sell something at a predeter-

Pipeline Hedging and Fallout Risk 13

mined price. In a mortgage lock situation, the applicant can *put*, or sell, the mortgage to the lender at the locked-in rate and price. Besides being an apt analogy, the option comparison provides a framework for classifying locks with respect to market conditions. An *in-the-money lock* has a rate and price combination that is more favorable to the applicant than the current market. In contrast, an *out-of-the-money lock* has a rate and price combination less favorable to the applicant than the current market. An *at-the-money lock* has a rate and price combination that is the same as that of the current market.

Option measurements that are more complex than simple in- or out-of-the-money calculations also have application in pipeline hedging. Nonetheless, before running too far with the option analogy, keep two thoughts in mind:

1. Because of the mortgage complexities noted previously, options on mortgages are more difficult to analyze with precision than options on other instruments.

2. Most option pricing models assume efficient exercise, meaning that in-the-money options are always exercised and out-of-the-money options are never exercised. However, few, if any, mortgage pipelines exercise with complete efficiency: Some applicants will exercise out-of-the-money locks and other applicants will not exercise in-the-money locks due to underwriting denials or other transactional barriers.

Fallout Measurement

Those mortgage lenders who bother to measure fallout typically do so by dividing loans that are ultimately funded by the loans which were originally put into process as applications. Applications may relock, change rates, switch programs or cancel and reactivate before they eventually close. Most lenders erroneously use this "eventual closing" rate for hedging purposes. Once a fallout rate is assigned, net lock-ins (total lock-ins less projected fallout) are managed as though they were closed loans.

While some lenders vary fallout rates according to market conditions, they still base fallout projections on eventual close rates:

- Eventual Closing Rate = $\dfrac{\text{Closings}}{\text{Applications}}$
- Eventual Fallout Rate = 100% − Eventual Close Rate

Enhanced accuracy results from measuring closing percentages on locks rather than applications. When a lock does not close, it counts as fallout. Consider a loan that locks at 8.00 percent. It then relocks at 7.50% and closes. Under the traditional eventual-closing approach, the closing rate would be 100% and the fallout would be 0 percent. One application yields one closed loan. Measuring the example using the lock method, the close rate would be 50% and the fallout rate also would be 50 percent. Two locks were necessary to close a single loan. The author refers to this approach as "lock-in termination."

All locks terminate in one of several ways:

- **Closing:** The loan can close and fund. A closing percentage should be calculated by dividing closings by lock-ins.
- **Cancellation:** The borrower or seller can cancel the application. Sometimes, cancellations reactivate and then relock.
- **Rejection:** Underwriting may reject the borrower's credit or the property based on its appraisal.
- **Expiration:** The lock-in may expire.
- **Relock:** The loan may relock. A relock can mean a change in rate, price, program or expiration date (an extension).

In the remainder of this chapter, the closing rate using the lock-in termination method will be referred to as "LIT closing rate." Likewise, fallout based on lock-in terminations will appear as "LIT fallout rate."

- LIT Closing Rate = $\dfrac{\text{Closings}}{\text{Lock-Ins}}$
- LIT Fallout Rate = 100% − LIT Closing Rate

The eventual closing measurement does not account for relocks and reactivations. However, these practices have tremendous cost, particularly on hedging activities. Applications may close, but at different terms from the original lock. For example, at one lender, eventual closing rates on applications run near 75 percent. However, LIT closing rates are closer to 55% and may go below 20% at some branches. If the 75% ratio was used for hedging, an overhedged position would often result. Further, because program and rate switches are not properly anticipated, the eventual-close approach can leave some product lines overhedged while others are underhedged. This hedge imbalance can occur even in a flat market.

Lenders often attempt to measure fallout on groups of applications. Attempts to accurately measure fallout without considering each individual loan application will fail. Further, individual lock-in transactions must be accounted for within loan level. Meaningful summaries can be generated only after the results from each lock are evaluated. The minimum variables that lenders should capture for each lock include:

- **Lock terms:** mortgage instrument (for example, FHA 30-year fixed rate), note rate, price or discount, lock period and lock number and type (for example, 1st lock, 2nd lock, extension)

- **Dates:** lock date, expiration date, high and low market price dates and *exercise date* (the date the lock closed or fell out)
- **Market prices:** price at lock date, price at lock termination date, high and low market prices during lock period and price at lock expiration date
- **Lock termination type:** closing, cancellation, rejection, expiration or relock

Besides the lock-level data, lenders should collect additional information on each application such as general source (retail, broker, correspondent), specific source (branch, loan officer, broker), loan purpose (purchase, rate refinance) and applicant demographics.

Pricing Fallout

Many lenders refuse to recognize the importance of lock-in exercise efficiency and fallout pricing despite the consequences they have on hedging success or failure. An example demonstrates the standard mortgage industry technique:

Pipeline	Fallout/ Close Ratios	Inventory Price
$1,000,000 @ 98	25%/75%	$750,000 @ 98

In this example, loans that close and become inventory are assumed to have the same price (98) as the beginning pipeline. In other words, the example assumes inefficient lock exercise and price random fallout. Except for underwriting rejections, the exercise of the lock option is seldom totally inefficient. Whenever possible, applicants will decide to close when their lock is better than the market and decide not to close if their lock is worse than the market. Because the prices of applications that fall out almost

Pipeline Hedging and Fallout Risk   17

always differ from the prices of applications that close, the final inventory price will seldom match the pipeline.

Table 1-2 shows the unlikely pipeline that experiences price random fallout. Table 1-3, a pipeline identical to the one in Table 1-2, shows an example of how efficient exercise of the lock option degrades final inventory price. Perfect exercise efficiency means that only those locks with prices equal to or better than the current

TABLE 1-2
Price Random Fallout

Beginning Pipeline	Locked Price	Closed Loans	Closed Price
$90,000	99.00	fallout	na
90,000	98.00	90,000	98.00
110,000	97.00	110,000	97.00
90,000	96.00	90,000	96.00
90,000	95.00	fallout	na
$470,000	97.00	$290,000	97.00

TABLE 1-3
Perfectly Efficient Exercise

Beginning Pipeline	Locked Price	Closed Loans	Closed Price
$90,000	99.00	$90,000	99.00
90,000	98.00	90,000	98.00
110,000	97.00	110,000	97.00
90,000	96.00	fallout	na
90,000	95.00	fallout	na
$470,000	97.00	$290,000	97.93

market close. Locks priced worse than the market do not close. Table 1-2 and Table 1-3 show the extremes of exercise efficiency. Most real- world pipelines are somewhere between perfect efficiency and inefficiency (price-random fallout). An efficient pipeline is much more difficult to manage than an inefficient pipeline. A very high degree of exercise efficiency almost guarantees disappointing hedging results.

In addition to considering lock exercise efficiency, it is important to calculate pipeline price dispersions. *Price dispersion* measures the price *spread*, or variance, of a specific segment of the pipeline. Price dispersion affects LIT closing ratios and the final weighted-average price of the closed-loan inventory. Table 1-4 and Table 1-5 are similar to the previous tables. Although the weighted average prices of the beginning pipelines are all identical, the price dispersions in Table 1-4 and Table 1-5 are lower. In the unlikely event that all fallout is price random, dispersion has no impact on the final price of the closed loans. Low dispersion mitigates some of the harmful effects of high efficiency. Note the price difference in the closed-loan totals between Table 1-3 and Table 1-5; the pipeline in Table 1-5 benefits from lower

TABLE 1-4
Price Random Fallout (low dispersion)

Beginning Pipeline	Locked Price	Closed Loan	Closed Price
$90,000	98.00	fallout	na
90,000	97.50	90,000	97.50
110,000	97.00	110,000	97.00
90,000	96.50	90,000	96.50
90,000	96.00	fallout	na
$470,000	97.00	$290,000	97.00

TABLE 1-5
Perfectly Efficient Exercise (low dispersion)

Beginning Pipeline	Locked Price	Closed Loans	Closed Price
$90,000	98.00	$90,000	98.00
90,000	97.50	90,000	97.50
110,000	97.00	110,000	97.00
90,000	96.50	fallout	na
90,000	96.00	fallout	na
$470,000	97.00	$290,000	97.47

dispersion. Like high lock-in exercise efficiency, high dispersion makes pipeline hedging more difficult.

Dollar-weighted standard deviation is one method of measuring pipeline price dispersion. Each dollar in the pipeline represents one observation. The standard deviation of price is calculated for all of the observations related to a single rate/product type. Do not combine rates or products; this calculation must be performed for each unique rate/product type in the pipeline. While calculating dispersions is a useful exercise, the best approach is to measure and project closing/fallout probabilities at loan level. Loan level probabilities handle the issue of exercise efficiency as well as dispersion. See Table 1-6 for an example of an inefficient exercise and Table 1-7 for an example of an efficient exercise.

Path Dependency

Over a given lock period, a lock originally priced at-the-money could subsequently become in- or out-of-the-money as a consequence of market price movements. Even in the absence of

TABLE 1-6
Price Random Fallout

Beginning Pipeline	Locked Price	Closing Probabilities	Expected Loans	Expected Price
$90,000	99.00	61.7%	55,532	99.00
90,000	98.00	61.7%	55,532	98.00
110,000	97.00	61.7%	67,872	97.00
90,000	96.50	61.7%	55,532	96.00
90,000	96.00	61.7%	55,532	95.00
$470,000	97.00		$290,000	97.00

TABLE 1-7
Efficient Exercise

Beginning Pipeline	Locked Price	Closing Probabilities	Expected Loans	Expected Price
$90,000	99.00	92.6%	83,348	99.00
90,000	98.00	74.0%	66,600	99.00
110,000	97.00	61.0%	67,872	97.00
90,000	96.00	50.8%	45,720	96.00
90,000	95.00	29.4%	26,460	95.00
$470,000	97.00		$290,000	97.46

market price movements, the convergence of forward and spot prices will cause an at-the-money lock to become out-of-the-money as the lock moves through time.

Figure 1-4 shows two price paths. Assume an application locks at a price of 100 (discount = 0). Path A represents an improving market (rates down/prices up). Efficiently exercising applicants would elect to not close (that is, to fall out) in a path

FIGURE 1-4

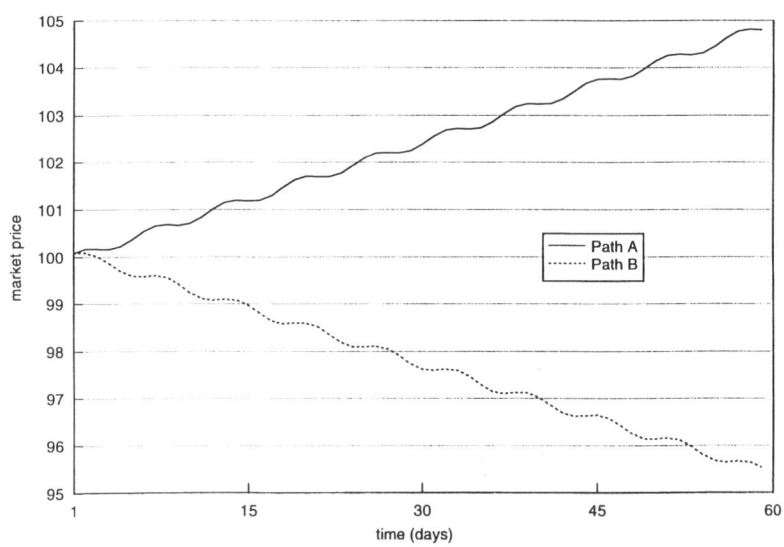

A market environment because their locks are out of the money. However, path B shows a deteriorating market situation. Efficient applicants would close their locks under path B circumstances. Figure 1-5 shows two price paths where the lock is in and out of the money at different times during the lock period.

Although efficient exercise is easy to define at any period in time, the lender may not be aware of the exact moment that locked applicants exercise. Applicants are not likely to inform the lender of their decision to lock at a better price with another lender. It is more difficult to characterize lock terminations as efficient or inefficient in "trendless" market environments such as the ones shown in Figure 1-5.

Unlike European-style options which can only be exercised at a single point in time, locks may exercise (close or fall out) any time during the lock term. Because of the ability to exercise early, lenders should consider the influence of pricing paths on applicant

FIGURE 1-5

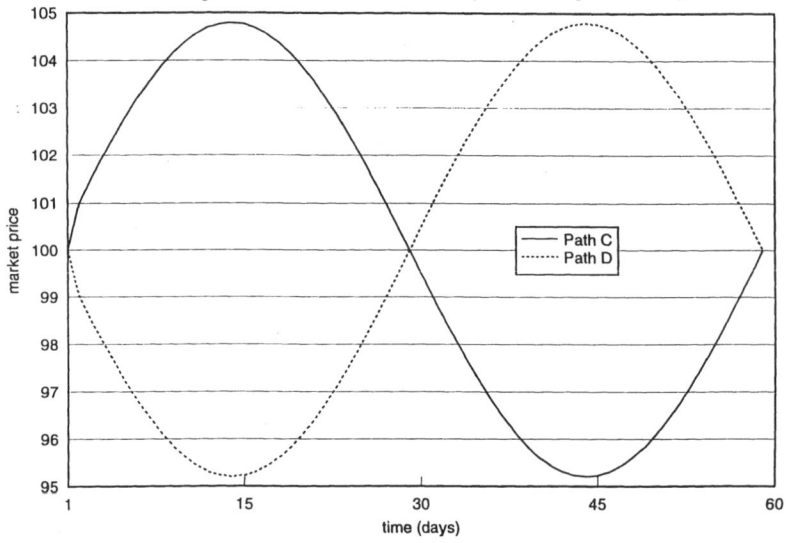

behavior. Knowing when applicants exercise and immediately reflecting this information on the pipeline management system are essential to effective hedging.

Hedging Strategies

Completing the steps described so far makes the process of selecting an appropriate hedging strategy less difficult. Unfortunately, many lenders attempt to hedge pipelines without fully completing some or all of the steps. Executing a pipeline hedging strategy consists of two steps:

1. Understanding and managing the long position.
2. Understanding, selecting and managing the optimal hedging vehicles.

Long Position Management

The warehouse and pipeline comprise the long position. Because the warehouse is made up of closed loans, it is less problematic to hedge. In most instances, the best hedge is forward sales of the exact instrument into which the warehouse loans will be delivered. A cross-hedge of portions of the warehouse may be called for in some instances. A thorough understanding of how prices for different mortgage instruments respond to changes in market conditions (interest rates, slope of the yield curve, volatility) makes a cross-hedge easier to execute.

The pipeline portion of the long position poses a greater analytical and management challenge. Accurate and timely pipeline data are crucial in assessing interest rate and fallout risk. Pipeline systems should incorporate controls to ensure that the exact status of each application and loan is correctly reflected. These data feed the models that calculate each lock's closing probability at any point in time.

Lenders employ policies and practices that can increase or decrease the lock exercise efficiency of their pipelines. While there is nothing inherently wrong with increasing pipeline efficiency, efficiency has significant impact on the cost and potential success of a lender's pipeline hedging activities. Said another way, high-efficiency pipelines are more risky and more expensive to hedge than low-efficiency pipelines. Therefore, lenders should carefully consider the benefits and costs of implementing or continuing to follow any practice that increases pipeline efficiency. At the same time, lenders should continually seek new methods to impede and reduce exercise efficiency. Surprisingly, few lenders seem to actively manage the variables that influence efficiency. Examples of decisions that affect pipeline behavior and are under the control of the lender include:

- **Lock periods:** Lenders determine what lock periods to offer to which production channels. Both common sense and the options analogy imply that longer lock periods are riskier and more difficult to hedge than shorter locks. Lenders should avoid offering longer locks to those applicants who exhibit higher efficiency, such as broker-originated and refinance applications.

- **Price subsidies:** Price subsidies affect pipeline behavior. It may make sense to subsidize shorter lock periods more than longer lock periods to encourage shorter locks. However, it may be wise to subsidize short locks less because applicants who can use shorter locks are ready to close and may be less likely to fall out for price related reasons.
- **Pricing policies:** Pricing policies exert enormous influence on pipeline behavior and lock exercise efficiency. Some lenders vigorously restrict relocks in falling rate markets while other lenders have programs encouraging the practice.
- **Pricing windows:** Some lenders provide overnight price protection whereby applicants can lock at yesterday's price. This practice obviously impairs the ability to match locks with hedges.
- **Channel mix:** Broker-originated applications tend towards higher efficiency than retail applications. Pricing policies should therefore differ by channel.
- **Compensation practices:** Loan officer compensation practices can help or hinder the pipeline hedging effort. Compensation practices should not encourage or reward efficient exercise.

A lender's initial hedging efforts should focus on analyzing, understanding, and managing the long position. Only after completing that task should the lender turn to selection of hedging instruments.

Hedging Instruments

Lenders use a variety of instruments to hedge interest rate risk in the warehouse and interest rate and fallout risk in the pipeline. The best instruments to use are the instruments that mirror the price-rate behavior of the warehouse and pipeline at the lowest possible cost and risk. Virtually all hedging instruments can be classified into two broad categories: short forward sales and put options. The simplest example of a short-forward-sale hedge is selling a particular closed loan for future delivery. Until this trade settles, the forward sale hedges the closed loan. MBS forward sales work in a similar fashion; a lender might sell a Ginnie Mae 7.0% coupon for future delivery against a warehouse of 7.5% note rate FHA and Veteran's Administration (VA) mortgages.

Short sales are often accomplished with similar, rather than identical, instruments. For instance, MBS at one particular coupon may be shorted to hedge the entire range of note rates in a pipeline. Cross hedges like the one described here are used for reasons of convenience and liquidity as well as to exploit potential basis opportunities. As MBS coupons move farther away from *par* (the face value), either higher or lower, liquidity tends to deteriorate. On the other hand, *premium* (above par) coupons can be desirable instruments to cross hedge mortgage pipelines. In a rallying market, heightened prepayment expectations tend to mitigate price appreciation on premium MBS. When the hedge is unwound and the mortgages are sold into their exact coupons, the mortgages being hedged may have appreciated more in price than the hedge instruments thereby creating a basis gain. Basis losses are also possible if the inappropriate instrument or the inappropriate amount of the appropriate instrument is shorted against the long position. This example underscores the necessity of understanding mortgage price behavior.

Because of the option-like characteristics of mortgage locks, lenders sometimes employ put options as hedging instruments.

As with the short sale, the simplest example of the purchased put is buying a put on the exact instrument into which a mortgage will be delivered. A short sale combined with a purchased call also creates a synthetic put. Puts can also involve cross-hedges. Many lenders purchase options on cash treasuries or options on treasury futures because these markets are more liquid than the MBS option market.

Puts can be replicated rather than purchased. Using replicated puts as a pipeline hedging vehicle is often referred to as *delta hedging*. A put is replicated by shorting an amount equivalent to the put delta times the notional amount. Delta is an option measurement, ranging from 0 to 1 for calls and from -1 to 0 for puts, that indicates how much an option will gain or lose in value compared to the underlying instrument. Suppose a purchased put on a Treasury bond (T-bond) with a notional amount of $1,000,000 has a delta of -0.5. That means that for a 1% price appreciation on the T-bond, the put will decline in value by 0.5%, and for a 1% price deterioration in the treasury bond, the put will increase in value by 0.5 percent. To replicate this put, one would do a short sale of $500,000 of the treasury bond ($1,000,000 x -0.5). Delta changes with changes in market variables, such as time left until expiration of the put option, market volatility, short-term interest rates and especially the price of the underlying instrument. The absolute value of put deltas decrease as the market price of the underlying instrument appreciates and increase as the market price of the underlying instrument deteriorates. This is because as a put goes farther out of the money, its delta approaches 0, and as a put goes farther in the money, its delta approaches -1; therefore, at expiration, a put's delta is 0 if it is out of the money or -1 if it is in the money. As a result, successful put replication requires that the hedger constantly adjust the short position as market prices and the put delta change.

There are several other considerations involved in delta hedging. The delta hedging strategy works especially well in "trending" markets similar to those shown in paths A and B of Figure 1-4. In an improving market like path A, the short position is reduced as market prices move higher and higher. Trading gains are very likely because the ultimate sales are executed at a time when market prices are high relative to the preceding hedge period and losses on the short position were diminished as a result of the short position being reduced as prices improved. The strategy works just as well in a deteriorating market like B because the short position is increased as market prices move lower and lower.

However, the delta hedging strategy does not work well in a "sideways" market such as that which is shown in Figure 1-5. In path C, the short position is initially reduced as the market improves. The short position must then be increased as market prices begin to deteriorate in the middle portion of the price path and are then reduced again as prices improve in the final segment of the price path. Using paths C and D, Table 1-8 shows the losses accumulated in a simple example of delta hedging.

Finally, calculating the correct delta for a pipeline is not an easy task. The complex nature of a mortgage's price-rate relationship was briefly discussed earlier in this chapter. In addition, lock options do not exercise with complete efficiency and differ from lender to lender and from one lock to the next.

Cost aside, most lenders would prefer to used purchased puts as their hedging vehicle. Unfortunately, purchased puts are usually one of the more expensive alternatives. Short sales are less expensive but less effective unless actively managed. While most pipeline hedging discussions focus on selecting and using hedging instruments, this element of pipeline hedging has little relevance without first completing the steps outlined at the beginning of this chapter: determining hedging objectives, understanding mortgages, understanding pipeline profits and losses, understanding pipeline behavior and fallout and understanding basic pipeline hedging strategies.

TABLE 1-8

Delta Hedging Example (locked applications = $10,000,000)

Time	Deltas		Short Position		Market Price		Gain/Loss for Adjusting Short Position		Note
	Path C	Path D	Path C	Path D	Path C	Path D	Path C	Path D	
1	-0.45	-0.45	(4,500,000)	(4,500,000)	100	100	$0	$0	
15	-0.25	-0.70	(2,500,000)	(7,000,000)	105	95	(100,00)	0	(2)
30	-0.50	-0.50	(5,000,000)	(5,000,000)	100	100	0	(100,000)	(2)
45	-0.75	-0.30	(7,500,000)	(3,000,000)	95	105	0	(100,000)	(2)
60	-0.55	-0.55	(5,000,000)	(5,500,000)	100	100	(100,000)	0	(2)
							$(200,000)	$(200,000)	

Notes:
[1] Initial short position = $10,000,000 x delta of -.45 = ($4,500,000)
[2] Loss on adjusting short position = position bought back x increase in market price.
[3] Deltas used in example are simplified.

2

The Optional Nature of Mortgage Rate Locks: Implications for Pipeline Risk Management

Stephen S. Harris, Vice President,
Mortgage Banking Group
Goldman, Sachs & Co.

Acknowledgment: The author wishes to thank Peter Niculescu for carefully reviewing drafts of this document and making many insightful suggestions along the way, to thank Kathleen Huber, Emma B. Rasiel, Vishal Gupta, and Roger Saks for their valuable contributions, and to thank Eric P. Schott of GMAC Mortgage for his helpful comments on earlier drafts.

The secondary market risk manager is operating in a completely new environment. Competition for every new loan is fierce and is often exacerbated by the combined pressure of commission-oriented loan officers, all-important real estate agents and increasingly sophisticated mortgagors. In many origination markets, the competition has become so intense that it forces production programs upon risk managers that may not be economically optimal. Often, the new loans are produced and the relationship with valued realtors is developed but at a significant cost to the secondary market risk manager. Further, the recent proliferation of rate protection programs — encompassing everything from extended lock terms to ratchet commitments and the ubiquitous lock-and-shop program — add some very real costs and risks to the institution offering the program. Unfortunately, the secondary market risk manager not only must comply with these competitive pressures but must also minimize the economic impact of the institution's exposure to the interest-rate markets that are usually associated with these programs.

We begin this chapter by investigating the extraordinarily competitive environment in which originators currently compete. Then, we examine the most popular option-based analytic tools that originators currently employ to measure and hedge the risks associated with their mortgage pipelines.

A New Environment

During the mid-1990s, the new loan origination environment changed significantly. No longer can independent regional originators compete with the larger, better capitalized and traditionally more aggressive national lenders. In fact, most regional originators have been consumed by their larger competitors, who, more likely than not, are subsidiaries of nationally chartered money-center banks.

Much of this consolidation is attributable to the compelling operating efficiencies and economies of scale that exist in mortgage banking. In addition, the newly promulgated accounting standards, in concert with the application of superior technology, have stratified the mortgage banking industry. This stratification occurs among institutions based on the size of their servicing portfolios, and there are three readily observable divisions. The first layer comprises the megaservicers that have servicing portfolios in excess of $100 billion. Next are the larger institutions with portfolios of at least $25 billion — these tend to be divisions of diversified financial service providers. The final group of originators comprises regional institutions with portfolios of less than $25 billion.

Technology and the Consolidation of an Industry
The immense capital and management costs associated with developing the automated systems required to efficiently originate and service residential mortgages have become a substantial burden for institutions that hope to compete in this consumer-item processing-intensive industry. In an environment where the servicing cost of an exceptional institution can be as low as $40 per loan per year and the cost for another more typical competitor may be in excess of $90 per loan, there are likely to be some striking dislocations. Often these dislocations manifest themselves in the form of strategic combinations or outright acquisitions of less efficient originators by those who excel. While technology alone does not define efficiency or determine the resulting processing costs, it certainly plays a significant role.

Servicing Technology and Efficiency
Residential mortgages have become commodity-like, consumer products that generally command little more brand- or originator-loyalty than do more traditional consumer products, such as bath soap. Consequently, when looking for a mortgage, mortgagors generally focus on price and, to a much lesser degree, service. It is no surprise, therefore, that the originator who offers the lowest price to the mortgagor will probably win the business

and close the loan. As the application of new processing technology — for example, artificial intelligence for loan underwriting, automated collections and online customer service — has reduced institutions' origination and servicing costs, mortgagors have benefited by receiving a greater choice of mortgage products with better service at lower prices. By extension, institutions that have made the necessary investments in technology and systems development are likely to benefit from the improved market share they will achieve by offering lower prices.

SFAS 122

The promulgation of accounting standard SFAS 122 in May 1995 fundamentally changed the mortgage banking industry. Specifically, the new accounting standard eliminated the accounting distinction between originated and purchased mortgage servicing rights (OMSR and PMSR, respectively). This had the effect of converting a historically valuable off-balance-sheet asset to one that could now be capitalized and even be included as part of an institution's regulatory capital.

Prior to SFAS 122, many mortgage bankers would routinely sell their originated servicing in favor of purchasing servicing assets of another institution in order to benefit from the preferential accounting treatment afforded purchased servicing. Now, however, originated servicing is generally retained by the originator and carried as an asset on its balance sheet. Exceptions to the retention of OMSRs often result from market conditions where the servicing can be sold at prices in excess of the originator's valuation or when cash is a preferred asset.

Commercial Banks and Opportunity

Commercial bank managers recognize that mortgage banking is an extension of the commercial bank's traditional data-intensive, cash-processing-oriented, consumer-lending franchise. As such, they have seized the opportunity to leverage these franchises by acquiring mortgage banks. Mortgage banks are desired for both their asset-laden servicing portfolios and for the new loan origination networks they typically possess. Further, as originated servicing now qualifies as a balance sheet asset, many commercial banks have purchased mortgage banks as a mechanism to produce additional assets — for example, cash from the escrow deposits and capitalized servicing — and to procure a consumer-based fee-generating business. Potentially more attractive to commercial bank managers though, are the opportunities for cross-selling the bank's other consumer banking products and services to the captive audience of a mortgage bank's servicing portfolio.

Competition and the New Realities of Origination

Because commercial banks have consumed many of their smaller, lesser-capitalized rivals, competition for new originations has become fierce for reasons of both fundamental economics and market share objectives.

Economics and the Value of Servicing
Loan pricing is a key factor in determining which institutions will attract new originations and gain market share. To be more competitive, some aggressive institutions artificially subsidize their loan pricing by inappropriately capitalizing an origination subsidy as a loan-closing cost that is then amortized over the life of the loan. The risk of this policy is that the periodic mark-to-market of the servicing, as required by SFAS 122, will indicate that the capitalized value is in excess of the market value and therefore must be impaired by an amount equal to the difference (the origination subsidy). Consequently, aggressive

institutions will pay for the origination subsidy through a loss when their loans are sold or when their servicing is marked to market.

More often, however, an institution will determine that it services for a lower cost than its competition or it may determine that it receives such financial dividends from cross-selling that it passes these efficiencies on to the mortgagor in the form of better loan pricing. Consequently, as efficient originators grow larger and their commitment to technology grows, it is likely that their efficiency will further increase, their pricing will become more competitive and their market share will continue to improve.

Market Share and Concentration

Perhaps the single most impressive change in the mortgage banking industry is the degree to which market share has consolidated over the past five years. In January 1990 and for much of that year, when Fannie Mae 9.5% mortgages were the current coupon, the top 25 mortgage originators controlled approximately 28% of the total single family origination market. For 1995, when Fannie Mae 7.0% mortgages were the current coupon for much of the year, the top 25 originators controlled approximately 41% of the total origination market.[1] This dramatic consolidation of market share is largely the result of commercial banks acquiring their independent mortgage banking competitors. More important, though, is that compelling economies of scale prevail in the origination industry and that these economies, in concert with the recognition of mortgage servicing as a balance sheet asset, have eliminated inefficient producers and given fuel to the acquirer's quest for market share.

---

1. Source: Inside Mortgage Finance Publications, Inc. The Mortgage Market Statistical Annual for 1996.

While the torrid pace of industry consolidation has certainly reduced the number of originators vying for each new loan, those who remain are generally better capitalized, more sophisticated and more competitive than in the past.

Loan Production Programs and the Quest for Market Share

In the present environment, historically appealing mortgage rates, in concert with high levels of housing affordability, are not bringing forth the number of new mortgages and refinances that the industry would expect. Consequently, many institutions have responded with production programs that may not optimize the economics of the enterprise but may attract incremental business.

Narrow Margins and Little Tolerance for Risk
Often, ambitious production programs are accompanied by extremely thin or negative profit margins. Consequently, there is little room for error in the pricing, hedging or delivery of these programs. An unfortunate result of these conditions is that secondary market risk managers are often faced with an almost certain marketing loss, even if they perform their function perfectly. Further, because there is so little profit margin in these aggressive programs, risk managers have limited latitude in applying their traditional risk management techniques and marketing skills. From the risk manager's perspective, extended lock programs, float-down programs and the like are examples of the loan production function taking precedence over the normal loan program's balance of production goals and marketing prudence.

In Pursuit of Refinance Business

Several years ago, mortgage originators began offering to refinance mortgages without the traditional fees and out-of-pocket expenses typically associated with this process. The mortgagor, in exchange for the originator's assumption of these costs, would be required to accept a slightly higher-than-market interest rate. The originator would in turn sell its above-market mortgages to investors at premium prices in order to recoup the out-of-pocket origination costs and expenses. These no-fee refinance programs, as they are known, had the effect of significantly reducing the mortgagors' aversion to the process and the expense of refinancing an existing loan.

The viability of these no-fee refinance programs is largely a function of investors' continued willingness to pay premiums for newly issued securities backed by mortgages with note rates in excess of the current market. The conditions prevailing in the bond market during 1993 had a sobering effect on premium mortgage investors. At that time, the yield curve was very steep; there was tremendous demand from CMO investors for mortgage collateral, which caused mortgages to out perform the Treasury rally; the rally itself exceeded the most optimistic forecasts; and perhaps most important, mortgage bankers recognized significant economies of scale in pursuing refinance business.

Because refinancing a mortgage became so financially efficient for the average mortgagor, a much greater number of mortgagors refinanced than the market had expected. Consequently, many premium MBS investors found themselves being repaid at par long before they anticipated such repayment; therefore, they incurred substantial losses on their investments.

The result of origination programs that improve the economic and logistic efficacy with which mortgagors can refinance their debt is a mortgage securities market that is now characterized by investors' general reluctance to pay premiums beyond a limited degree. Their unwillingness to pay such premiums causes the spread between mortgage coupons to compress tighter than in the past (all other variables held constant) and affords much less value to the incremental income of higher coupons because the life expectancy of these loans is also much lower than in the past. Figure 2-1 illustrates this by comparing the coupon spreads prevailing in the mortgage market on December 11, 1995 (when the 10-year note was yielding 5.706%) with the coupon spreads that prevailed on November 18, 1993 (when the 10-year note was also yielding 5.706% and no-fee refinances were just coming into vogue). Consequently, today's mortgagors who refinance their loans through no-fee programs are forced to pay — in exchange for the originator assuming all the refinance fees and costs — an interest-rate premium above the prevailing market that is much greater (in relative terms) than the differential used before investors lost so much money on the unanticipated refinances of their premium securities.

For secondary market risk managers, hedging the market and pipeline risks associated with these no-fee refinance programs is made far more difficult by the investor's disdain for premium mortgage securities and the "elastic" nature of these typically price-hypersensitive mortgagors. The investor's disdain for new-issue premium securities creates an asymmetric risk profile for these refinance mortgages because the risk manager's potential upside in selling the mortgage is severely limited by the investor's refusal to pay prices much beyond 102. The potential downside is significant, as deterioration in the bond market will extend the anticipated average life and duration of these loans, causing their price to drop sharply. A further complication is that most no-fee refinance mortgagors are extremely sensitive to changes in the bond market. Their price sensitivity guarantees a high level of pipeline fallout when the bond market rallies and almost certainly greater-than-expected levels of loan closings when the market deteriorates. Therefore, even the most proficient risk managers will find themselves short in a rallying market, as

FIGURE 2-1

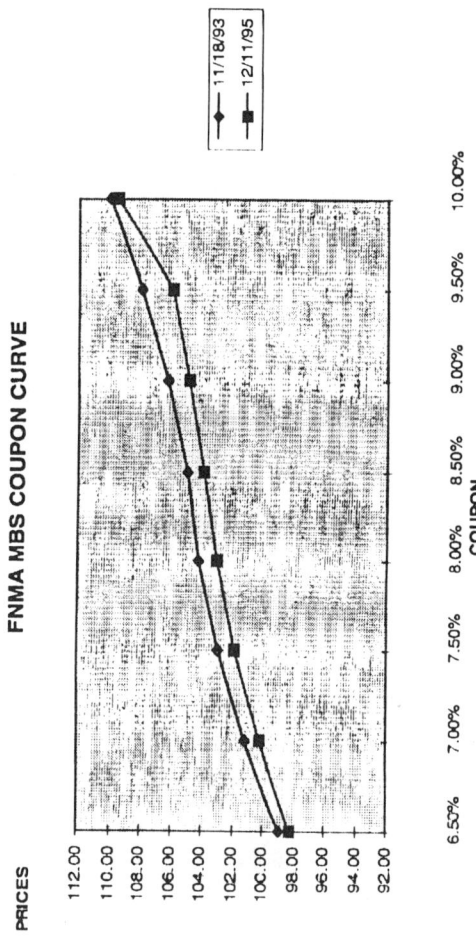

loans fall out and the pipeline evaporates, and will find themselves long in a deteriorating market, where every loan commitment is effectively in the money.

Proliferation of Lock Options

Today's competitive environment requires originators to offer a plethora of extended rate-lock and production-enhancing programs in order to effectively compete and, at minimum, retain market share. What many originators fail to realize, however, is that each of these new production programs is literally, in its most basic economic form, a capital market option that is either given away in the hope of producing incremental business or sold to a mortgagor at a price that only modestly compensates for the risks embedded in the option.

An *option* is an agreement between two parties that gives the purchaser the right, but not the obligation, to buy or sell a specific asset at a specified price during a specified period of time. The seller, or writer, of the option typically receives a payment, called a *premium*, in exchange for the promise to perform under the specified characteristics of the option if the option purchaser elects to exercise the right acquired by purchasing the option. A call option gives the purchaser the right to buy an asset, or call it away, and a put option gives the purchaser the right to sell an asset, or put the asset back to the seller. Figure 2-2 depicts the typical return profiles of standard call and put options.

Production Programs — Options Sold Short

When you evaluate a new production program for pipeline and interest rate market risks, often it is helpful to adopt the perspective of a Wall Street options trader. From such a perspective, each feature of the program can be reduced to an issue of economic risk versus economic reward. Generally, we find that

FIGURE 2-2
Payoff Charts of Long and Short Calls and Puts

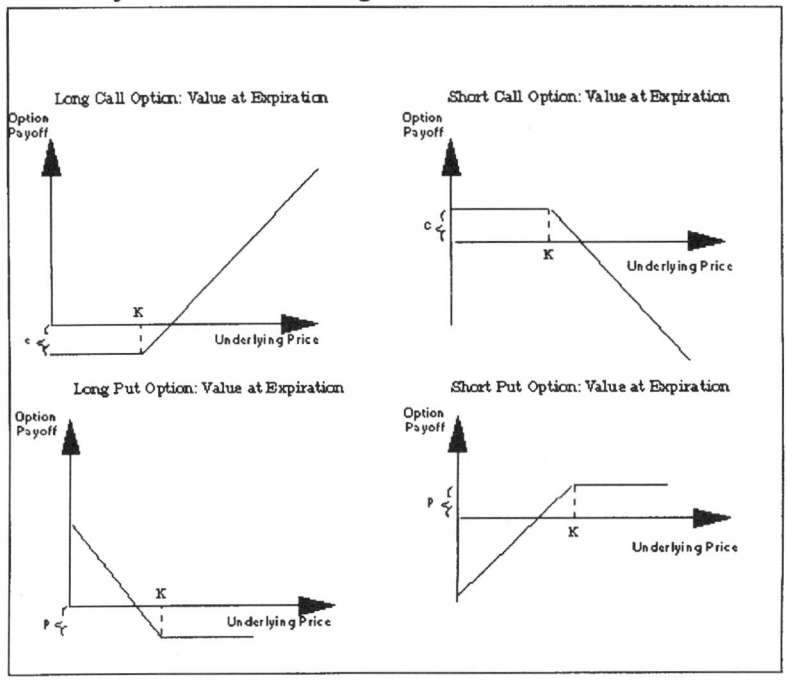

many mortgage production programs feature characteristics that are simply marketing twists of actively traded Wall Street capital market options.

A good example of a popular production program is the ubiquitous "lock-and-shop" program. In this example, we assume that the prospective mortgagor is given a 90-day commitment, or loan lock, for a property that they have yet to select. Obviously, the commitment is for an unknown loan amount, and most important, is for a specified maximum interest rate and maximum discount points. Additionally, the mortgagor typically has the right to convert his loan pricing at any time during the lock period from its initial pricing characteristics, or ceiling, to the pricing that prevails at the time of the conversion. In other words, if the interest-rate market improves subsequent to their application, the mortgagor will benefit. If however, the interest-rate market deteriorates, the mortgagor is protected by the cap feature or "lock" component of the program.

Measuring the Cost of Originator Options
From a Wall Street dealer's perspective, this production program is actually an elaborate, and accordingly expensive, capital market option. In essence, it is a capital-market option that the originator has written for the mortgagor's benefit with the expectation that incremental business will follow.

Wall Street dealers offer this option as well, albeit in a somewhat more structured form. They offer it as a long-dated American-style put option with a conversion or knockout feature. There is, however, one major difference between the Wall Street version and the version offered by mortgage originators: Wall Street dealers charge a significant premium for these options, while most originators receive little or no premium from their mortgagors.

The value of these mortgagor-friendly options can be great. As shown in Figure 2-3, depending on implied price volatility levels, this option for the typical lock period of 60 days could cost as little as 15/32nds of 1% when price volatility is 3% and 14/32nds of 1% when price volatility is 7 percent. Typically, price volatility fluctuates in a range between 3% and 7 percent. It is possible, though, for price volatility to move significantly higher or lower in a very short period following or proceeding some significant market-moving occurrence.

Similarly, many other popular production programs are actually capital market options crafted in such a manner to attract mortgagor interest and the likely origination business that fol-

42   Handbook of Secondary Marketing

FIGURE 2-3

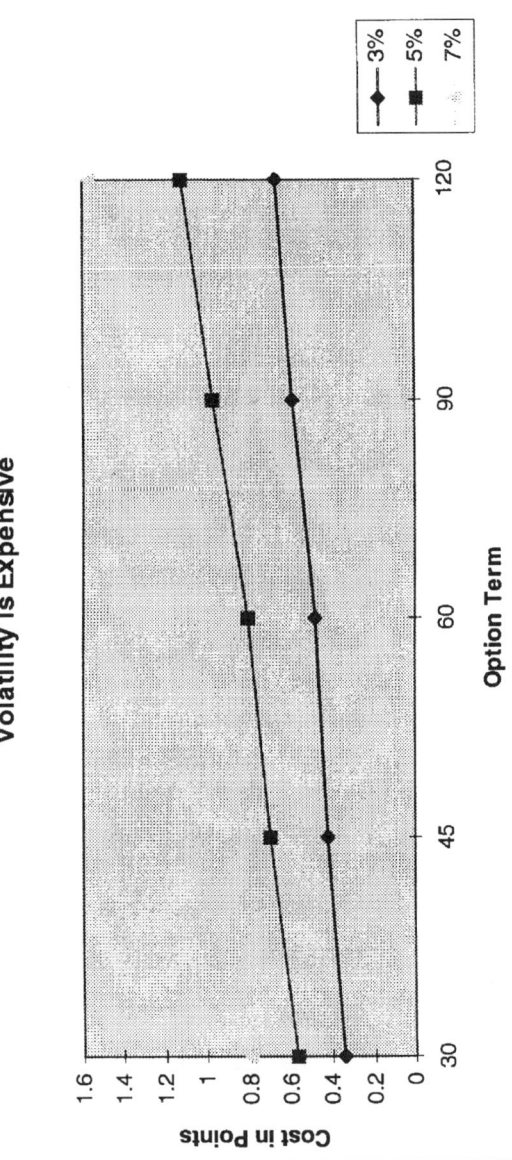

lows. As such, it is possible to determine the explicit cost of these options, based again on the Wall Street option dealer's perspective. All dealers, and many sophisticated originators, use computer-based models to determine the actual financial cost or value of the capital market options they buy or sell.

Most of today's popular option pricing models are based on the evolutionary work of Black-Scholes, Cox-Ross-Rubinstein, Merton and Black-Derman-Toy. While it is beyond the scope of this chapter to detail the complete mathematical foundation of these models, we will introduce some of the basic concepts and explain their application to mortgage pipeline and mortgage servicing hedging.

In a path-breaking paper published in 1973, Fischer Black and Myron Scholes derived an analytical formula for pricing European-style call options on non-dividend-paying stocks.[2] Later, Robert C. Merton extended the Black-Scholes model to price American-style call options on non-dividend-paying stocks by mathematically demonstrating that an American-style call option should have the same price as a European-style call option if the underlying stock pays no dividend.[3] This common price results because there is no economic incentive to exercise the American-style call early.

The related concept of put-call parity was further formulated to detail the relationship between calls and puts on an underlying security. *Put-call parity* means that a portfolio which is long a call and short a put, with both options having the same strike price and the same time to expiration, is equivalent to a long forward position in the underlying asset that has the same forward price as the strike of the two options. This concept is illustrated in Figure 2-4. The major relevance of put-call parity stems from its

---

2. Fischer Black and Mylom Scholes, "The pricing of Options and Corporate Liabilities," Journal of Political Economy, 81, May – June 1973, pp. 637–659.

3. Robert C. Merton, "Theory of Rational Option Pricing," Bell Journal of Economics and Management Science, 4, Spring 1973, pp 141–183.

FIGURE 2-4

Put/Call Parity (European Style)

A portfolio that is long a call and short a put (with the same strike and expiration) is equivalent to a long forward position whose settlement price is equal to the common strike of the options.

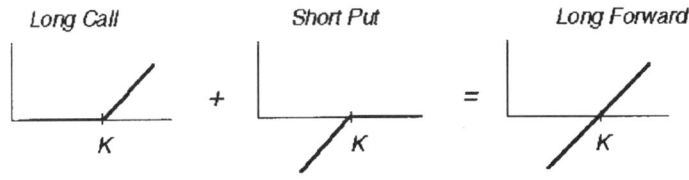

character as a relationship that is independent of any model valuation assumptions.

However useful these incremental modeling advances may have been, the Black-Scholes analytical models were difficult to apply when attempting to determine the option values of interest-bearing securities.[4] Black-Derman-Toy solved this problem using a stochastic interest rate rather than the constant rate approach utilized in the Black-Scholes model.[5] Because there are so many different theoretical methods for determining interest rates and the effect they have on options, many option-pricing models have further evolved. Some of these models are available commercially (some are even available free of charge on the Internet) and are widely used by market participants.

4. See. for example, John C. Cox, Stephen A. Ross, and Mark Rubinstein, "Option Pricing: A simplified Approach," Journal of Finanacial Economics, 7(3), 1979, pp.229–264.

5. Fischer Black, Emanuel Deeman, and William Toy, "A One-Factor Model of Interest Rates and Its Application to Treadury Bond Options", Financial Analysts Journal, 46(1), 1990, pp.33–39; originally distributed as Discussion Paper 1, Financial Strategies Group, Goldman, Sachs & Co., June 1988.

It may seem obvious that commercially available option-pricing models are not a holy grail and do not alone determine the success of an institution using them for speculation or hedging. The user must know enough about the model's critical elements and assumptions to properly understand its applications and limitations.

To use a typical option-pricing model, the following security and market-based valuation inputs are necessary for the model's basic processes to function accurately:

- Current price of the security
- Coupon of the security
- Repurchase rate or financing rate of the security
- Strike price of the option
- Time to expiration of the option
- Implied volatility of the security
- Discount rate

The preceding valuation inputs are for fixed-income securities, but we can easily substitute the mortgage characteristics of any rate lock — for example, the current price of the mortgage, its coupon, and its repo rate. The secondary market risk manager must be aware of the relative levels of these market-based factors when pricing a production program or hedging a mortgage pipeline. These factors ultimately determine the cost of the options the institution is giving away or selling to the mortgagor.

Option Delta

In addition to helping users determine the economic cost of extending a rate lock to a mortgagor, option models also produce a useful approximation of the probability that an option will be exercised or, more specifically for mortgage originators, that a mortgage rate lock will ultimately conclude as a closed loan. The approximate measure of this probability is called the *option delta*; by extension, it is generally referred to as the *hedge ratio* of the option as well. Simply stated, we may define an option's delta as the rate of change of the option premium, or its present market value, with respect to changes in the price of the underlying asset. The best way to think of it, though, is as a measure of the sensitivity of an option's price to a change in the price of the underlying asset.

Mathematically, the definition of the option delta is the slope of the curve of the option price as a function of the underlying asset price, or the first derivative of the option price with respect to the underlying asset price. With either definition, the formula looks like this:

$$\text{Delta } (\Delta) = \frac{\text{Rate of Change of the Option Premium}}{\text{Change of Price of the Underlying Asset}}$$

For call options, the delta is capped by a value of one and floored by a value of zero. The converse is true for put options where the delta is capped by a value of zero and floored by a value of negative one. The graph in Figure 2-5 illustrates how the call delta is the slope of the call price curve. The graph in Figure 2-6 shows how the delta of a call moves from approximately zero when the option is significantly out of the money to approximately one when the option is significantly in the money. For put options, the curve and delta profiles would demonstrate the same behavior as for calls except that the values would be negative for the put options.

Returning to mortgage banking and managing a mortgage pipeline, we note that the delta has many applications. Perhaps the most significant application is its usefulness as a method to predict the probability that a particular loan with specific rate lock guarantees will close.

FIGURE 2-5
How to Calculate Delta

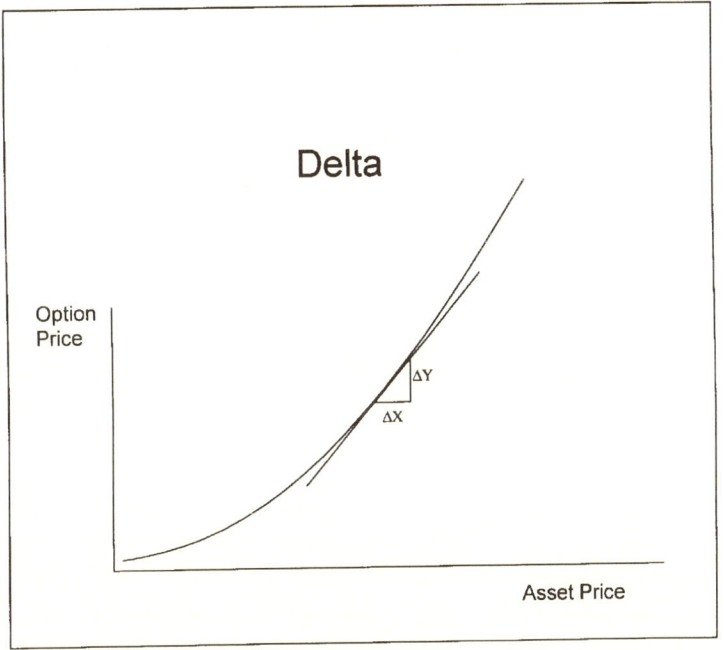

The Likelihood that a Loan Will Close

Recognizing that a mortgage rate lock is really just a capital market put option extended to a mortgagor, we can apply our option pricing models to these rate lock agreements and determine both their values and their deltas. We consider a mortgage rate lock to be a put option because the originator has extended to the mortgagors the right, but not the obligation, to put (close) their mortgage at its specified rate and price to the originator. By extension, therefore, determining how likely it is that mortgagors will close their loans can be as simple as calculating the delta of the rate lock.

FIGURE 2-6
What Delta Measures
Delta measures the sensitivity of an option's price to a change in the

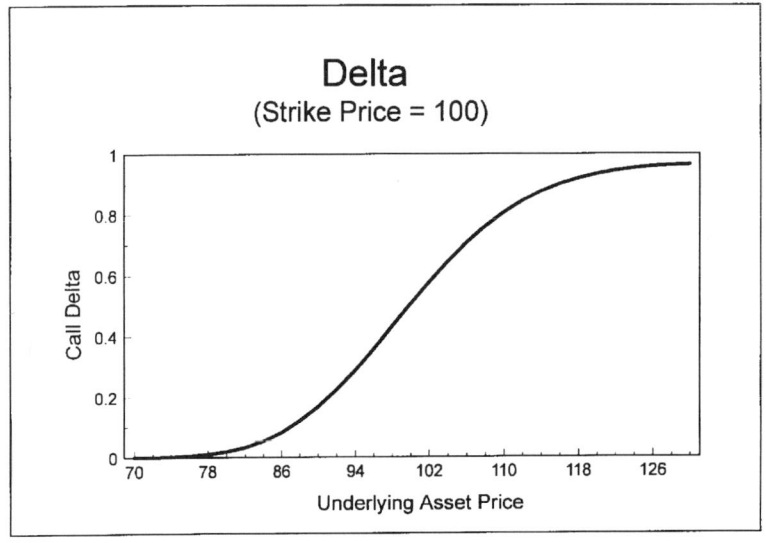

Because the delta is a measure of the probability of an option being exercised, the delta of a rate lock is a convenient measure of the approximate probability that the mortgagors will exercise their right to close the loan. In the example in Figure 2-7, at the time an at-the-money option or rate lock commitment is written, it has a delta of approximately 0.5. This means, in effect, that the probability of the option being exercised at expiration is 50 percent. This makes sense intuitively, as there is a 50% chance that rates may go higher and a 50% chance that rates may go lower. Further, an option with a delta of 1.0 is very much in the money and therefore is very likely to be exercised. The opposite can be said of an option with a delta of close to 0.0, as it is very unlikely to be exercised.

The Optional Nature of Mortgage Rate Locks   49

FIGURE 2-7

Normal Distribution of Interest Rates
Normal distribution of interest rates means an equal chance of higher or lower rates. A call option struck at the money forward has a 50% chance of being in the money at expiration.

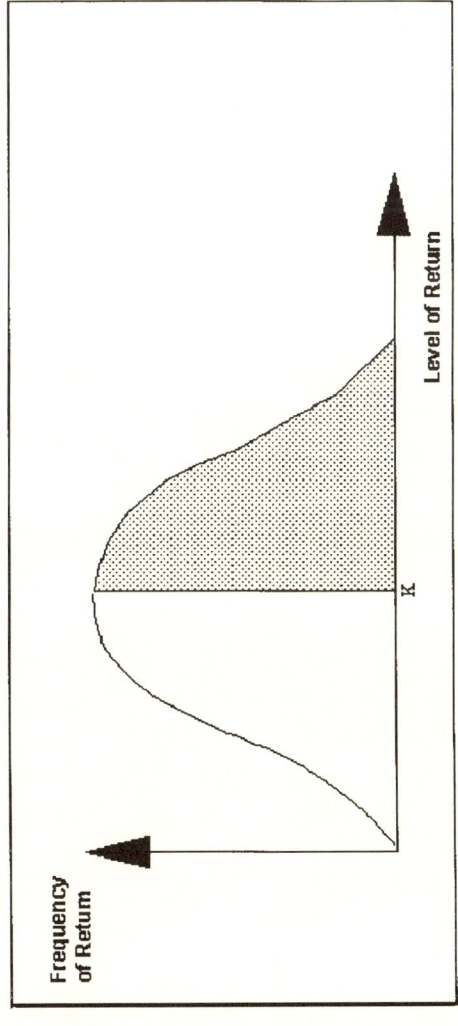

When using delta analysis to approximate the mortgagors' probability of exercising their rate lock, keep in mind that delta analysis assumes that mortgagors will behave in an economically rational manner. While this assumption is necessary to accurately measure the probability of the mortgagor closing the loan at the agreed-upon conditions of the rate lock, it may not always be realistic. There are many noneconomic variables that, from time to time, do influence mortgagors' decisions to close a loan.

For example, mortgagors with rate locks that are in the money may fail to close. This economically suboptimal decision may come about because the mortgagors decide that they really don't want the home, or because they suffered an adverse credit event during their lock period. Conversely, mortgagors whose rate lock may be out of the money may still close their loans. Again, this is an economically suboptimal action, given that the mortgagors could ask for the benefit of the improved market or simply submit their loan application to another institution in order to take advantage of the market improvement.

However, over the long term, in diverse market conditions, many sophisticated originators have found the delta of an option, or of a mortgage rate lock, to be a reliable approximation for estimating the probability that mortgagors will close their loans.

When using the delta of an option to approximate the probability of exercise, also keep in mind that as the price of the underlying asset changes, so too does the delta. Therefore, the delta of an option must be recalculated with changes in the price of the underlying asset and should not to be considered a static or constant value. Figure 2-8 and Figure 2-9 illustrate this concept. As we will see shortly, the fact that the delta of an option changes with the price movement of the underlying asset can become a very valuable characteristic when applied in a properly designed hedge.

The Optional Nature of Mortgage Rate Locks 51

FIGURE 2-8

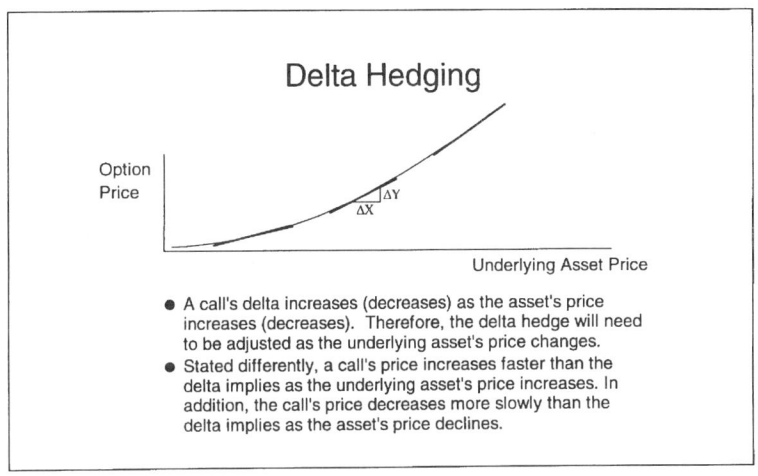

FIGURE 2-9
Variation on the Delta of a Call and a Put as the Underlying Price Changes

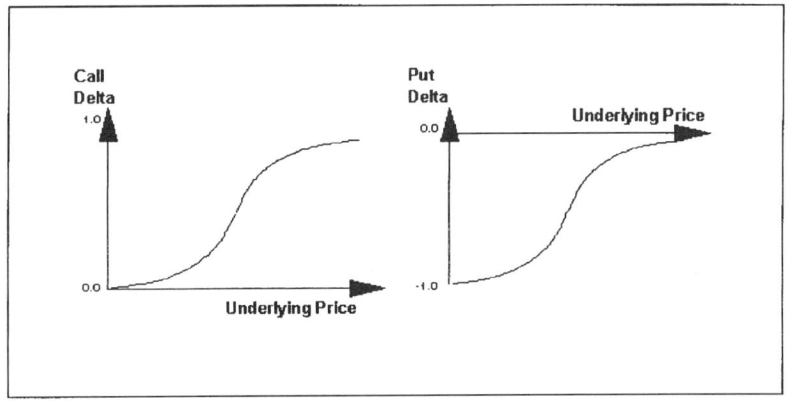

Measuring Option Risk in a Pipeline Context

In certain circumstances, it may be helpful to calculate the delta of a particular rate-locked loan or mortgage commitment, thereby approximating the probability that the loan will close. However, for large originators with commensurate-sized pipelines, it often is not practical to calculate the delta on a loan-by-loan basis. Neither is there much value in the data that result from an excessive number of individual option valuations. Consequently, several commercial vendors have developed pipeline-based option pricing models that can efficiently calculate the delta of the pipeline as a whole, as well as the individual deltas for many different loans.

Delta as a Hedge Ratio

A useful application of the delta valuation that option-pricing models provide is the ability to use these data for the construction of a hedge that is both market-neutral and, in many respects, self-adjusting to small or moderate moves in the price of the underlying asset. The use of option deltas to construct such a hedge is called *option-inclusive delta hedging*, or *synthetic put hedging*. In certain circles, this strategy it is referred to as a "riskless hedge" because of its self-adjusting nature. This strategy is a modification of traditional delta hedging, which gets its name from its primary goal of crafting a hedge by replicating the delta of an option without actually purchasing any options.

At this point, it is important to review two very basic hedge strategies, before introducing the more sophisticated delta-based hedging strategies: Assume an originator has a particularly successful production program, similar to the extended rate lock discussed earlier, and commits to $10 million of rate locks during the day. The originator has realistically given away put options to prospective mortgagors in order to win these $10 million of rate locks. As pure capital-market options, the puts have a delta of 0.5 at the time of lock-in, and by extension have a 50% probability of closing.

The secondary marketing risk manager now finds himself long $10 million of mortgage commitments and therefore at risk should the market change. Consequently, the risk manager must determine the proper hedge for his newest commitments. As typically found in the industry, the risk manager desires to include cash sales as a significant component of his hedge program. This allows him to commit to the forward delivery of their production and to satisfy senior management's requirements that hedging vehicles be as close to the characteristics of the loan production as possible without exposing the institution to additional risk.

Table 2-1 outlines the simplest way to hedge the $10 million of rate commitments is to sell an adjusted amount, incorporating the expectation of fallout, of Fannie Mae 7% MBS forward, and then let the hedge remain in effect until the loans close or fall out. This strategy will expose the risk manager to even greater risk should the market rally (or decline) and therefore cause the fallout to exceed (or fall short of) expectations.

An alternative strategy, which again is rather extreme, is to simply hedge the pipeline by purchasing from a Wall Street dealer

TABLE 2-1

Lock Rate	=	7.5%
Lock Price	=	100
Lock Term	=	45 days
Lock Delta	=	0.5
Underlying MBS	=	Fannie Mae 7%
Underlying MBS Price, 60 day delivery = 100 At-the Money Call on Fannie Mae 7% with 45 days to expiration = 18/32nd of 1%		
Call Delta	=	0.5

capital-market put options with characteristics similar to the rate locks. The primary problem with this second strategy is that it can be very expensive, particularly if the risk manager chooses to cover the entire pipeline with puts. Further, while this strategy does provide interest rate and fallout protection, it can often lull the risk manager into a false sense of security. The pipeline may be undergoing significant stress in terms of coupon compression and product swap spread disruptions caused by changes in the underlying collateral market.

The two strategies outlined above are employed in varying forms by many institutions that try to keep their hedging strategies simple to implement and easy to maintain. However, these two strategies create pronounced risks of their own and may make the risk manager's job more difficult and more expensive. A better strategy, option-inclusive delta hedging, is one that combines the ease of our first example, where mandatory Fannie Mae MBSs are sold, and the efficiency of our second example, where capital market options are purchased.

Mechanics of Delta Hedging

We can create an almost "riskless hedge" through the purchase of a call option and the sale of its underlying security. The performance of these two trades executed in concert will closely replicate the theoretical payoff of the lock option given away by the originator. In fact, the purchase of the call and sale of the underlying security produce a performance profile similar to that of a put option.

As discussed earlier, an option's delta is constantly changing with movements in the price of the underlying security. This automatically adjusting delta is the primary advantage of using the option-inclusive delta hedging strategy; it allows you to construct a hedge that, independently of additional trading or manipulation, can adjust its delta to mirror the theoretical change in the delta of the pipeline. For example, assume that our risk manager initiated his hedge by shorting $10 million of Fannie Mae 7.0% securities and purchasing $10 million of at-the-money calls expiring in 45 days. Recall that when an option is purchased at the money, with time remaining to expiration, it has a delta of 0.5. As Figure 2-10 shows, when this call option is purchased and the underlying asset is sold short, the combination has the effect of creating a synthetic put option.

FIGURE 2-10
Creating a Synthetic Put

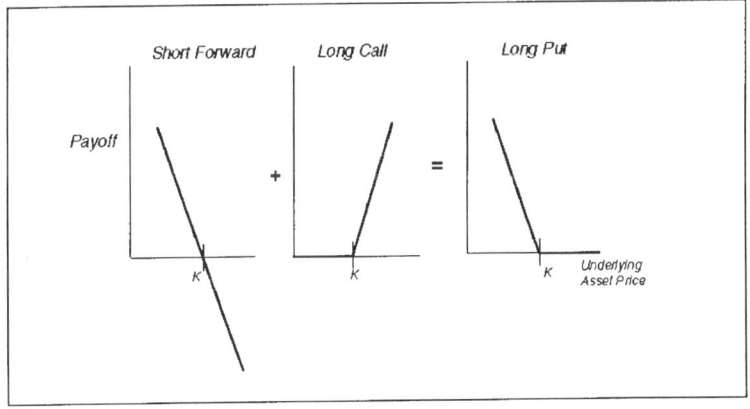

Example A:

At initiation of hedge:
- Rate-locked $10 million mortgage commitments, 45-day locks, at the money (that is, long the market). Hedge value

is: + $5 million. (Recall that rate commitments are simply put options that have a delta of 0.5 at the time of commitment: $10 million ' 0.5 delta = $5 million.)
- Sold $10 million of Fannie Mae 7% = $10 million of mandatory coverage (that is, short the market). Hedge value is: -$10 million.
- Bought $10 million of Fannie Mae 7% Call at the market with a 0.5 delta (that is, long the market). Hedge value is: + $5 million.

Position Summary:

Pipeline:	+$5 million)	($10 million x 0.5 delta)
Fannie Mae 7% MBS:	- $10 million	(Sold $10 million short)
Fannie Mae 7% Call:	+ $5 million	($10 million x 0.5 delta)
Net Hedged Position:	$0.00 million	(Flat the market)
Net Hedge Delta (Hedge Ratio):	0.5% of pipeline covered	

In this example, we are essentially at the beginning of a process that may or may not result in a mortgagor exercising his rate lock option and closing his loan. At this stage of the rate lock's life, most risk managers would agree that the probability of it closing successfully is approximately 50 percent. Therefore, it is intuitively satisfying to know that the delta of our pipeline, at this point, is approximately 0.5, as is the delta of our hedge.

Example B:

The mortgage market has rallied and Fannie Mae 7% MBSs are now trading at 102.

The pipeline, a series of originator-written put options, is now out of the money by 2 points. Consequently, the pipeline delta now falls to 0.076, as calculated using Goldman Sachs' proprietary option-pricing model.

The Fannie Mae 7% MBS that we sold short at 100 now has a 2 point loss. The Fannie Mae 7% call, however, has increased in value to approximately 22/32nds, and the delta of the option has also increased accordingly to approximately 0.912.

Position Summary:
Pipeline: + $0.76 million   ($10 million x 0.076 delta)
Fannie Mae 7% MBS: - $10 million   (Sold $10 million short)
Fannie Mae 7% Call: + $9.12 million   ($10 million x 0.912 delta)
Net Hedge Position: - $0.88 million   (-$10 million + $9.12 million)
Net Hedge Delta: - 0.088% of pipeline covered
(Hedge Ratio)

In this example, we see that the market has significantly rallied, and therefore the likelihood of our rate locks closing has declined in a commensurate fashion. Further, we see that the delta of our pipeline has decreased to reflect the out-of-the-money nature of the put options the institution wrote to the mortgagors. The effective coverage ratio of our hedges has declined as well, as measured by the declining delta. Notice that our hedges automatically reduce their coverage without any intervention from the risk manager.

Example C:

The mortgage market has deteriorated and Fannie Mae 7% MBSs are now trading at 98.

The pipeline is now in the money by 2 points. Consequently, the pipeline delta has increased to 0.955, as again calculated using Goldman Sachs' proprietary option-pricing model.

The Fannie Mae 7% MBS that we sold short at 100 now has a 2 point gain. The Fannie Mae 7% call, however, has decreased in value to approximately 1/32nd, and the delta of the option has also decreased accordingly to approximately 0.041.

Position Summary:
Pipeline: + $9.55 million   ($10 million x 0.955 delta)
Fannie Mae 7% MBS: - $10 million   (Sold $10 million short)
Fannie Mae 7% Call: $0.41 million   ($10 million x 0.041 delta)
Net Hedge Position: - $9.59 million   (-$10 million + $0.41
                                           million short the market)
Net Hedge Delta: - 0.959% of pipeline covered
(Hedge Ratio)

Example C demonstrates how the interaction of the short MBS and the long call automatically adjusts the coverage ratio. This increases the effective hedge percentage as the market deteriorates and more of the pipeline's loans are coming into the money and are therefore more likely to close.

The preceding examples show the dynamic nature of an option's delta and how it can be applied to pipeline hedging. To summarize the strategy: As the market fluctuates, the delta of an option also fluctuates. The option delta is both an effective hedge ratio and an approximation for the likelihood that an option is going to be exercised (or the likelihood that a loan closes). For this reason, we can construct a pipeline hedge using long options and short mandatories (such as MBSs) that automatically adjust their effective percentage of coverage, or hedge ratio, as the market fluctuates. with little or no intervention from the risk manager.

These examples are a bit extreme, as they utilize a strategy of covering the pipeline with 100% of both calls and mandatories. In reality, most risk managers would use a mix of both instruments to craft an appropriate coverage delta and minimize transaction costs. The examples do serve to demonstrate the manner in which a synthetic put can be utilized to produce a self-adjusting pipeline hedge.

Rebalancing the Option-Inclusive Delta Hedge

Typically, risk managers will remain free from rebalancing their option-inclusive delta hedge until such time as more specific information regarding the status of the individual loans becomes available. Once risk managers know that specific loans have requested closing documents or have fallen out of the pipeline, they can modify the hedge.

The primary reason for rebalancing is to limit the amount of call options and mandatories incorporated in the hedge. Options are like ice cubes because they decay with the passage of time (all other things being equal) as the graph in Figure 2-11 shows. This decay results from the option losing a key component of its value: the time remaining to expiration. Consequently, the longer an institution owns an option, the more value is consumed as time passes (all other variables remaining the same).

Therefore, if risk managers know that specific loans are going to close (or not), they can lift the part of the hedge that is

FIGURE 2-11

Time Decay of an at-the-Money Call Option
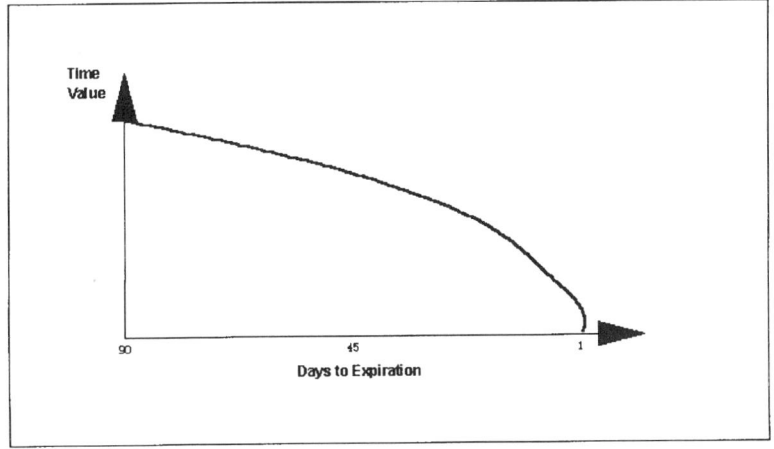

no longer needed. For example, they can buy back the MBS short and sell out the call for those loans that have fallen out of the pipeline. Another alternative is to sell the call on those loans that are definitely going to close and then deliver them into the forward MBS trade.

The ease of rebalancing this hedge strategy to reflect changes in the pipeline is a significant reason why option-inclusive delta hedging has become a popular pipeline hedging technique. In our preceding examples, we have chosen to use synthetic put options in order to include the actual delivery of product, through the MBS sale, as an integral part of the hedge. The end economics of using long puts as the primary hedge vehicle, instead of synthetic puts, will be the same. However, the overriding objective when adjusting an option-inclusive delta hedge is to conserve the time value of the options you own. Options can be very expensive. Consequently, sophisticated risk managers buy options only when necessary and sell them back as soon as their utility is exhausted.

Replicating an Option with Traditional Delta Hedging

During periods of high volatility and therefore expensive option premiums, many delta hedgers will try to replicate the performance of an option's delta through an active and dynamic hedging strategy by exclusively utilizing forward MBS sales. As a convenient example, let's return to the point in the loan application process where we first decide to hedge our pipeline. Initially, we know that the delta on our pipeline is approximately 0.5 because the applications are brand new. Consequently, a traditional delta hedger would begin the hedging process by selling 50% of the pipeline forward in the form of mandatory commitments using the Fannie Mae 7% MBS. This initial hedge would create a coverage ratio of 0.5 which approximates the pipeline delta.

As time progresses and the market cycles higher and lower, the dynamic delta hedger will regularly recalculate the pipeline delta and adjust the coverage ratio to reflect any changes.

Let's go back to our examples from above where $10 million of rate locks are committed, and at initiation, the risk manager sells forward 50% of the rate locks. If the market were to immediately rally two points (a far-fetched example but suitable for our purpose here), the likelihood of our pipeline closing would decline significantly (as the rate locks are now out of the money), and the pipeline delta would fall to 0.076. Consequently, the risk manager would repurchase a sufficient quantity of forward MBS sales at this higher market level to reduce the short position to $0.76 million. This position reduction will decrease the coverage ratio to a level that approximates the new delta of the pipeline.

Conversely, if the market were to immediately decline by two points (again a bit far-fetched), the likelihood of the rate locks closing would increase because all the commitments are now in the money. Accordingly, the pipeline delta would increase to 0.959. To remain properly delta hedged, or "delta neutral," the risk manager must sell more MBSs at this lower market level to bring the coverage ratio approximately equal to the new delta.

Interestingly, if the volatility level implied by the high option prices should equal actual volatility, the costs that arise from buying back hedges when the market has rallied and selling additional hedges when the market has deteriorated are likely to equal or exceed the cost of the expensive option the risk manager is attempting to replicate. This is because of transaction costs, such as the bid/ask spread.)

In summary, as the market continues to cycle, delta hedging risk managers must continually adjust their coverage ratios to reflect their pipeline's changing delta and any specific loan closings or fallout information that becomes available.

A Delta Hedging Caveat

The paradox of using a pure delta hedging strategy is that most often risk managers will utilize this strategy to replicate the performance of an option and its delta when implied price volatility is high and option premiums appear expensive. Unfortunately, though, high volatility should be a warning: Along with high volatility comes exaggerated short-term price moves and greater risk of a particularly volatile market pattern, called a *whipsaw*. Whipsaws are exaggerated market moves in one direction that are followed shortly thereafter by equally extreme moves in the opposite direction. For delta hedgers, volatile markets and whipsaw patterns equate to a high level of trading and retrading the hedge positions in order to regularly rebalance coverage ratios to better reflect the constantly changing deltas of their pipelines. Risk managers should buy options rather than incur additional risk by attempting to trade themselves out of a volatile market.

In volatile markets, some delta hedgers will try to restrict their trading and position rebalancing by setting limits or market levels that must be penetrated before they will execute a trade. These limitations on trading, often called *market collars*, do instill some additional discipline and strategy on risk managers. However, they actually expose risk managers to even greater risk of loss should the market continue in one direction when a restricted hedge has not been adjusted.

Observations of a Wall Street Dealer

My group of colleagues specializes in covering the mortgage origination industry, so we regularly observe the manner in which many institutions define their risk management goals, design policies to implement their goals and choose what hedges they ultimately execute. With regard to their risk management programs, we can generally separate the institutions into three broad categories: technologically advanced risk managers, market speculators and pipeline hedgers.

Improve Data to Ensure Effective Hedging
The critical element that consistently separates these three groups is information — the quality, timeliness and depth of the information they receive about the loans contained in their pipelines. Pipeline information is the most important determinant of which institutions will have successful risk managers and successful risk management programs.

Identify the Risk
The most effective risk managers have a strong understanding of the specific loan and market characteristics that constitute the risk of their pipeline. Typically, the most successful risk managers know where the individual loans were originated — retail, wholesale or correspondent — and how each origination channel has performed in getting locked loans to close during periods of adversity. These risk managers will generally hedge each origination channel in a different manner or to a different degree. This is because retail originated loans tend to have the highest probability of closing, above what would be expected based solely on their option delta; correspondent originations, followed by wholesale originations, tend to have a much lower probability of closing. In the lexicon of risk managers, this loan closing rate, as a percentage of the pipeline, is generally referred to as the "pull-through rate." In an ideal hedging environment, the delta of the pipeline, the coverage ratio of their hedges, and the pull-through rate of all loans in the pipeline would be equal.

The next critical element that successful risk managers often analyze when determining how to hedge their pipeline — and to what degree — is the loan purpose. For example, purchase loans tend to benefit from the mortgagor's emotion of purchasing a new home and the accompanying pressure from the seller and real estate agents to close the deal as soon as possible. This potent combination of emotion and desire typically motivates new mortgagors to enthusiastically process their loan applications and close them quickly in accordance with their specified terms. On the other hand, refinance loans tend to be very sensitive to changes in the interest rate market and generally close less frequently than their deltas would imply. This again makes sense intuitively, as there is little emotion or outside pressure (other than the desire to reduce monthly expenses) to motivate the refinancing mortgagor to close on time and at the contracted rate.

Another significant component of successful hedging programs is the ability to analyze the pipeline as a function of the lock periods granted individual loans. Institutions with limited risk management costs tend to have much shorter lock periods than do institutions that provide long-dated commitments. Long-dated commitments, by virtue of their more complex nature and greater expense to hedge, have a tendency to compound the usual pipeline risks by distracting risk managers and consuming their traditionally limited resources.

Hedge the Risk

It appears that successful institutions commit a great amount of time and capital to developing the systems and management tools necessary for identifying the risks embedded in their pipelines. They then try to hedge these risks as simply and inexpensively as possible. In contrast, less successful institutions tend to commit little time and capital to their systems and therefore spend an inordinate amount of time and effort trying to understand the smallest details of each interest rate market event rather than focusing on their pipelines. While it is certainly important for risk managers to be aware of market-moving events and for them to have an understanding of how their pipelines will react, this seems to be subordinate to understanding and hedging the risks involved.

We have further observed that consistently successful risk managers stratify their pipelines by loan characteristics (as discussed earlier), and then group the loans based on their likelihood of closing. This final aggregation is predicated upon the delta of each stratum and typically results in three separate groups of loans. Each group is hedged in a different manner and to a different degree. The first group includes loans that have great certainty of timely, as-committed closure. Generally, this group comprises retail-originated purchase loans with lock periods of less than 45 days, where the mortgagor has agreed to pay discount points. Risk managers generally expect 85% to 90% of these loans to close and therefore hedge them with a significant amount of MBS mandatories. The mandatories usually work well because there is less "optionality" with these loan locks than with others.

The next group of loans is a mixture of wholesale and correspondent production, with a large concentration of refinances. These tend to have longer-dated locks and fewer discount points attached to them than do the loans in our first group. Consequently, this second group is trickier to hedge because it has more "optionality" than the first group. It is also usually the group where capital market options, such as the synthetic put or long puts, are used in concert with MBS forwards.

The last group comprises those loans over which the risk manager has the least control and therefore the least confidence in their closing. This group usually has a significant concentration of refinance loans with cash out and high loan-to-value ratios. Further, this group is usually dominated by wholesale originations with long-term rate locks that are often associated with no-fee refinance programs. Risk managers view this group of loans as the most problematic because they contain the most "optionality"; these mortgagors close their loans only when the economics of doing so are optimal.

Consequently, risk managers typically utilize a significant amount of options and few (or no) MBS forwards to hedge this group. Often, the options utilized are out-of-the-money puts or synthetic puts struck out of the money. However, both methods are predicated upon determining and regularly monitoring the delta of the group and adjusting the coverage ratio as necessary. This group is the most closely scrutinized of the three, as it invariably closes "en masse" when it is most advantageous for the mortgagor and least advantageous for the risk manager.

Administrative Methods for Hedging

An increasingly popular method of pipeline hedging is the administrative hedge. The idea is to institute a compensation program that rewards loan officers and correspondents for the quality of loans they produce and for the risk characteristics of the rate locks that their clients select. For example, a loan officer may receive a maximum commission of 75 basis points (bp) of the loan amount if the mortgagor chooses to eschew a rate lock and float with the market until the loan closes. On the other hand, if the mortgagor chooses a long-term rate lock, say 90 days, and is very slow in providing the necessary credit information and documentation to process the loan successfully, then the loan officer would receive only a small commission of 25 bp or so. The goal of this program is to shift as much of the market and processing risks as possible onto the mortgagor.

Another popular administrative risk management program involves refunding fees to mortgagors upon the successful closing of their loans. In those areas where the origination market will allow the collection of an up-front lock-in fee, many institutions have begun using the potential return of such fees as a vehicle for keeping the mortgagor involved in the loan underwriting process and discouraging the routine selection of rate locks from those mortgagors who may not be serious about closing.

3

Real-World Secondary Marketing Strategies

Douglas D. Foster, Chief Operating Officer
Fidelity National Mortgage Corporation

As director of secondary marketing for Cooperstown Mortgage Company, Abby Doubleday believes her effectiveness is directly related to how well she is able to combine a variety of disciplines into one cohesive marketing strategy. Not only does she need to be knowledgeable in all facets of the mortgage business — loan origination, processing, underwriting and closing — but she must combine this knowledge with a keen understanding of fixed-income investments, economics and marketing. She knows that there is no single source she can rely on for direction. She has to make up the rules as she goes along.

Abby and Cooperstown Mortgage are, of course, fictional, but the challenges they face are real-life examples of those encountered by many medium- to medium-large mortgage banking enterprises today. In fact, the combined experience of several current secondary marketing managers has been used to create Abby's reasoning and decision-making process.

The strategic and operating decisions made by Abby are those she believes to be right for her and her company; these examples are not intended to serve as rules for decision making. Just as all firms have their own unique corporate blueprint, so too must all secondary marketing managers find what works best for their own circumstances. These "real world" strategies are meant to provide helpful ideas that can be adapted accordingly.

Marketing Policy and Objective

Cooperstown's marketing objective is to accurately measure, evaluate and mitigate the risk inherent in the process of originating mortgage loans, while effectively managing the sale and delivery of such loans to permanent investors. The most difficult risk to manage in this process is that of making forward price commitments to mortgage applicants whose decision to close may be affected by the subsequent movement of interest rates.

This objective is clearly stated in Cooperstown's written marketing policy guide, which has been approved by the board of directors. Along with the statement of objective, the guide sets forth the following:

- Acceptable hedging practices
- Authorized types of hedge instruments
- Accounting and mark-to-market requirements
- Trading authorities and limitations
- Maximum allowable interest rate risk exposure
- Maximum allowable dealer exposure

The marketing policy requires that a marketing committee, consisting of members of senior management, meet on a regular basis to monitor the activities of the marketing department and make specific recommendations when appropriate.

Cooperstown's marketing objective is consistent with that of most mortgage bankers: Its primary focus is on risk management. Abby is herself aligned with this focus. Her financial background and education has led her to believe that it is extremely difficult, if not impossible, to consistently call the market. She reasons that the only ones who profit in the long run from the speculative mentality are those who are lucky and the brokers. She and senior management are in complete agreement that the fortunes of Cooperstown Mortgage will depend upon how well it performs in its core business — mortgage lending and servicing — and not on the market.

That being said, Abby will be very quick to point out that in many ways the secondary mortgage market is inefficient, and that arbitrage opportunities exist. She knows that she can add real value to the firm by using her skills to exploit these opportunities without putting the firm at undue risk. She wisely does not confuse a conservative risk management philosophy with closed-mindedness and paralysis.

But Abby also understands that exploitation of market opportunities never includes breaking the commitments she has made. For example, she would never pull a lock she has committed to a best efforts delivery to one investor and deliver the loan to another at a better price because the market has improved. She knows that in the long run the strength of her relationships with her investors will be important to Cooperstown's success. She believes that short-run profit is never justified at the expense of long-term relationships.

Her reconciliation of a conservative risk management philosophy and a market-opportunistic approach is what sets her apart from many mortgage bankers. Many in the industry pair a focus on risk management with a goal of break-even financial performance. Abby sets her sights higher, believing that prudence means exercising good judgment with total awareness.

Cooperstown's Hedge Strategy

Abby's risk management focus is in hedging the firm's bottom line (profit and loss, or P&L), not in matching contract amounts between the long and short positions. Her goal is to get risk protection across a wide range of interest rate fluctuations at the lowest possible cost. She is trying to construct a hedge with a P&L profile that most closely matches, in the opposite direction, that of the position created through the mortgage origination process. She knows that the hedge has a cost and that her job is to minimize it.

Pipeline Coverage: Mandatory/Optional Mix

Abby uses a combination of different types of both forward mandatory commitments and options in her hedge strategy. Her decision of how much mandatory and how much optional coverage to use is based on the characteristics of her pipeline. For closed loans — and for a percentage of unclosed loans that she is certain will always close no matter what happens — it makes sense to use mandatory coverage. By doing so, she saves on option premiums. At the same time, there is a percentage of loans that she knows will never close no matter what happens. For those she needs no coverage. What's left is a group of loans for which she simply cannot predict what will happen. For this percentage, she uses optional coverage.

For example, if her pipeline consists of 20% closed loans and another 40% she knows will close under any circumstances, she will be 60% covered with forward mandatories. She also knows that no matter what happens, 20% of her pipeline will never close. She therefore chooses to be 20% covered in options (80% - 60%), as shown in Table 3-1. Next, she must decide which instruments she will use in constructing her hedge.

TABLE 3-1

Optional versus Mandatory Coverage

Status	Mandatory Coverage	Optional Coverage	No Coverage	Totals
Closed	20%			20%
Certain to Close	40%			40%
Uncertain		20%		20%
Certain not to Close			20%	20%
	60%	20%	20%	100%

Mandatory Forward Coverage

For mandatory forward coverage on fixed-rate conforming loans, Abby has a choice between MBS forwards and treasury futures contracts. (For this analysis, we will assume that her intent is to hedge the closed loans until she has enough product to optimize her delivery execution).

If she can sell MBS forwards and fill them with her pipeline, she has no basis risk. Assuming that the market is liquid, MBS forwards will be the best choice. However, the market for some MBS, such as extremely high or low coupons, or *balloons*, is illiquid and therefore likely to be less efficient. If she sells these forward and then cannot deliver the exact amount and type of coupon or loan needed for the MBS, she will likely pay a high bid/ask spread when she pairs off the commitment.

Treasury futures contracts offer the highest degree of liquidity, and therefore the lowest transaction costs, but they do introduce *basis risk*. This is the risk that the observed relationship between the price behavior of the instruments changes such that losses on the instrument being hedged are not completely offset by gains on the hedge instrument.

Abby is aware that some who use these instruments in mortgage hedging will monitor yield spreads between mortgages and treasuries. When spreads appear to be out of balance, they will trade treasuries rather than MBS in an attempt to profit from arbitrage. For example, if the yield spread between treasuries and MBS has widened, these individuals may choose to short treasury futures rather than MBS in hedging their pipelines.

However, in Abby's view, the potential gains from treasury/mortgage arbitrage outweigh the risks; a wide treasury/mortgage spread may simply continue to widen, resulting in losses on the net hedge position. She therefore decides to hedge all of the conforming fixed-rate mandatory long position, including the illiquid mortgages, with liquid MBS forwards, adjusting for differences in duration. She realizes that she is still exposed to some risk (such as a yield-curve shift) but believes that this strategy best meets her risk/return objectives. For jumbo fixed-rate loans, she also uses duration-adjusted conforming MBS as her hedge, but only when she views the spread between MBS and the jumbo whole loan forward market as favoring MBS as the best hedge vehicle (that is, when the spread between MBS and jumbo yields is relatively high). She firmly believes that inefficiencies in the jumbo whole loan market mean that profitable low-risk arbitrage opportunities exist and can be exploited through prudent cross hedging.

Options

For options, Abby has a choice between over-the-counter (OTC) MBS or exchange-traded (CBOT) options on treasury futures contracts. (Note: CBOT stands for Chicago Board of Trade. It is not the only futures exchange used in hedging by mortgage banks; however, it is the futures exchange Abby uses in her decision making). Since the instruments underlying CBOT options are treasury futures contracts, Abby again must consider the basis risk. However, there are different factors to consider here than with mandatory forwards — factors which directly affect the choice of instrument.

These factors are related to the dynamic nature of the pipeline and the need to be concerned not only with the absolute level of option contracts, but also with the *delta* of those contracts. *Delta* is the change in the value of an option relative to the change in the underlying instrument. But first, it is important to understand why you would cover with options at all.

For the three groups of unclosed loans in the pipeline — those that will never close, those that will always close, and those that are uncertain, Abby considers which factors might determine when a loan closes and when it does not. All except one of the reasons why loans will or will not close are fairly constant and predictable over time. Denials, contracts that fall through, holding the "feet to the fire" — the percentages of these occurrences are not likely to change dramatically over a short period of time.

The unpredictable situation is when the decision to close is affected by the subsequent movement of interest rates. While it is possible to predict the percentage of loans for which the decision to close is so affected, it is not possible to know what the decision will be. This is because such decisions are based entirely on future changes in interest rates which cannot be known in advance. For these borrowers, the rate lock is a put option which is more likely to be exercised the closer the price is to being in the money, and more likely to expire the closer to being out of the money. In giving rate locks to borrowers, Cooperstown has offered free put options. Unless Abby covers the risk by taking an offsetting position in options, she has written a "naked" put option subject to unlimited risk.

But an offsetting option position is not accomplished simply by purchasing the right face amount of options. Abby must also be sure that any deterioration in her pipeline value due to the borrowers' rate-lock options is offset by equal improvement in the value of her option hedge. In other words, she cannot cover an in-the-money rate lock with an out-of-the-money put option and expect to come out whole. In essence, she must *delta-match* her rate locks with her option hedge: The change in value of the options making up her hedge must offset the change in value of the pipeline.

Further complicating the matter is the dynamic nature of the pipeline. Cooperstown is constantly taking in new locks as older ones expire or close. To delta-match her option hedge, she must adjust it regularly, which leads Abby back to the question of OTC MBS options versus CBOT options on treasury futures.

Because of the need to regularly adjust optional coverage, liquidity is extremely important. For this, she just can't beat CBOT options. Also, CBOT options trade in as little as $100,000 contracts, versus $1 million minimums for MBS OTC options. She must still contend with basis risk, but her downside on the option contracts is limited to the option premium.

Another significant opportunity with CBOT options is a strategy known as a *synthetic put* (sometimes referred to as a *convexity put*). This involves hedging a high percentage of the pipeline with MBS forward sales, while hedging against pipeline fallout with the simultaneous purchase of CBOT call options. If interest rates rise, Abby can deliver into the MBS forwards and let the calls expire. If rates fall, she will likely have to pair-off a portion of the forwards due to pipeline fallout. However, gains on the call options will offset pair-off costs. In some cases, Cooperstown will even come out with a net profit when rates decline; gains on the call options will more than offset losses from MBS forward pair-offs. As shown in Figure 3-1, this is because the probability of increasing prepayments limits price appreciation on premium MBS (a phenomenon known as *price compression*, or *negative convexity*), while prices on treasury securities appreciate at an increasing rate when interest rates decline (a phenomenon known as *positive convexity*).

Abby believes the advantages of CBOT options outweigh the risks. She uses an option pricing model to run a best execution between CBOT and OTC MBS options, but unless there is a

FIGURE 3-1

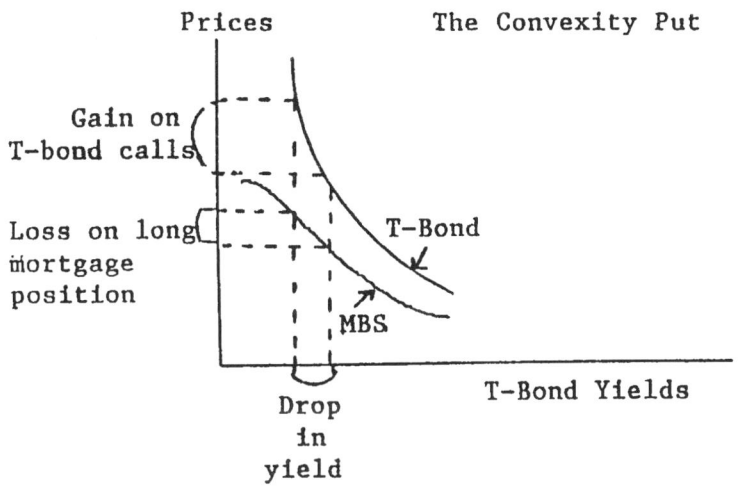

significant pricing discrepancy favoring OTC options, she normally hedges with CBOT options.

Purchase of Options versus the Delta Hedge

Some hedgers, instead of buying options, employ what is known as a *delta-hedge* strategy. A delta hedger, saving on option premiums, replicates optional coverage by constantly adjusting forward coverage to delta-match the pipeline. In a rising-rate market, the delta hedger increases forward coverage to match the increasing delta of the pipeline as locks go further in the money. Conversely, in a falling-rate environment, coverage is reduced as locks fall out of the money.

A delta hedge can be a profitable strategy when actual market volatility is less than that which is implied in actual option premiums. In fact, assuming that the addition of new locks can often be substituted for pair-offs when rates drop, it may even be more profitable in periods of slightly greater volatility, as long as the delta hedger is disciplined in maintaining the "right" level of forward coverage.

Abby prefers the purchased option strategy. She is concerned about the risk of being one step behind a volatile market and being unable to adjust coverage fast enough to avoid big losses. She is also concerned about high transactions (bid/ask) costs involved in constantly trading in and out of forward coverage. Finally, she likes the "self-adjusting" nature of purchased options. She reasons that her job is stressful enough without the constant worry of adjusting coverage levels. Although option levels must be adjusted regularly, the option-purchase strategy does not require as intense a level of management as the delta hedge.

Fallout Analysis

Knowing that the key to an effective hedge strategy is understanding fallout, Abby places great value on having a system capable of providing her with meaningful fallout reporting. The most significant component of her hedge cost is options expense. The amount she must spend on options is entirely dependent on the efficiency with which the borrowers' "free put" is utilized. Thus, the more accurate she can be in predicting the market sensitivity of her pipeline, the better her chances of minimizing her hedge cost. She knows that there are several variables which can be directly correlated with efficient use of the free put, including:

- Refinance versus new purchase
- Source of business (wholesale versus retail)
- Rate lock period
- Type of loan

- Locked price relative to market price
- Market volatility
- Stage of processing

Making the task more difficult is that many of these factors are, to varying degrees, interrelated. For example, a loan that is one percent in price above current market is more likely to close above market (inefficiently) if it has already been approved and sent to the closing agent and if it's a purchase loan rather than a refinance (refi) loan.

To the extent that Abby can predict the percentage of efficient closings, she saves money. Over the long term, if she's consistently wrong in either direction, it will cost her money. In evaluating risk management software, Abby was careful to select a system that could provide her with both historical and predictive fallout modeling capability. She knew it would do little good to have one without the other. The predictive modeling also had to be build into the sensitivity or *rate shock analysis* (a report showing net hedge results given significant movements upward and downward in interest rates), since this is the report she uses in deciding how much and what type of hedge to construct.

Cooperstown's Delivery Strategy

For Cooperstown, the sales decision is a separate one from the hedge decision. Even though the hedge decision will sometimes dictate how the loan will be sold, the two decisions are based on different information. The hedge decision is based on lowest cost risk management, while the sales decision is based on best execution. Only when the lowest cost risk management instrument also represents the best sales execution do the two become the same. When the two are different, this is a cross hedge.

Often however, the hedge and delivery vehicle are the same. Part of the cost of the hedge is the cost of unwinding it, represented by the bid/ask spread. Thus, Abby will only decide to cross hedge when the cost of using the cross hedge instrument is lower than the deliverable instrument by at least the bid/ask spread.

Fannie Mae/Freddie Mac Master Commitments

For the sale of conforming fixed-rate loans, Abby periodically negotiates master commitments with both Fannie Mae and Freddie Mac. The master commitment sets forth the terms under which Cooperstown may deliver loans to the two agencies over the term of the commitment (usually about six months). The terms include acceptable loan types, variances to standard lending guidelines, the servicing option selected, guarantor fees on MBS and guarantor fee buy up/buy down grids.

Virtually all of the terms of the master agreement are negotiable, and because Abby is dealing with the majority of her loan production over the next six months, she works hard to negotiate the best deal possible. For example, on a $1 billion master, a 1 bp difference in guarantee fee is worth nearly $1/2 million to Cooperstown's bottom line. Abby has trouble understanding why mortgage bankers would accept what they were offered without working hard to negotiate a better deal. Even a 1 bp guarantor fee difference on a deal of $50 million is worth over $24,000.

Abby uses a best execution model developed by an outside software vendor to compare guarantor fees under different servicing options offered by Fannie Mae and Freddie Mac. She is looking for the servicing option that will maximize corporate profits given expected prepayments, float utilization and the expected slope of the yield curve. It is very important to Abby that she maintain good relationships with both secondary market agencies. She knows that to do so she must deliver quality products and avoid alienating the agencies. In the long run, a damaged relationship with either agency will impair her ability to use competition between them to get the best deal.

Servicing Retained versus Released

Like most mortgage bankers, Cooperstown maintains a large servicing portfolio to help balance it's financial position. When interest rates rise and production slows down, a slowing of prepayments on the servicing portfolio keeps servicing revenues high. When rates fall, profits from increased production offset lost value due to higher runoff.

Cooperstown believes that the market for loan servicing is inefficient and therefore offers profit opportunity. The company has a servicing acquisition group that buys and sells servicing according to it's return objectives and capacity constraints.

Similarly, Abby's decision to sell loans with servicing retained or released is one of best execution, pure and simple. If she is able to sell the servicing at a higher price than that offered her by the acquisition group, she will do so. The acquisition group is actually treated as just another investor. As such, the group is free to shop the servicing market for the best deals it can find. The net result is that the company profits from lower investment in the servicing asset and/or higher production revenues.

Fixed-Rate Conforming Loans

Abby uses a spreadsheet-based best execution model to arrive at the best all-in price for delivery of conforming loans. The model compares MBS and whole loan pricing, buy up/buy down fees, guarantee fees, excess servicing values, SRPs (including those from the loan acquisition group), warehouse spreads, funding fees and other fees related to specific loan attributes such as geographic location, loan-to-value ratio (LTV) and occupancy.

The model features live pricing feeds from her financial information sources, so it is always up-to-date.

Each loan is tested against the model prior to disposition. If the cost of pairing out of an unfilled deliverable hedge commitment is less than the additional benefit of an alternative delivery, the commitment is fully or partially paired out and the loan delivered to its best execution.

Today, many experts feel that the mortgage business is rapidly becoming a commodity business. To the extent this happens, Abby reasons, the most successful companies will be the lowest-cost producers. The continuous form of best execution modeling ensures that Abby is always getting the very best price the market has to offer. This in turn helps Cooperstown to be a low-cost producer.

Jumbo Loans

Abby looked into jumbo securitization but concluded that her current volume is not sufficient to make it a profitable alternative. Even so, she knows that the larger the pool of closed loans she can accumulate, the greater her chances for a pickup in execution over the posted prices of some of the jumbo investors.

For pricing purposes, Abby runs a daily best execution between several large jumbo investors. For hedging and delivery purposes, she tracks the price spread between conforming MBS and jumbo best execution because the market for fixed-rate jumbo loans is less efficient than the conforming market. Therefore, unless the price spread is unusually tight, she will normally hedge jumbos with MBS until she has a pool of at least $5 million. She then stratifies the pool in such a way as to again enhance the overall execution. Then, when she has accumulated the closed loans and the spread is favorable, she puts the loans out for bid with eligible investors.

Conclusion

First and foremost, Abby sees herself as a risk manager. In her eyes, a conservative approach to risk does not mean having blinders on when it comes to the exploitation of market opportunities. She takes pride in her ability to add significant value to the firm by applying the skills she has developed. However, she tempers this pride with the humility of knowing that the game is always changing and there will always be new rules to make up.

4

An Analysis of Popular Hedging Strategies

Madeline Johnson-Oler, Secondary Marketing Consultant
Donald R. Palumbo, Senior Secondary Marketing Consultant
Mortgage Dynamics, Inc.

"I'm a delta hedger..."
"I'm a cross hedger..."
"I'm a proponent of core mandatory coverage..."

Assemble a group of secondary marketing managers and this is what you will hear proclaimed proudly. Yet, if you look at the substance behind their statements, you will find that many managers are leaving money on the table and exposing their companies to potential losses and unnecessary costs.

This chapter examines the risks and benefits of some of the most popular hedging strategies over the full range of interest rate and market conditions that secondary marketing managers have faced in the 1990s. It tests the exclusive use of each strategy under various market conditions and concludes with what the authors consider to be the optimum tandem use of strategies. Our mission is to shed some objective light on using these strategies while adhering to what should be every secondary marketing manager's goal: to maximize net proceeds and simultaneously minimize and control risk.

An Overview of Popular Hedging Strategies

Secondary marketing managers typically select one of three risk management strategies:

- Extensive use of nondeliverable crosshedge instruments such as futures and options on futures
- Delta hedging
- Hedging using deliverable instruments such as mandatory forwards and options on MBS securities

In our experience as management consultants, we have seen each of these strategies in operation under a wide range of market conditions. Each has its strengths and weaknesses, and each works best under certain market conditions. No single strategy consistently outperforms the others under all market conditions.

Implications of Hedging
Before selecting a hedging approach, it is critical for senior management to understand the implications of hedging risk and how day-to-day secondary marketing hedging strategies support or violate management's profit maximization and risk minimization objectives. More frequently than not, we find that the actual hedging strategies utilized are not in line with the company's overall risk management objectives and policies.

Unfortunately, there is no single instrument or strategy that is always effective and efficient no matter what the market scenario. To successfully hedge risk over time, managers must proactively develop dynamic hedging strategies that effectively perform in changing market conditions.

To perfect a dynamic hedging strategy, managers must know when it is appropriate to modify existing strategies based on a number of factors, including changes in current market scenarios, agency pricing and products, production, historical fallout analysis, competitiveness and product menus.

They must monitor these factors constantly and make adjustments to offset changes in the market as necessary.

Secondary marketing managers may devise several different strategies to minimize hedging risk. These strategies may employ:

- Forward mandatory sales based on core mandatory coverage requirements
- Delta hedging
- Cross hedging with exchange-listed futures and options
- OTC options on MBSs

Most senior managers desire risk management plans that yield consistent results. The key to successfully achieving this goal is to employ a strategy which maintains deliverability and optionality. For example, cross-hedging mortgages with futures was commonplace in the mid-1980s. However, when the basis widened between the hedge vehicle and the underlying delivery instrument, many companies suffered tremendous losses due to the inconsistent relationship between the hedge vehicle and the delivery instrument. These cross hedges did not have deliverability or optionality, and therefore, they failed to produce a consistent result.

Cross Hedging
Some secondary marketing operations use cross-hedging strategies for their entire mortgage pipeline, and others cross hedge only the nonconforming pipeline. Many companies that choose to retain servicing on nonconforming production will cross hedge this portion of the pipeline with MBS forwards, Treasury futures or exchange-listed options. Since these instruments are not a perfect match for all mortgages in a pipeline, such a strategy presents considerable basis risk that must be managed properly.

Futures transactions carry risks associated with the company's ability to meet margin-call requirements as the instruments are marked to market. If the relationship between mortgages and options on futures remains the same, substantial profits would be realized in a rallying market and moderate losses would be incurred in a worsening market.

Some companies have employed complex strategies designed to generate windfall profits. However, a prudent secondary marketing corporate hedging policy should clearly state that speculating for profits is not allowed. It also should set forth limitations on transaction vehicles and dollar amounts outstanding and establish predefined exit parameters. In the 1980s, many companies discovered the risks associated with speculative trading in the futures market. In some cases, these companies seriously impaired their parent institutions.

Since all cross hedges are nondeliverable, it is essential to constantly monitor the basis and know the correct beta correlation for the underlying instruments. Some companies are effectively using cross-hedging strategies to hedge their jumbo pipeline. Others find that the costs associated with certain nondeliverable instruments on agency products outweigh the benefits.

Cross hedging with nondeliverable instruments on agency products may limit the best execution opportunities currently available with deliverable instruments. Since market opportunities change on a daily basis, it is important for the trader to have the flexibility to improve the value of the hedge at any opportune time during the life of the hedge. By employing best execution on deliverable instruments on a daily basis, the trader can analyze coupon and agency swap opportunities in the MBS market and improve net proceeds, risk free. (An example of an agency/coupon swap is presented in Appendix 4-1 at the end of this chapter.) It can be difficult and costly to execute these trades for nondeliverable instruments on a daily basis as the original hedge must be lifted. This frequently involves pair-off expenses. In addition, such instruments do not provide the trader with delivery variance.

Delta Hedging
Another strategy in the secondary marketing manager's hedging alternatives is or *delta hedging*, which focuses on the analysis of duration and option characteristics. *Option delta* is the degree to which the option price changes given a change in the price of the underlying security. Delta hedging tries to match the delta of a mortgage position with the delta of a hedge position such that price movements will offset each other. The underlying hedge theory requires coverage only for a portion of the pipeline that will close at a loss to the lender.

The risk exposure is measured as the probability that the loans are at the money or in the money when the rate lock expires. This type of approach frequently yields tremendous gains in a falling rate environment. This is due, in some part, to the underlying theory that when rates fall, efficient borrowers will exercise their right to walk away from the rate lock. Since not all borrowers are efficient, profits can be derived in a falling rate environment as these loans are eventually sold at higher market prices. Most traders, however, establish company-specific fallout price-elasticity tables to analyze the expected level of pull-through associated with each product type, rather than assuming perfect borrower efficiency.

Volatile Markets
A delta hedging strategy combined with the assumption of perfect borrower efficiency often allows the trader to have a substantial long pipeline position in a falling rate environment. This produces large gains on the loans that eventually close.

Some companies utilize a modified delta approach to lessen the effects of wide increases and decreases in coverage ratios and to adhere to the minimum and maximum levels of coverage mandated by corporate policies. Such a strategy is vulnerable to rapidly alternating increases and decreases in interest rates — zig-zag market patterns. Coverage in this type of market may be added and then paired off at losses or may be paired off and then re-established at lower levels.

If we were able to predict the direction of interest rates, the delta hedging strategy would seem to be the logical approach to take in a falling rate environment. This type of strategy yielded substantial profits for many lenders during the 1991 to 1993 rally. Taking a look back over the last 10 years, however, the market rallied over 100 bp in yield only two times within a typical 60-day lock period.

To see if this approach would work well in a sideways market or a market with wide swings in both directions, let's review the historical occurrence of interest rate changes during a typical 60-day period during the 1992 to 1994 time period. According to the Chicago Board of Trade in its 1994 publication, *Concepts and Applications*, rates increased or decreased by 25 bp in yield 82% of the time, and by 50 bp 39% of the time. These sharp movements in the market during the 60-day lock period would dictate constant adjustments to coverage percentages and would leave the company exposed to erratic gains and losses.

As consultants, one of the first items we review in a secondary marketing department is risk management performance results and consistency of earnings. Wide swings in month-to-month gains or losses on sales raise questions about the risk manager's effectiveness. Furthermore, dramatic monthly profit and loss swings tend to be problematic for banks and other companies which require stable and consistent results.

Mandatory Forwards and Options
One of the most commonly used strategies, based on the number of companies using it, is the mandatory forward sale of MBS securities combined with some level of OTC options.

By simply utilizing a percentage of core mandatory forward coverage based on pipeline pull-through assumptions, the trader can inexpensively cover the pipeline for the duration of the lock period. Relying entirely on mandatory forwards, however, while seemingly an easy and cheap method of hedging, falls short of the risk manager's goal because of the variability of pipeline fallout. For this strategy to be effective, companies must perform routine historical fallout analysis by loan characteristics and price sensitivity.

Frequently, the analysis being performed does not quantify all of the factors properly, and a global approach must be taken to determine pull-through percentages. Incorrectly assessing the level of coverage in a falling rate environment can cause the lender to be short, creating pair-off risks and losses. These losses can be severe, especially during periods of sharp market rallies. During late 1992 and early 1993, for example, lenders experienced tremendous pair-off losses as a result of the significant decline in interest rates. Conversely, during late 1993 and early 1994, many lenders experienced losses as a result of being undercovered when interest rates rose.

To come closer to the optimum level of coverage needed to combat risk in differing interest rate scenarios, successful lenders have implemented a more refined approach. This strategy involves the use of core mandatory coverage in combination with optional coverage. In addition, security delivery tolerance can be utilized as well. This allows the trader to have more flexibility in making minor modifications to coverage levels based on market conditions and fallout analysis. It is impossible to correctly predict the direction of the market and, subsequently, the exact amount of coverage. The trader must begin by establishing a starting point for the most appropriate percentage of mandatory coverage based on historical experience and fallout analysis.

Traders who are familiar with their pipelines, products, and fallout history can adequately determine the appropriate level of mandatory coverage. They must evaluate their coverage levels against market conditions, coupon and agency spreads, product mix and fallout analysis on a routine basis. Then, they can use optional coverage and delivery tolerances to offset any changes in market conditions that would require subsequent coverage changes. This strategy adheres to a more consistent approach to risk management as it provides deliverability both on a mandatory and optional basis. Therefore, the hedge is not subject to basis risk, and pair-off risks can be minimized.

Options
OTC options, as well as exchange-listed options, are used by most traders at some point in the hedging process. OTC options are frequently more expensive on a relative basis than exchange-listed options due to the negotiated nature of the OTC market versus the efficiency of an exchange-listed market. They can be purchased either at the money or slightly out of the money and can be a straight or split-fee structure. Exchange-listed options appear to be more efficiently traded than OTC options, but do not provide deliverability or delivery tolerance. Exchange-listed options expose the hedge to basis changes and, therefore, risk.

One effective use of options occurs just after the market rallies and has leveled off for several days. At that point, the trader increases the levels of mandatory coverage and purchases call options. This mitigates the effects of fallout if the rally resumes. At the same time, the high levels of mandatory coverage can minimize losses if the market suddenly deteriorates.

The use of put options can help cover the part of the pipeline that closes only when rates rise. This strategy uses a lower percentage of mandatory coverage combined with put options.

Measuring the Impact of Volatility
A preferred method of measuring the effectiveness of any particular hedging strategy is to generate a "rate shock" report. This report would measure the effect of interest rate movements and corresponding pull-through percentages against the current hedge position. However, it is critical to design the report such that incremental movements are depicted as actual yield curve changes instead of as linear shifts in interest rates.

Successful hedging strategies will achieve three goals:

1. They will maximize the use of deliverable short positions in combination with various options.
2. They will minimize risks and maximize proceeds in the current and other high-probability market scenarios.
3. They will meet senior management's expectation of consistent monthly performance results.

These goals can be accomplished by a diligent hedging approach that maintains deliverability and optionality in most market scenarios.

To effectively manage risk, it is essential that an adequate risk management computer-based system with analytical capability be in place. This system must efficiently analyze historical fallout, quickly produce position reports, calculate mark-to-market valuations, run best execution models and produce sensitivity or "rate shock" reports.

Test-Driving Hedging Strategies

No matter which hedging mechanisms you prefer, it pays to test (on a theoretical basis) the "other" strategies occasionally. Remember: No single strategy consistently outperforms the others.

Testing other strategies helps us reacquaint ourselves with the factors that influence the appropriateness of a hedging strategy under various market conditions (rallying, tanking and flat). This section discusses the implications of deliverable (core mandatory) and nondeliverable (cross-hedging) strategies for agency product in the above three market scenarios.

To demonstrate the risks and results of exclusive use of one strategy, we will use a pure mandatory hedging strategy and a pure optional hedging strategy in the case studies that follow. The optional strategy will incorporate the use of nondeliverable instruments.

Nondeliverable Cross-Hedging Strategies

Nondeliverable cross-hedging strategies include the use of instruments such as Treasury futures and options on futures. The Chicago Board of Trade (CBOT) is the exchange that actively trades these types of instruments. Typically, most mortgage bankers do not enter into futures contracts to hedge the interest rate and fallout risk in their pipeline. Due to the risks inherent in the futures market, it is much more common and practical for mortgage bankers to purchase exchange-listed options on Treasury futures.

For those mortgage bankers who participate in the Treasury markets, put options are the primary options vehicle used to hedge interest rate risk. Exchange-listed call options are not commonly purchased by mortgage bankers for pipeline hedging purposes. However, they can be used effectively to hedge against fallout risk and servicing prepayment risk.

An Analysis of Popular Hedging Strategies 93

A common crosshedge for fixed rate mortgage pipelines is options on Treasury note futures, particularly the 10-year T-note. This is due to the closer duration match between the 10-year T-note and mortgage prepayment expectations.

Although CBOT Treasury futures and options markets are extremely liquid and transaction costs are low, their use presents additional risks, such as basis risk, intermarket risk and yield curve risk, that are not incurred with deliverable instruments.

Basis risk occurs when the yield-to-price relationship between the underlying instrument and the hedge vehicle changes. As Figure 4-1 illustrates, in December 1989, spreads between the MBS and the 10-year T-note had widened to 145 bp in yield. These spreads narrowed to 90 bp between June 1990 and December 1991. This dramatic narrowing of the spreads severely affected the performance results of futures positions during this time frame.

Intermarket risk refers to the risk associated with changing prepayment patterns, volatility or relative supply and demand conditions that cause the prices of mortgages to be different from those of Treasuries.

FIGURE 4-1

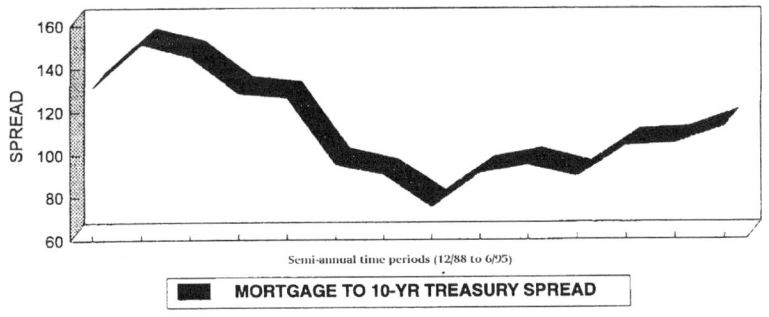

The increased prepayments in the refinance rally of 1993 caused spreads to narrow from 101 bp in September 1993 to 89 bp in December 1993. This sharp movement in the spreads increased basis risk as the underlying instruments did not correlate to the hedge vehicles.

Yield curve risk refers to the effect of changes in the yield curve on the relative price movements in the two markets. During the refinance boom in 1993, prepayment speeds increased dramatically, and as a result, MBS pools moved to a shorter duration and a different position on the yield curve. Subsequently, a 1% change in yield did not have as significant an effect on price as it would for a long term Treasury instrument. This is because Treasury instruments do not experience price compression caused by anticipated prepayment risk. In addition, in a market rally, price compression and negative convexity affect investors' perceptions, limiting the degree of premium pricing on mortgage-backed securities.

The differences between a cross-hedging, nondeliverable, optional strategy and a deliverable, mandatory strategy are striking when you examine their use in the three different market scenarios that follow. Manager A is an advocate of nondeliverable cross-hedging strategies. Manager B uses core mandatory coverage.

Case 1: Tanking Market

In August 1994, rates were fairly stable. From early September to late November, market prices declined sharply and interest rates rose. At that point, mortgage bankers had several choices:

- Maintain the same coverage levels.
- Increase coverage levels with mandatory forward sales.
- Increase coverage levels with optional sales (either OTC or exchange listed).

Figure 4-2 displays the movement of price and spread in the market during this time frame.

The size of the pipeline on day one was $100 million. The note rate was 8.75 percent. For simplicity, we analyzed the effects of the hedging strategies on this isolated pipeline during the 60-day lock period and assumed no additional locks were added over the life of the hedge. Fallout parameters were based on a hypothetical lender's fallout history in a worsening market environment.

Manager A believed that the market might continue to decline and chose to utilize a cross-hedging strategy with at-the-money put options on 10-year T-note futures. Manager A assumed on day one that pull-through would be 75%, and after calculating the hedge ratio, purchased $50 million in puts to cover the pipeline.

In contrast, Manager B devised a mandatory forward deliverable strategy using a relatively high amount of mandatory coverage — 75 percent.

FIGURE 4-2

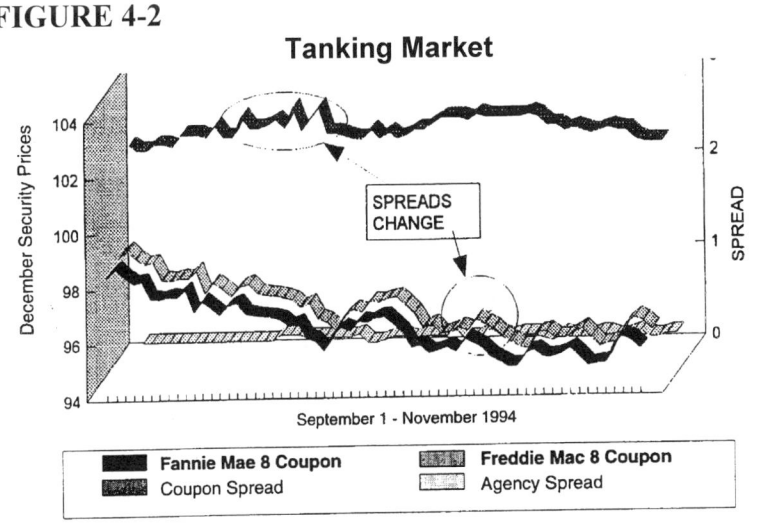

Analysis Methodology. Using an at-the-money put on CBOT 10-year T-note futures, we calculated and tracked the liquidation value of the net position over the 60-day period. Each day, the options' intrinsic and/or time value was determined to calculate the short position gain or loss. The value of the long position was computed based on daily best execution results for the 8.75% loans. We assumed that, on day one, the loans had a buy price close to current market prices.

The mandatory forward position was marked to current market prices each day as well. The long position was marked to best execution pricing, while the short position was marked to current market securities for the forward sale made on day one.

Results. Over the course of the 60-day coverage period, the market deteriorated rapidly. The actual fallout was less than both managers expected. Therefore, the amount of loans that pulled through above their initial expectation was marked to market at a loss.

As shown in Figure 4-3, Manager A's nondeliverable put option strategy yielded positive results at only a few points in time. Despite the fact that the put was purchased at the money, pull-through was higher than expected, and the net position was marked at a loss

FIGURE 4-3
Crosshedge vs. Deliverable (Tanking Market)

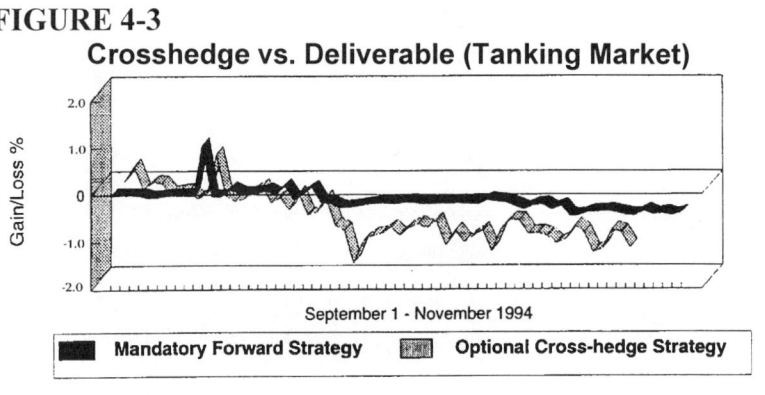

over most of the hedge period. The value of the position was most erratic late in the hedge period. This time frame corresponds with the period when most of the loans would be expected to close. If Manager A had chosen to liquidate the option position during this period, substantial losses would have resulted.

In contrast to Manager A's approach, Manager B used a deliverable hedging strategy and was able to improve the value of the mandatory forward position by performing swaps. The deliverable mandatory strategy yielded more consistent results because mandatory forward coverage was sold on day one and later improved, using best execution techniques as agency and coupon spreads continued to widen. On October 18, Manager B was able to perform an agency swap to increase proceeds. In addition, the effect of delivery variance on each trade allowed the position to improve 3 bp over the life of the hedge.

Case 2: Rallying Market

Case 2, illustrated in Figure 4-4, covers a 60-day period beginning in late April 1995, after the market had been steadily

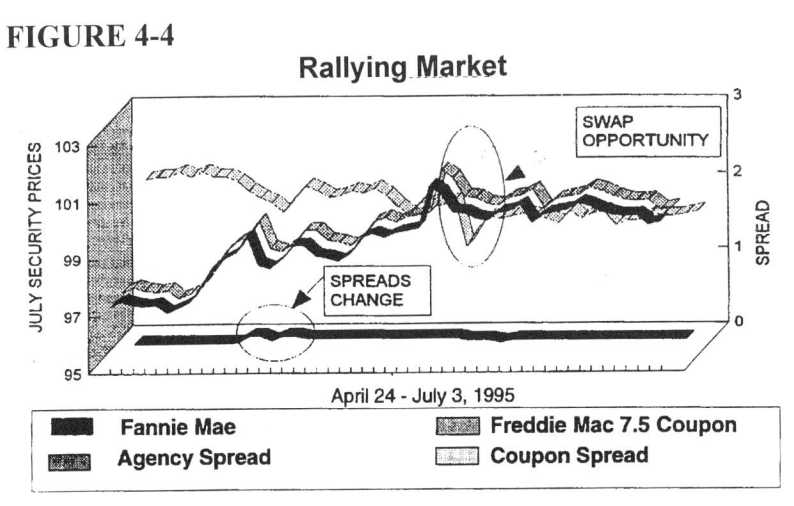

FIGURE 4-4
Rallying Market

improving. Mortgage bankers once again were faced with a dilemma: Should they reduce coverage levels or maintain the current levels? In this case, both managers were bullish, but concerned about the market deteriorating. Both maintained coverage levels at 70% of the pipeline.

Using the nondeliverable strategy, Manager A decided to purchase put options on 10-year T-note futures at one point out-of-the-money. Manager A calculated the hedge ratio and determined that $46 million in out-of-the money put options were required.

Manager B's deliverable strategy required mandatory forward sales of 70% of the pipeline. Using this strategy, the pipeline remained at $100 million; however, it contained 8.25% loans. Both managers assumed pull-through on day one was 70 percent.

Results. Just like in Case 1, a daily liquidation value for the net position was determined for each strategy. As Figure 4-5 shows, the optional put strategy (cross hedge) yielded favorable results almost every day of the 60-day hedge period. During this time, the market rallied substantially. Despite the cost of the premium paid for the put option, the price improvement of the rally more than recovered the fee paid for the option.

FIGURE 4-5
Crosshedge vs. Deliverable (rallying Market)

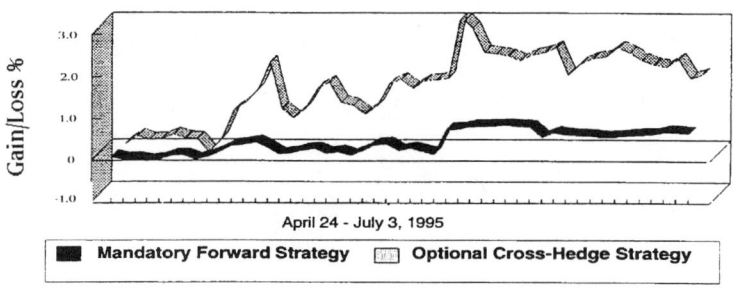

Manager B's deliverable strategy produced a substantial gain over the period, but it did not outperform the crosshedge strategy due to the effects of fallout against mandatory forward sales. Since Manager B initially expected more loans to pullthrough, excess coverage had to be paired off at the end of the lock period. However, Manager B was able to improve the hedge using best execution and delivery improvement swaps as shown in Figure 4-4. On June 2, Manager B was able to perform a coupon swap from 8.0% to 7.5% to increase proceeds.

Case 3: Flat Market

Case 3 covers a 60-day period from October 1 through November 30, 1995. The market had experienced several different scenarios, rallying in the spring and early summer, then tanking in July and August. As you can see in Figure 4-6, it had leveled off by late September.

The pipeline consisted of 7.75% loans. Since both managers were concerned that the market might deteriorate, they chose to maintain coverage ratios at 72 percent. Manager A calculated the

FIGURE 4-6

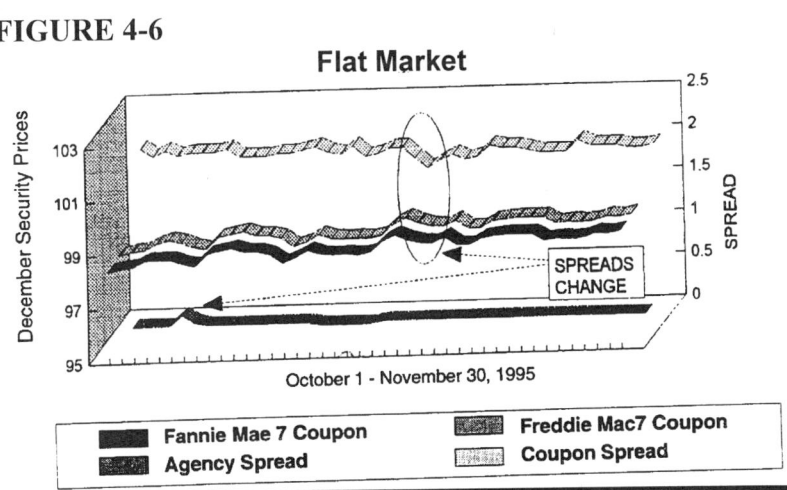

FIGURE 4-7
Crosshedge vs. Deliverable (Flat Market)

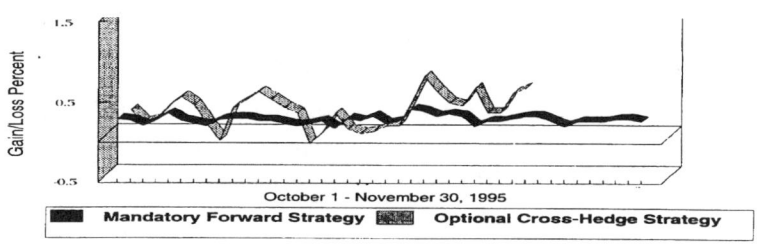

hedge ratio and purchased $48 million in at-the-money put options. Manager B sold forward $72 million.

Results. During this time period, the market remained within a tight range and was relatively flat. Using best execution swaps, Manager B's deliverable mandatory strategy yielded a consistent gain over the 60-day hedge period since pull-through levels met expectations, as shown in Figure 4-7. On November 2, Manager B was able to perform an agency swap to further increase proceeds.

The nondeliverable optional strategy produced wide swings in position value over the hedge period. Although the market remained relatively flat, most of the cost of the put premium was lost. In addition, delivery improvement strategies could not be utilized until the crosshedge position was liquidated.

Conclusion
Analysis of the above cases indicates that the deliverable strategy using mandatory forward sales works best in two of the three market scenarios. However, our goal is to achieve the greatest

An Analysis of Popular Hedging Strategies 101

amount of proceeds with the least amount of risk in *all* market scenarios.

The mandatory forward strategy allows deliverability, delivery tolerance, best execution and delivery improvement, but not optionality. It also produces more consistent results over the coverage period than the crosshedge strategy as shown in Figures 4-3, 4-5 and 4-7. However, to achieve consistent results in all market scenarios, an appropriate amount of optional coverage is a required component in the hedging equation.

Optionality + Deliverability + Measuring Tools = Success

A hedging strategy of combined levels of deliverable mandatory and optional instruments performs better than cross hedging or the exclusive use of options or mandatories. However, it is crucial to have an accurate system to measure pipeline value and to support a systematic method for determining the amount of coverage and when to purchase OTC puts versus calls.

A properly designed option strategy should limit the severity of hedge losses resulting from swings in fallout with minimum hedge costs. Keep in mind that excessive use of options unnecessarily increases hedge costs and reduces opportunities to increase proceeds through swaps of deliverable mandatory forwards.

The next step is to examine the effects of coupling deliverable mandatory coverage with varying "layers" of OTC puts or calls, as opposed to exchange-listed options. Although exchange-listed call options can be used effectively to hedge against fallout risk, we now focus specifically on using OTC options in all scenarios to provide deliverability and to eliminate the additional cross-hedging risks discussed earlier.

The following cases illustrate the results of using one strategy exclusively in the three market scenarios reviewed above.

These cases demonstrate the pitfalls of blindly using a single strategy in all scenarios instead of systematically defining a strategy based on market conditions. The cases compare two different hedging strategies against each other:
- Manager A is an advocate of lower levels of mandatory coverage with OTC puts.
- Manager B uses higher levels of mandatory coverage with OTC calls.

Case 1: Tanking Market

The short-lived stable rate environment in August 1994 deteriorated quickly from early September through late November. Using a combination of mandatory forward sales and options to cover December settlements, let's review the following two strategies:
- Strategy A: Reduce mandatory coverage and purchase a wider band of OTC puts.
- Strategy B: Increase mandatory coverage and purchase a layer of OTC calls.

The scenarios analyzed were performed using an isolated pipeline of $100 million worth of 60-day locks taken in September 1994, with a note rate of 8.75 percent. All comparisons assumed that no additional locks were added during the coverage period. All fallout projections were based on a loan-level price-sensitive historical analysis compiled into fallout grids.

On day one, the loan-level fallout analysis determined a closing ratio of 76 percent. Manager A thought the market could improve and chose to reduce mandatory coverage to 60% of gross lock-ins and simultaneously purchased a wide band (20%) of OTC put options on Fannie Mae 8s, one-half point out-of-the-money. Using 60% mandatories plus 20% puts resulted in a potential coverage range between 60% and 80 percent.

Meanwhile, Manager B believed the market would continue its bearish trend, but also wanted protection against a sudden rally. Therefore, Manager B increased mandatory coverage to 85% of gross locks and purchased a 10% layer of at-the-money OTC calls on Fannie Mae 8s. This created a potential coverage range between 75% and 85 percent.

A liquidation value was computed and plotted daily for each position: The loans were marked to best execution instruments, the mandatory short was marked to market and the option position was matched with its intrinsic and time values. Total mark-to-market results for each strategy were then compared.

As shown in Figure 4-8, market prices had declined 2 points over a 60-day period. Both managers purchased too much optional coverage on day one since neither manager had a systematic method for determining the amount and when to purchase a put versus a call. Note that Manager A's strategy of reduced mandatory coverage, coupled with a wide band of put options, produced substantially greater losses than Manager B's strategy.

Although the actual fallout experienced by both managers was not much greater than anticipated, the bullish use of manda-

FIGURE 4-8

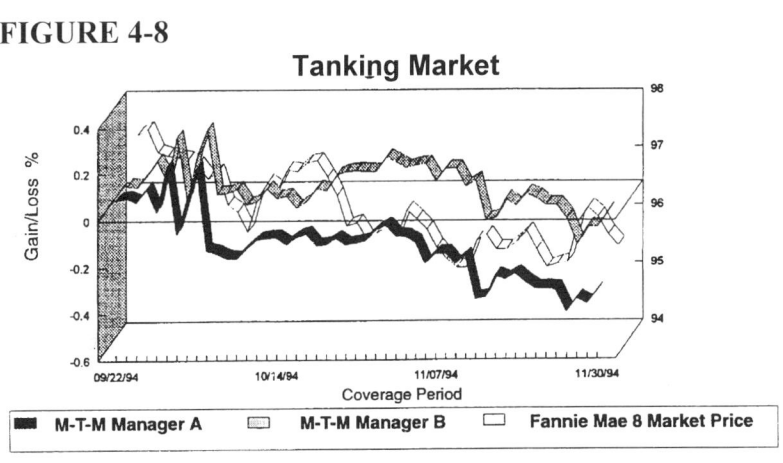

tories on day one required Manager A to sell the unexpected pull-through (nearly 6%) at a loss of 1.84 points. The overuse of put options on day one contributed further to the loss with unnecessary premiums.

In this scenario, where Manager A clearly overcovered in puts in a tanking market, the prudent step would have been to save the time value by increasing mandatory levels and pairing off the puts. On the positive side, the use of OTC puts on MBS forwards provided the much needed "deliverability" factor. Without the ability to exercise and deliver into the optional coverage in a tanking market, the pipeline would have been subject to the effects of the intermarket risk described earlier in this discussion.

Deliverability is key factor. As shown in Figure 4-8, in a tanking market environment, the higher level of mandatories, coupled with a layer of calls on deliverable forwards, produces a much better result. The additional value was realized through delivery of the higher pull-through into the existing mandatory coverage. Although the layer of calls provided the necessary protection against a sudden rally, this layer was too wide as a starting point on day one when the pipeline was at the money.

A call is purchased to limit the damage of greater fallout. Therefore, in a tanking market with a pipeline that continues to decline in value, it would have been better to pair off the excess call options as quickly as possible to recover some of the fees paid.

Both managers were able to take advantage of the risk-free opportunity on October 18 to increase the value of their existing mandatory coverage through an agency swap.

Again, this analysis shows that deliverability is a key factor. Maximizing delivery tolerance on settlement also improved the short position by an additional three basis points. Compared to the wide gain/loss swings of +/- 100 bp on the crosshedge strategy, the combination of deliverable mandatory and options used by both managers in Case 1 provided more stability.

Case 2: Rallying Market

In April 1995, secondary marketers were faced with a different challenge due to a steadily improving market. Manager A established the hedge on July settlements with the same method of substantially reduced deliverable mandatory coverage (60%) coupled with a wide band (20%) of half-a-point-out-of-the-money OTC puts. This strategy placed Manager A in a position to profit from a significant rally while simultaneously guarding against sudden price declines.

Although somewhat bearish on the market, Manager B reduced the coverage ratio from the usual 85% to 80% and added a 10% layer of at-the-money OTC calls. Since Manager B's analysis of historical fallout experience showed an expected closing ratio between 70% and 75%, this bearish approach was designed to provide stop-loss protection down to a pull-through ratio of 70% if the market should rally.

The pipeline contained $100 million of 8.25% loans. A market value for each position was computed daily in the same manner described for Case 1. The resulting gain/loss totals were then analyzed. As shown in Figure 4-9, market prices increased 4 points in 30 days and then backed down to an increase of 3 points over the last 30 days. Manager A's lower mandatory

FIGURE 4-9

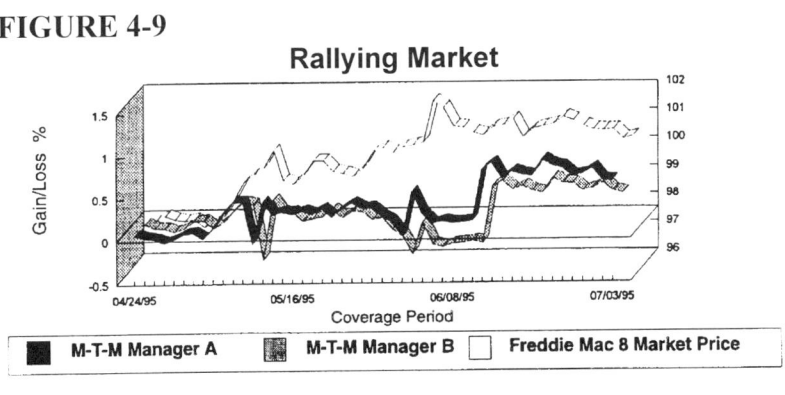

coverage and puts significantly out-performed Manager B's higher mandatory coverage and calls. As anticipated, both managers experienced a pull-through ratio of 69 percent.

Since the sharp rally more than twice recouped the put premium (which expired 3.5 points out of the money), Manager A's closings above 60% were sold at a gain of 3 points. This portion of the pipeline alone contributed 14.5 basis points of total additional gain. Even though the strategy worked well, it would have been better to layer out-of-the-money or split-fee puts as the pipeline value moved deeper in the money.

In contrast, Manager B's strategy only covered the downside caused by fallout and excessive mandatory coverage. Due to Manager B's bearish tendency with the level of mandatory coverage, the strong increase in market prices had a detrimental impact. Although the 10% layer of at-the-money calls moved quickly in-the-money, they were exercised on notification to satisfy the requirement for inadequate product.

On the positive side, without the calls, Manager B would have suffered a massive 3 point pair-off loss on $10 million. The net result is the loss of the option premium (28 ticks) and the remaining 9% of the pipeline was settled at a price 3 points less than that of Manager A.

Once again, although neither approach is optimal, it is important to notice the stability of these deliverable strategies when compared to the volatile swings of the cross-hedging strategy cited earlier. In addition, while not included in this analysis, both managers were able to take advantage of a best execution coupon swap from 8% to 7.5% on June 2.

Case 3: Flat Market

The rally in the Spring of 1995 turned to a worsening market in the Summer, and a flat pattern of sideways waffling from late September to December. The performance of each strategy

An Analysis of Popular Hedging Strategies 107

against a flat market scenario was analyzed during this period for December settlements of 7.75% loans. Although market prices gradually improved by 1 point during this period, most of the increase was due to normal roll-up price appreciation. As December moved nearer to being the front month delivery, the value of the drop was naturally picked up.

As shown in Figure 4-10, the results of each strategy are nearly identical. However, since neither manager implements a systematic method for determining the proper level of optional coverage, we see that both managers over used options on day one and continued through the coverage period.

Similar to the actions in Cases 1 and 2, Manager A's strategy of using extremely low mandatory coverage and a 20% band of OTC puts is excessive when the loans are at the money or near the money. Manager A was trying to address risks that are typically inherent in a maturing bull market after the pipeline has substantial gains.

In flat rate environments such as this, the normal price appreciation of the underlying instrument for 60-day puts will result in them being worthless at expiration. Once dealers write OTC options, they typically attribute little or nothing to time value for the option. As a result, the tradeability of the OTC

FIGURE 4-10

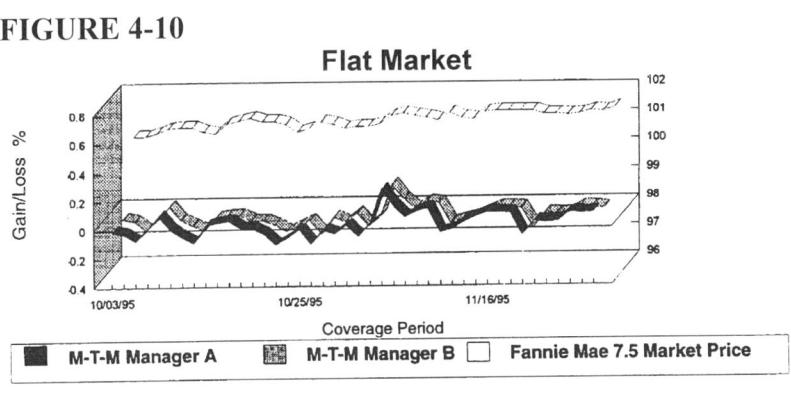

option, unlike an exchange-listed option, is limited. This places a higher level of importance on initially obtaining the correct amount and type of OTC options.

In this scenario, the 22.75% of gross pipeline that closed over and above the established 60% mandatory coverage was sold at current market prices for a 1 point gain.

In addition, Manager B's strategy of establishing high mandatory coverage and a 10% layer of OTC calls on day one is also excessive. In this scenario, the call options were completely paired off to capture the intrinsic value only to recoup the original premium cost.

Summary

The analyses performed in this chapter indicate that a strategy of combined levels of deliverable mandatory and optional instruments performs better than cross-hedging or the exclusive use of options or mandatories.

Three keys to establishing and maintaining a correct mix of mandatory and optional coverage are:

- Knowing the proper amount of mandatory coverage to maintain.
- Knowing the amount of optional coverage to purchase.
- Knowing when to switch from one combined optional and mandatory strategy to the other.

Processes built on intuition and preset approaches not sensitive to market conditions should be replaced with methodically applied techniques based on quantifiable factors. This can only be accomplished with the use of an integrated system.

Manager A and Manager B need to implement a systematic method for determining the coverage amount and timing for purchasing OTC puts versus calls. Critical to this process is the

An Analysis of Popular Hedging Strategies 109

ability to accurately determine the value of the pipeline in relationship to the market. Gains and losses in the pipeline can be ascertained through the use of a loan-level fallout analysis or a loan-level mark-to-market of the at-risk long position.

Using this information, the successful secondary marketing manager can effectively determine the value of the pipeline in relationship to the market. This will provide the necessary insight for making decisions about required coverage amounts and the use of a put versus a call.

In addition, when combined with a rate shock analysis, the results provide an indication of your position's greatest exposure to market price swings. This valuable information can assist the practitioner in refining the coverage band.

Deliverable mandatory coverage with a layer of optional OTC coverage will yield more consistent results in all market scenarios, as well as allowing more flexibility in adjusting coverage ratios. The above analyses clearly illustrate the axiom: No one strategy works best all the time.

Appendix — Chapter 4

EXAMPLE OF AN AGENCY/COUPON SWAP

In the following example, the trader intends to take advantage of coupon spread relationship changes in the marketplace. The trader recognizes that due to premium compression, the spreads between higher coupon MBS have narrowed. In addition, due to the market rally, 8.0% coverage is no longer best execution for a 8.25% note rate. The pipeline requires 7.50% coupon coverage for best execution. Therefore, the trader recognizes an opportunity to swap 8.0% Freddie Mac PC coverage for 7.50% Fannie Mae MBS coverage.

Date	Vehicle	Coupon	Trade Price	Market on April 24	Market on June 2
4/24	Freddie Mac PC	8.00	99.40625	99.40625	102.7500
6/2	Fannie Mae MBS	7.50	101.5625	97.37500	101.5625

Swap 8.0 Coupon for 7.5 Coupon
1. Determine 8.0 coupon spread (current market – original trade): 3.34375
2. Subtract spread from 7.5 coupon price on 6/2 <u>98.21875</u>

112 Handbook of Secondary Marketing

	Original Trade	Improved Trade
Notes Rate	8.25	8.25
Coupon	8.00	7.50
Price	99.40625	98.21875
Beginning Guarantee Fee	.22	.22
Net Guarantee Fee	-0-	.42
Buy Down Ratio	4.5	
Buy Up Ratio		4.3
Buy down/up Cost	-.99	.86
Total Cash	98.41625	99.07875
Excess Servicing	-0-	0.08
Cap 4:1	-0-	.32
Total Book	98.41625	99.39875

98.21875 is now the new trade price. (The loss of 3.34375 on the sale of the Freddie Mac 8.0 coupon PC is subtracted from the price of the Fannie Mae 7.5 coupon MBS to derive the net all-in price on the new hedge vehicle.) This is an improvement of .84375 over the price of 7.5 coupon MBS on 4/24.

Note that the improved trade involved buying up the guarantee fee by 20 bp. This left 8 bp of excess servicing (0.75 gross spread less 0.42 guaranty fee less 0.25 servicing fee), which the mortgage banker capitalized at 4:1 for a value of 32 bp. The total all-in improvement over the original trade was 0.9825 percent (99.309875-98.41625).

5

Pricing Profitability Analysis How Much Are You Really Making?

Stephen R. Rigsbee
Sirri S. Ayaydin
Charles A. Richard
Quantitative Risk Management Group

The authors would like to thank Sharif Shakhshir for his assistance in producing this chapter.

Pricing for Profits

In days past, when there was less competition and lower rate volatility, secondary marketing performance benchmarks were often very simplistic. The mandate frequently was to break even in terms of security execution, thereby leaving 50 bp of servicing on the table as "gravy." Some less competitive markets allowed for significant profits to be built into their loan pricing strategy.

An occasional month of secondary marketing losses was tolerated — after all, gross profit margins were high, and servicing assets were valuable enough that small pieces of the servicing portfolio could be broken off to subsidize secondary marketing losses. And, if there was a thrift or banking parent, it may have been possible to bury losers in the portfolio. This strategy, of course, never made economic sense because unreversed market value losses, by definition, eventually come back over time in the form of reduced earnings. Another equally unsuccessful strategy was to attempt to trade out of bad pricing decisions, speculating on the future course of interest rates. This option only served to create even greater volatility of earnings.

In today's competitive market all-in spreads are much narrower, interest rates are more volatile and servicing values are lower. Mortgage bankers who manage their operations and their risks more effectively are building a formidable advantage over the more loosely managed operations of their competition.

Pricing strategies followed by mortgage bankers differ significantly from one institution to another, sometimes — though not always — reflecting competitive forces. We have seen some midwestern institutions charging a point up front to lock the rate on a mortgage application. This typically reflects a greater overall spread earned by the mortgage banker (adding together upfront points and points at closing). It also results in a lower fallout in virtually all rate-change scenarios because the borrowers must forfeit the fee if they walk away from the commitment. This means that a greater rate decline is needed to provide the consumer with enough incentive to take their mortgage elsewhere. The reduced sensitivity of fallout to interest rate changes results in a lower hedge cost. However, the increased profitability gained by charging the upfront fee almost always reduces loan volume substantially.

In many markets, imposing an upfront fee would all but dry up origination volume because of the fierce competition for loan

Pricing Profitability Analysis 117

product. This competition has led mortgage bankers to offer more complex rate locks with features that are more favorable to the borrower and even more costly to the lender. Examples include several versions of float-down, floating subject to a cap and the "Lock and Shop" rate locks. The float-down rate lock provides borrowers with the benefit of any rate decline during the life of the rate lock, often subject to a point or rate "hurdle." The floating-subject-to-a-cap floats in both directions, but cannot move above a preset maximum cap rate. "Lock and Shop" rate locks give borrowers the ability to lock a rate before they have even identified a specific house. These rate locks dramatically increase the cost of hedging. Unless the business is done at a substantially higher spread, offering these types of rate locks clearly has a negative effect on the lender's profitability. Whether it makes sense to offer these types of rate locks depends first upon whether these rate locks are profitable at all and second upon the extent to which offering such a rate lock increases volume or makes it more predictable.

The interest rate volume environment of the early and mid 1990s has significantly increased the volume of refinance applications and the demand for purchase loans. Pricing a refinance rate lock profitably is particularly challenging because refinance borrowers are less likely to close the loan if rates fall, but are more likely to close if rates rise during the rate-lock period. Refinance rate locks typically have more upside value potential than the float-down rate locks because borrowers are not automatically entitled to a lower rate as rates decline. Some mortgage bankers attempt to maintain the same net level of profitability on refinance and exotic applications as on other applications by charging a fee to lock the rate. This fee, in theory,* is charged to cover the increased cost of hedging the refinance and exotic rate locks.

In our observations of the industry, it has been surprising to see how infrequently mortgage bankers go beyond basic analysis and rigorously analyze the all-in profitability implications of their own pricing decisions and rate-lock strategies. Although it is widely known that rate locks are hybrid forms of options, analysis is rarely used to determine the cost of hedging or the cost of extending rate locks.

Quantifying Quandaries

The building blocks of profitability are well known, but systematic analysis is often inhibited because it is not always easy to quantify some important elements. For example, how does a mortgage company's hedge cost vary among different product types? Or, how much more should a mortgage company charge for a 60-day lock than for a 30-day lock? How does preapproval effect hedging costs? Should the company structure and price refinance rate locks differently than purchase rate locks? Should the company structure exotic rate locks to meet or surpass the ones offered by their competition? How does the value of servicing vary among product types and rates, and for that matter what is the correct method to evaluate servicing? Being able to answer these questions is key to making economically sound pricing decisions, which in turn is key to survival in today's marketplace. This chapter will discuss the components of the profitability equation and set forth a practical methodology for accurately computing rate-lock profitability.

Practitioners typically have the most trouble trying to quantify hedge costs (or sometimes, simply understanding why there are hedge costs). Fortunately though, most mortgage bankers realize that in making rate-lock commitments to borrowers, they are issuing a form of a put options. To accurately determine the value of a rate-lock put option, you must understand basic option theory and modeling. Unfortunately, while some may be familiar with the valuation of Treasury options and perhaps even MBS options, few have the tools to quantify the value of the options that they are giving away in a rate lock. In this discussion, we will show how to determine the value of the rate-lock option given away using an example that compares two different rate-lock types — purchase versus refinance — with different lock periods.

Determining the value of servicing can also be difficult. Current implied market prices, agency buy-up and buy-down ratios and servicing-released premiums may be readily available. However, if a mortgage lender intends to retain the servicing, it must also establish an accurate appraisal of the economic value the servicing holds. This should be based on the lending institution's own cost of capital and cost of servicing. It is still a common practice for many institutions to use an arbitrary internal servicing transfer rate in their pricing profitability analysis. This over-simplified method could lead to poor pricing decisions.

The Profitability Equation

This section describes the rate-lock profitability equation and includes a table that quantifies all the variables of the equation. All-in profit will be calculated for both government and conventional loans of different expiration dates for both refinance and purchase rate locks.

Profit from loan origination is determined according to the following equation:

All-In Profit=(Gross Spread at Close x Expected Closing Ratio) - (Income and Costs of the Rate Lock)

Gross Spread at Close = Forward price of underlying mortgage
  +Value of excess servicing created
  +Interest accrued from closing date to forward settlement date in excess of interest paid on warehouse line-
  Buyprice (par minus discount points collected at closing)

+Value of base servicing created- Commission points paid to intermediaries such as loan brokers or agents- Overhead costs associated with loan closing

Income and Costs of the Rate Lock=
+"Junk" fees collected upon application
(par minus discount points collected at closing)
+ Overhead costs associated with loan origination
- Cost of hedging interest rate risk during rate-lock commitment period

Now that we have established the profitability equation, we will review an actual example. Table 5-1 shows a profitability analysis for ABC Mortgage Company for typical mortgage loan rate locks with the variations that were described earlier. In our example, the mortgage banker is following a simple strategy of pricing rate locks "to the screen" (that is, equal to the likely settlement month at forward-market security prices). The analysis is based on the market conditions present on February 2, 1996.

Interpreting the Numbers

Table 5-1 highlights three important generalizations:

1. The cost of hedging refinance mortgages is substantially higher than for purchase mortgages. This is because refinances carry greater fallout risk — that is, they are more "put option-like" — than purchases. (See Figure 5-2 for closing ratio assumptions.)
2. The value of servicing declines as the note rate increases. This reflects the greater prepayment risk for higher interest rate mortgages of higher interest rates.
3. Rate locks of longer time periods cost more to hedge.

Pricing Profitability Analysis 121

TABLE 5-1

ABC Mortgage Company Product Pricing Analysis

	DESCRIPTION				PER CLOSED LOAN												STATIC	STATIC	PER RATE LOCK			
	COM TRM	NOTE RATE	CLOSNG POINTS	STLM MONTH	SEC RATE	SEC PRICE (+)	EXCESS SRVCG BPs	SRVCG VALUE (+)	INT SPRD (+)	BUY PRICE (-)	MKTG P/L (=)	BASE SRVCG BPs	BASE SRVCG VALUE (+)	FEES PAID (-)	COST PER CL (-)	GROSS SPRD AT CLOSE (=)	CLSNG RATIO% (x)	P/L PER CL (=)	FEES COLL (+)	COST PER RL (-)	HEDGE COST (-)	ALL IN PROFIT PER RL (=)
PURCHASE COMMITMENT																						
1	15	7.000	2.500	Mar-96	6.50	97.406	2.50	0.102	0.031	97.500	0.039	47.50	0.920	0.25	0.25	0.459	75	0.344	0.375	0.25	0.033	0.436
2	15	7.250	1.500	Mar-96	6.50	97.406	2.50	0.102	0.045	98.500	0.054	47.50	0.903	0.25	0.25	0.457	75	0.342	0.375	0.25	0.050	0.417
3	15	7.500	0.375	Mar-96	7.00	99.469	2.50	0.092	0.060	99.625	-0.004	47.50	0.820	0.25	0.25	0.316	75	0.237	0.375	0.25	0.028	0.334
4	15	7.750	-0.500	Mar-96	7.00	99.469	2.50	0.092	0.074	100.500	-0.004	47.50	0.807	0.25	0.25	0.348	75	0.261	0.375	0.25	0.023	0.363
5	30	7.000	2.500	Apr-96	6.50	97.313	2.50	0.102	0.041	100.500	-0.033	47.50	0.920	0.25	0.25	0.387	75	0.290	0.375	0.25	0.077	0.338
6	30	7.250	1.500	Apr-96	6.50	97.313	2.50	0.102	0.052	98.500	-0.013	47.50	0.898	0.25	0.25	0.385	75	0.289	0.375	0.25	0.071	0.343
7	30	7.500	0.500	Apr-96	7.00	99.344	2.50	0.093	0.076	98.500	-0.013	47.50	0.830	0.25	0.25	0.367	75	0.275	0.375	0.25	0.067	0.333
8	30	7.750	-0.500	Apr-96	7.00	99.344	2.50	0.093	0.100	99.500	-0.037	47.50	0.830	0.25	0.25	0.273	75	0.205	0.375	0.25	0.058	0.272
9	45	7.000	2.500	Apr-96	6.50	97.313	2.50	0.102	0.124	97.500	-0.034	47.50	0.807	0.25	0.25	0.273	75	0.273	0.375	0.25	0.128	0.270
10	45	7.250	1.500	Apr-96	6.50	97.313	2.50	0.102	0.030	97.500	-0.055	47.50	0.820	0.25	0.25	0.365	75	0.264	0.375	0.25	0.111	0.278
11	45	7.500	0.500	Apr-96	7.00	99.344	2.50	0.093	0.043	98.500	-0.046	47.50	0.898	0.25	0.25	0.352	75	0.243	0.375	0.25	0.104	0.264
12	60	7.750	-0.375	Apr-96	7.00	99.344	2.50	0.093	0.057	99.500	-0.006	47.50	0.830	0.25	0.25	0.324	75	0.268	0.375	0.25	0.092	0.291
13	60	7.000	2.625	Apr-96	6.50	97.188	2.50	0.099	0.071	97.375	-0.038	47.50	0.807	0.25	0.25	0.345	75	0.258	0.375	0.25	0.178	0.216
14	60	7.250	1.625	Apr-96	6.50	97.188	2.50	0.099	0.057	97.375	-0.031	47.50	0.890	0.25	0.25	0.359	75	0.269	0.375	0.25	0.178	0.216
15	60	7.500	0.625	May-96	7.00	99.188	2.50	0.090	0.083	98.375	-0.005	47.50	0.899	0.25	0.25	0.394	75	0.295	0.375	0.25	0.161	0.259
16	60	7.750	-0.375	May-96	7.00	99.188	2.50	0.090	0.110	99.375	0.013	47.50	0.830	0.25	0.25	0.313	75	0.235	0.375	0.25	0.149	0.211
17	60	7.750	-0.375	May-96	7.00	99.188	2.50	0.090	0.137	100.375	-0.053	47.50	0.806	0.25	0.25	0.253	75	0.190	0.375	0.25	0.130	0.165
REFINANCE COMMITMENT																						
18	15	7.000	2.500	Mar-96	6.50	97.406	2.50	0.102	0.031	97.500	0.039	47.50	0.920	0.25	0.25	0.459	60	0.275	0.375	0.25	0.066	0.334
19	15	7.250	1.500	Mar-96	6.50	97.406	2.50	0.102	0.045	98.500	0.054	47.50	0.903	0.25	0.25	0.457	60	0.274	0.375	0.25	0.062	0.337
20	15	7.500	0.375	Mar-96	7.00	99.469	2.50	0.092	0.050	99.625	-0.004	47.50	0.820	0.25	0.25	0.316	60	0.189	0.375	0.25	0.051	0.282
21	15	7.750	-0.500	Mar-96	7.00	99.469	2.50	0.092	0.074	100.500	0.041	47.50	0.807	0.25	0.25	0.348	60	0.208	0.375	0.25	0.051	0.282
22	30	7.000	2.500	Apr-96	6.50	97.313	2.50	0.102	0.052	97.500	-0.033	47.50	0.920	0.25	0.25	0.387	60	0.232	0.375	0.25	0.131	0.226
23	30	7.250	1.500	Apr-96	6.50	97.313	2.50	0.102	0.076	98.500	-0.013	47.50	0.898	0.25	0.25	0.385	60	0.232	0.375	0.25	0.122	0.245
24	30	7.500	0.500	Apr-96	7.00	99.344	2.50	0.093	0.100	98.500	-0.037	47.50	0.830	0.25	0.25	0.367	60	0.220	0.375	0.25	0.115	0.230
25	30	7.750	-0.500	Apr-96	7.00	99.344	2.50	0.093	0.124	100.500	-0.034	47.50	0.807	0.25	0.25	0.273	60	0.171	0.375	0.25	0.102	0.194
26	45	7.000	2.500	Apr-96	6.50	97.313	2.50	0.102	0.030	97.500	-0.055	47.50	0.920	0.25	0.25	0.365	60	0.219	0.375	0.25	0.196	0.148
27	45	7.250	1.500	Apr-96	6.50	97.313	2.50	0.102	0.043	98.500	-0.046	47.50	0.898	0.25	0.25	0.352	60	0.211	0.375	0.25	0.179	0.157
28	45	7.500	0.500	Apr-96	7.00	99.344	2.50	0.093	0.057	99.500	-0.006	47.50	0.830	0.25	0.25	0.324	60	0.194	0.375	0.25	0.167	0.152
29	45	7.750	-0.375	Apr-96	7.00	99.344	2.50	0.093	0.071	100.375	-0.038	47.50	0.807	0.25	0.25	0.345	60	0.207	0.375	0.25	0.151	0.181
30	60	7.000	2.625	Apr-96	6.50	97.188	2.50	0.099	0.059	97.375	-0.031	47.50	0.890	0.25	0.25	0.359	60	0.215	0.375	0.25	0.259	0.081
31	60	7.250	1.625	May-96	6.50	97.188	2.50	0.099	0.083	98.375	-0.005	47.50	0.899	0.25	0.25	0.394	60	0.236	0.375	0.25	0.241	0.120
32	60	7.500	0.625	May-96	7.00	99.188	2.50	0.090	0.110	99.375	0.013	47.50	0.830	0.25	0.25	0.313	60	0.197	0.375	0.25	0.224	0.098
33	60	7.750	-0.375	May-96	7.00	99.188	2.50	0.090	0.137	100.375	-0.053	47.50	0.806	0.25	0.25	0.253	60	0.159	0.375	0.25	0.198	0.086

Bond Volatility: 9.45%

From the analysis, it is evident that the example mortgage banker, who has priced all his loans "to the screen," is, perhaps unknowingly, building in a substantially smaller profit margin on some rate locks than on others.

Producing a pricing profitability table like this should be a daily ritual at every mortgage banking company. Its production can be greatly facilitated by creating direct links to market price information using computer spreadsheets.

Let's look at a couple of specific examples from Table 5-1. Each line represents a different possible rate lock that could be offered to loan applicants. Table 5-1 is comprised of two major categories, each exhibiting unique profitability characteristics: a purchase rate lock and a refinance rate lock. Within each block are different commitment term and note rate combinations that loan applicants might choose.

For example, in the outlined row #7 of the purchase commitment section is the pricing analysis for a commitment on a 7.5%, 30-year, conventional-purchase, fixed-rate mortgage with a 30-day rate-lock period. ABC Mortgage Company requires 15 days, on average, to process a loan from closing to settlement against a forward commitment. Therefore, given a current date of February 2, this loan can be ready by the Public Securities Association (PSA) standard for security settlement date in the month of April. As previously stated, the pricing rule followed by this mortgage banker is to quote "screen prices," allowing a 50 bp servicing spread (including the guarantee fee). In other words, given a note rate of 7.5%, minus a base servicing fee of 25 bp, minus a base guarantee fee of 22.5 bp, minus a coupon of 7.00%, plus a credit for the value of the excess yield (2.50 bp) of 9.3 bp, the borrower is quoted 7.5% rate and 50 bp of discount (par, less security price of 99.344, plus .093 excess servicing value, rounded up).

This pricing follows the old break-even rule which suggests that a loan's discount should be the discount of the underlying security (in consideration of the appropriate coupon and likely delivery month) minus the value of any excess servicing. Unfortunately, this is where many mortgage bankers stop in making their pricing decisions. In addition to the above, mortgage bankers need to give proper attention to the following items:

- Value of the servicing created.
- Net interest earned from the expected loan closing date to the MBS settlement date.
- Cost of hedging interest-rate-related fallout risk.
- "Junk" fees collected or paid.
- Origination and overhead costs.

While these items often vary considerably from one commitment to another, our hypothetical mortgage banker is pricing all his commitments strictly on the basis of forward-market prices plus the value of excess servicing. Up to this point, the mortgage banker is expecting that his loan is worth the sum of the price of the underlying security (99.344) plus the value of the excess servicing (9.3 bp), which equals 99.437.

However, to continue the analysis of the all-in profitability of the 7.5%, 30-day, conventional-purchase mortgage commitment, the mortgage banker needs to add the interest spread earned (10 bp) from the expected loan closing date to the forward-commitment settlement date — this is equal to the difference between the interest earned on the mortgage and interest paid on the warehouse line of credit — and subtract the buy price of the loan (par minus discount collected = 99.5) to derive a marketing P/L of 3.7 bp.

If our hypothetical mortgage banker stopped here, it would still be an incomplete analysis. The value of the base servicing (25 bp), calculated via a model that correctly accounts for the increased likelihood of prepayments on higher rate loans, comes out to be 83 bp. Then there are commission fees paid (25 bp) and other costs related to loan closing (25 bp) that result in a gross spread of 36.7 bp.

But, do all rate locks close? Of course not. While it would be convenient to assume that the gross spread of a rate lock is as good as "money in the bank," it is not truly "deposited" until that loan closes. In this example, given zero price moves (appropriate, since we are looking at a brand new lock), the mortgage banker expects 75% of the locks to close. Therefore, of the 36.7 bp gross spread expected if all locks close, only 27.5 bp are actually given credit.

Lastly, there are "junk fees" (approximately 37.5 bp), other uncompensated costs of loan origination (25 bp) and hedge cost (6.7 bp), which is probably one of the most difficult values to quantify. The all-in profit on this rate lock, given the above assumptions, is 33.3 bp. Now, using this analysis, our mortgage banker has the information needed to work with production and maximize the profit-per-loan-times-volume equation.

The real insights into the benefits of an all-in profitability become apparent when we compare key values of longer-dated locks and refinance locks to our base case of a 30-day purchase lock (line #7). First, let's look at the effect upon hedge costs when the lock period increases. Focusing on line #11, a 45-day purchase commitment has a hedge cost of 10.4 bp — a 55% increase in the cost of reversing risk profile of this more "option-like" commitment. Many mortgage bankers charge borrowers only the interpolated drop between security months. For instance, given an 8-tick drop between months, they would charge 4 ticks for each additional 15 days of lock period. However, the actual costs of each additional 15 days is hardly static. Notice the increase in hedge costs for the 7.5% lock from 15 to 60 days. The cost moves from 2.8 to 6.7 to 10.4 to 14.9 bp. Therefore, on top of the incremental drop for the extension of lock period, the profit-minded mortgage banker must charge an incrementally higher hedge cost even when the incremental lock period is constant.

Now let's look at the effect of an Option-Adjusted Spread (OAS) analysis — or Monte Carlo simulation, as it is also called — upon the valuation of servicing values. Upon reviewing base servicing values for lines 1-4, it appears that a constant base servicing cannot be assumed to have the equivalent long-term value. Here, 25 bp of servicing (the 47.5 bp shown includes a 22.5 bp guarantee fee) on different note rates is valued at a high of 92 bp for a 7% note rate (an effective 3.68 ratio) to a low of 80.7 bp for a 7.75% note rate (a 3.23 ratio).

Lastly, let's look at the effect of loan purpose upon hedge costs. Figure 5-1 compares the hedge cost of our base case on line #7 for a 30-day purchase commitment to the hedge cost for a comparable refinance commitment. Notice that the hedge cost increases from 6.7 bp to 11.5 bp — an increase of 4.8 bp. Further, when we compare purchases versus refinances on a 60-day lock, we see the hedge costs jump from 14.9 bp to 22.4 bp — a 7.5 bp increase. If our hypothetical mortgage banker priced a 60-day refinance the same as a 60-day purchase, over one year's time, $500 million worth of locks have been taken, and the hedge cost that has not been compensated for could amount to $375,000! Clearly, the cost and time spent on such

FIGURE 5-1

	Purch	Refi	Flt Dwn	MBS Put
15	0.03	0.06	0.17	0.39
30	0.07	0.12	0.35	0.55
45	0.10	0.17	0.48	0.68
60	0.15	0.22	0.67	0.77

an analysis, even if done weekly, would pay for itself many times over.

To produce the same expected profit, the mortgage banker would have charged approximately 25 bp more for more discount points at closing on the refinancing lock than on the purchase lock. (It may be more complicated than this, however, if charging the additional 25 bp changes the fallout function.) At any rate, the optimal approach to pricing involves simultaneous consideration of profit margins per commitment and volume.

How to Use Profitability Analysis to Set Prices

Determining the cost of producing a loan is the first step in determining the price at which it should be sold. Obviously, the goal of a mortgage bank is to do better than break even and maximize profits. Different pricing levels imply different volume levels, as well as different profits per loan. Trial and error will help you determine the effect of price levels on loan demand; prices should be increased to the point that the profit-per-loan-times-volume equation is maximized. But to do this, it is necessary to accurately quantify total profit per loan as a function of price.

Mortgage product is complicated to evaluate because of the hedge cost and servicing elements. Even though the mortgage loan may be sold into the secondary market, the servicing revenue stream will continue for as much as 30 years. The pricing of less generic products, such as refinance loans, jumbo product, balloons, mortgage-broker-originated business and builder commitments, is more complex. Many mortgage bankers in competitive markets play "follow the leader" when setting prices. This could lead to problems if the competitors being followed have lower costs of servicing or origination or are managing risks more effectively. While "follow the leader" pricing may maintain or increase overall loan origination volume, it can often be at the expense of long-term profitability.

Each mortgage banker should establish a minimum cut-off price for each product, below which the lender simply will not offer that particular product. Above that level, pricing should be set to maximize the profit-per-loan-times-volume equation. It is clearly not possible to carry out this approach without a detailed, disciplined, daily profitability analysis.

How to calculate the hedge costs and servicing value pieces of the equation is an important final aspect of this pricing discussion. To explain how we arrive at hedge costs, we will need to step back a little and review some fundamental issues in modeling a mortgage pipeline.

Mortgage bankers are well aware of the asymmetric risk involved in making rate-lock mortgage commitments. When interest rates rise, a higher-than-average number of commitments close. When interest rates fall, a lower-than-average number of commitments close. As a result, the "upside" in mortgage origination is smaller than the "downside." Because of inefficiencies in the way that borrowers exercise their option to "walk away" from rate locks, the rate-lock option is less valuable than a market put option. While it is significantly cheaper to reverse than a market put option, a rate-lock option is also more complicated to replicate, simply because of the need to capture the essence of the inefficiency. Therefore, it is a mistake to view the rate-lock commitment as a simple put option. Doing so invariably increases the cost of the hedge and leads to less consistent profitability.

The key to evaluating different types of commitments is determining the sensitivity of their fallout ratios to interest rate changes. This task entails estimating a conditional relationship between interest rate changes and commitment closing ratios (adjusted for partial rate concessions) for a broad range of interest rate movements, up and down. Once this is accomplished, it is then possible to determine associated commitment profit-and-loss profiles.

The level and shape of the fallout function determine the commitment profit-and-loss profile. For a given market scenario, unhedged profits per commitment will, by definition, equal: Closing Ratio x (Initial Spread + Change in MBS Price). The initial spread is the difference between the commitment price (par minus points deducted at closing) and the forward-delivery MBS price, at the time the commitment is made. The graphs in Figure 5-2 illustrate this.

The cost of hedging is ultimately computed by determining the purchase price of the portfolio of hedge instruments needed to reverse the commitment profit-and-loss profile. The larger the downside relative to the upside (that is, the more asymmetric the profile), the larger will be the cost of the hedge. Thus, it will cost more to hedge refinance than purchases, because refinance applicants are more likely to "walk" in a falling rate scenario than purchase mortgage applicants.

Value of Servicing

Cash flows to mortgage servicing rights are not deterministic — that is, they are not known in advance — but rather vary depending on the course of interest rates. Therefore, to arrive at a true economic value, a stochastic pricing model must be used. A stochastic pricing model randomly generates hundreds of interest rate scenarios that are constrained to be consistent with the current term structure of interest rates and current market volatility. The most widely accepted stochastic model is the OAS model.

Within this framework, it is possible to model ancillary revenues and costs on a functional basis related to percentage of loans remaining, current balance, declining balance, payment amounts and prepayment amounts. Payment, escrow and prepay-

FIGURE 5-2

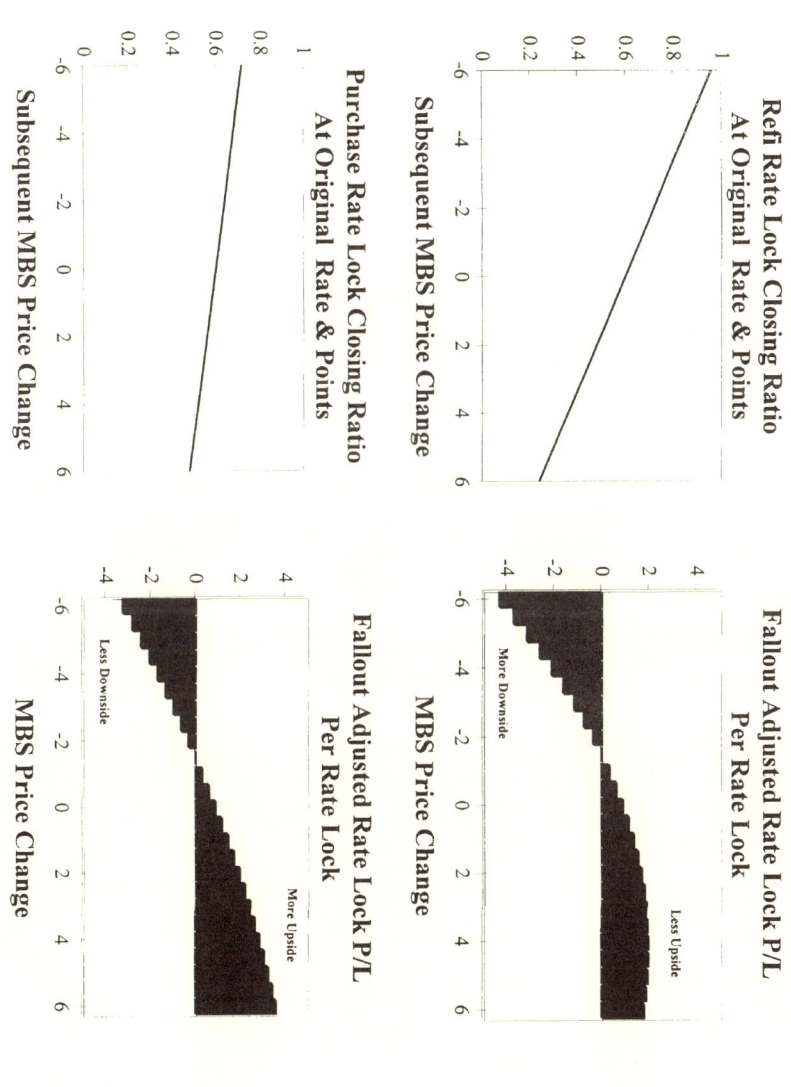

ment float earning rates are pegged to simulated periodic interest rates. Escrow and cost growth over time can be functionally related to inflation, which in turn is modeled relative to future interest rates (assuming a constant real rate of interest). A prepayment function may be based on national averages or may be one specific to the experience of the institution. Such a model can determine the current economic value of servicing, as well as the sensitivity of that value to changes in interest rate levels. This is done by averaging the results of hundreds of randomly- generated interest rate scenarios.

At this moment, OAS-based servicing evaluation analysis is not widely available commercially. Institutions that do not have the ability to generate such analyses in-house may be able to gain access to this type of model through experienced consultants or Wall Street investment firms that use stochastic models.

It is well understood that the right to service a 30-year, fixed-rate mortgage is more valuable than the right to service a 15-year, fixed-rate mortgage. It is also well known that, for a given mortgage type and remaining maturity, the right to service a higher-note-rate mortgage is less valuable than the right to service a lower-note-rate mortgage. However, more subtle factors can also have a large impact on servicing value.

For example, there is a good reason to believe that borrowers who, given the choice, prefer a higher- note-rate/lower-point combination at origination expect to remain in their house for a shorter period of time — that is, they expect to prepay sooner. Thus, the probability that such a mortgage will be prepaid is much higher no matter what the interest rate scenario is. The effect of this on relative servicing values can be dramatic: as much as $1\frac{1}{4}$ to $1\frac{1}{2}$ cents per basis point of retained servicing (after guaranty fee), under the extreme assumption of a 10% increase in CPR. This would translate to a 0.40 per 100 reduction in servicing value for a typical package. The increased prepayment bias can thus have a significant effect on the previously presented analysis, which assumed a constant prepayment function (the prepayment rate was assumed to be a function of the spread between the mortgage note rate and the prevailing refinance rate).

This potential tilt strongly reinforces the point that mortgages of higher note rates carry lower servicing values, thus requiring that the mortgage banker not cut the discount points charged on such loans as much as differences in security prices alone would dictate.

In the current environment of consolidation, low cost megaservicers, rapidly changing systems technology and constantly shifting customer preferences and prepayment behavior, it is necessary for all types of financial institutions to extract maximum profit from their operations. Rational pricing of rate-lock mortgage commitments will continue to increase in importance in determining the success of mortgage banking operations.

6

Analyzing Interest-Rate Trends

David Beadle, President
Bestrates, Inc.

Mortgage professionals are known for keeping one eye on origination volume and the other on interest rates. Despite this vigilance, over the years, many shops have repeatedly been caught leaning the wrong way both in their pipeline coverage and in adjusting their product mix to meet the needs of consumers and mortgage brokers. Rather than staying ahead of the pack, a host of lenders have been playing catch up and losing market share as a result. However, with some careful planning, you may be able to join the winners, no matter which direction rates move in the future.

This chapter begins with a summary of historical trends, and then provides an overview of both technical and fundamental approaches to forecasting the future direction of interest rates.

A Historical Overview

As you will note from Figure 6-1, the period from April 1994 through February 1995 included all three possible price scenarios: up, down and sideways. This instability made it extremely difficult to maintain adequate origination levels because lenders usually do not have all product bases equally covered at any one time.

While many have observed that the February/March 1994 downturn was more severe than any in memory, much lower buyprice levels had been seen before, and mortgage bankers were still able to conduct business. The hyperinflationary period of the late 1970s offers a good example. The difference in early 1994 was the speed with which prices plunged, combined with the relatively rapid and repeated changes of direction as the market stabilized during 1995.

There are basically three strategies for coping with the various price scenarios. In order to know which one to use, you have to achieve a more comprehensive understanding of the market environment. The next sections of this chapter provide a

FIGURE 6-1

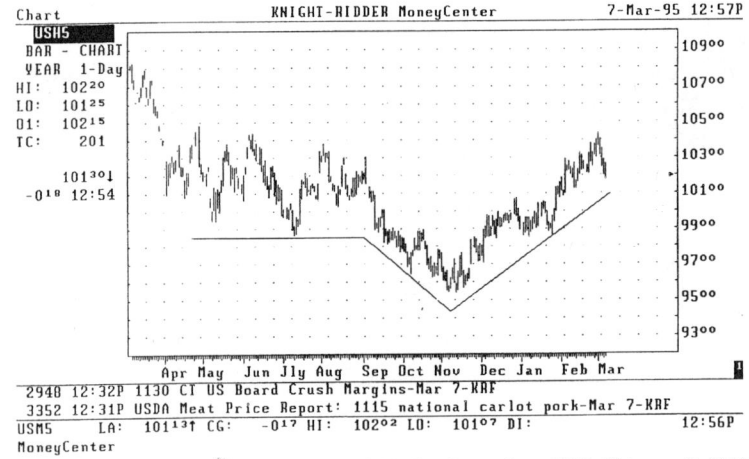

Reprinted with Permission, © *Bridge, 30 South Wacker Drive, Suite 1810, Chicago, IL 60606*

brief review of what has transpired since the 16-year bull market run began in 1981.

The 1980s

When Ronald Reagan took office as President of the United States in January 1981, times were tough in the housing market. During the first year of his presidency, rates soared to over 15% as measured by the U.S. 10-year T-note depicted in Figure 6-2. The historically high rates were the result of efforts by then Federal Reserve Chair Paul Volker to control runaway inflation. Fortunately, things did not get any worse. In response, the secondary market developed the first ARM products to make it possible for at least some Americans to afford a home.

There were more scares along the way, notably in 1984 and again in 1987. During this second "bounce" in yields, 30-year conventional fixed-mortgage rates momentarily hit 12%, before the stock market gave way with a 500 point crash in October

FIGURE 6-2

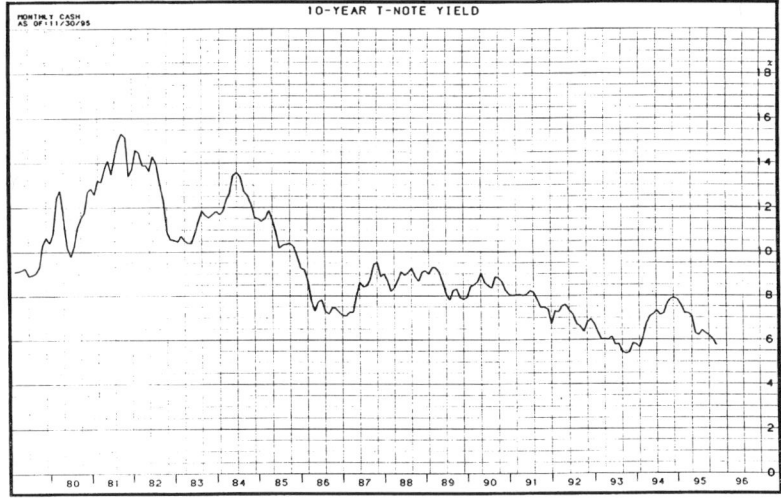

Reprinted with Permission, © *Bridge, 30 South Wacker Drive, Suite 1810, Chicago, IL 60606*

1987. From there, it was all downhill. By the end of 1989, interest rates had hit 8%, hinting at the coming recession.

The 1990s

What many thought was the cycle low in interest rates occurred on October 15, 1993. The 10-year T-note descended to less than 5.50 percent. On Friday, February 4, 1994, the first Federal Reserve Board (Fed) tightening in years caused panic in the trading pits. As you will notice in Figure 6-2, the yield pattern began to take on the look of a jet fighter in a steep climb. However, the change in policy by the Fed, in the face of a 1993 fourth quarter Gross Domestic Product reading of a robust and potentially inflationary 7.0%, had the desired effect. Inflation was cut off at the pass by an eventual doubling of the Federal Funds rate from 3% to 6%, and long term yields gradually fell back toward their 1993 lows.

The Federal Funds rate is the rate that one bank charges another for an overnight loan. The Federal Reserve Bank of New York conducts open market operations weekdays at 10:30 a.m. Eastern Time to either add or drain reserves from the banking system to maintain Fed Funds at the target specified by the Federal Open Market Committee (FOMC). The FOMC meets every six weeks to review interest rate policy.

The Inflation Factor

By their very definition, bonds are fixed-income instruments. When you buy a 10-year T-note with 1991 dollars, all future earnings are measured in terms of the value of that cash at the time of purchase. For example, if the 1991 T-note is secured at 8%, and inflation during the period in question averages 3%, then the real rate of return is only 5 percent. That's because throughout the holding period, the 8%

Analyzing Interest-Rate Trends 137

interest payments are constantly being eroded by a 3% reduction in value caused by inflation.

For this reason, it is easy to see why price pressures as measured by the Consumer Price Index (CPI) and other gauges can have a dramatic impact on the value of Treasury and mortgage-backed securities. Figure 6-3 illustrates the close relationship. The dotted line represents inflation in the form of the Knight Ridder Commodity Research Bureau (KR-CRB) index and the solid line constitutes the yield on the bellwether 30-year cash treasury bond.

The KR-CRB was created by combining futures prices from 17 different markets in a variety of categories. Agricultural commodities are heavily represented, which has caused a number of analysts to discount the accuracy of the KR-CRB's prognostication power due to the volatility of food prices. However, the index has consistently been an excellent lead indicator of interest-rate

FIGURE 6-3

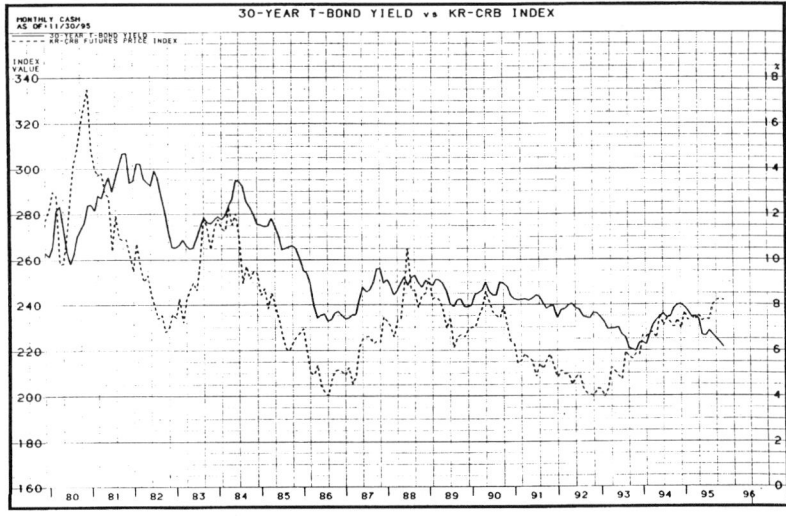

Reprinted with Permission, © *Bridge, 30 South Wacker Drive, Suite 1810, Chicago, IL 60606*

direction, as the 15-year chart history presented in Figure 6-3 demonstrates.

Cyclical Considerations

A rather unusual symmetry in the bond market was evident during the period from late 1992 through the end of 1995. Referring back to Figure 6-2, a nearly straight-line rally took place from November 9, 1992 until October 15, 1993, a period of 340 days. The bear market commenced from that moment until November 11, 1994 — 392 days. From there, another bull run ensued for a further 390 days to December 6, 1995, and completed a perfectly shaped mountain formation on the aforementioned yield chart.[1]

Product Considerations

Historical review may place matters into perspective, but as in the case of science, pure research must eventually result in a practical application of the principles involved to be thoroughly useful. For that reason, we shall now focus on a specific period in time and analyze what happened and why.

Rising long-term rates combined with relatively low short-term rates were the norm during the period from October 1993 through September 1994. And during the summer of 1994, ARMs were king.

To be sure, 1-year Treasury Bill (T-bill) yields were rising quickly, but they were starting from lower levels, as shown in Figure 6-4. And that initial 2% spread gave them the edge.

---

1. Information on the September 1992-October 1993 rally duration furnished by Steven W. Poser, New York Technical Analyst, Deutsche Morgan Grenfell. Information on October 1993–November 1994 and November 1994–December 1995 symmetry furnished by Richard Harding, New York US Government Bond Trading Department, Deutsche Morgan Grenfell, on December 11, 1995. Data used with their permission.

FIGURE 6-4

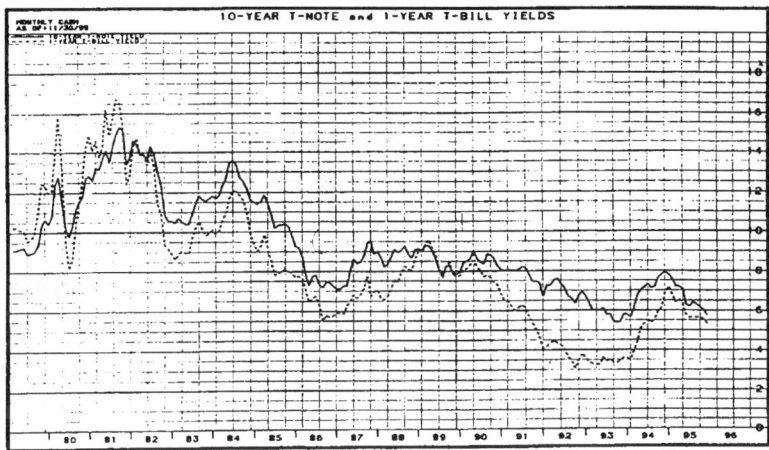

Reprinted with Permission, © Bridge, 30 South Wacker Drive, Suite 1810, Chicago, IL 60606

The ARM Factor

The problem was that many mortgage bankers did not have competitive ARM products, because Fannie Mae prices could not compete with the offerings of the local thrifts. Fannie Mae and Freddie Mac money was coming from the secondary market with a high price tag attached, whereas thrift cash was being derived from customer deposits and in some cases, private investors. Because the cost of the latter funds was comparatively low, the thrifts were able to put one-year convertible ARMs on the street at a retail price of 4.99% with zero points to the consumer. Even worse, these were convertible to a fixed product at some future point in time at the option of the borrower.

As Autumn 1994 arrived, numerous mortgage banking operations were finally able to secure non-Fannie Mae/Freddie Mac money and price more aggressively. But as you can see from Figure 6-5, they were too late, because short-term treasury rates

FIGURE 6-5

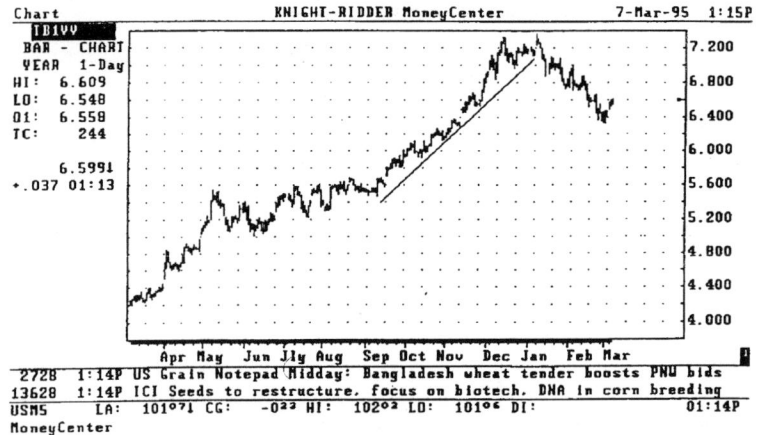

Reprinted with Permission, © Bridge, 30 South Wacker Drive, Suite 1810, Chicago, IL 60606

began a meteoric rise of two full percentage points during that three month period.

The result was a rapidly compressing yield curve which actually inverted for a time in late December. In other words, 5-year T-note yields exceeded 10-year T-note yields, and the 10-year to 30-year T-bond yield spread shrank to zero. As a result, ARMs quickly fell out of favor.

Buydowns

With rate compression in effect, the preferred vehicle of January 1995 became the zero-point lender-funded buydown. A *buydown*, as used in this chapter, is a type of loan with an elevated final note rate which a borrower takes in order to temporarily make a lower monthly payment for a set period of time. The advantage for the applicant is a lower qualifying rate and easier payments during the early years of the loan.

A lender-funded 2-1 buydown requires that a mortgage banker use roughly 2.6 points from an excess yield-spread premium to fund an escrow account. This cash, which amounts to $2,600 on a $100,000 loan, makes it possible for the home buyer to get an interest rate discount for two years before paying at the full note rate. For example, a borrower might pay at the rate of 7.5% the first year, 8.5% the second year and 9.5% from year 3 through 30 without being charged any origination or discount points at the time of closing or afterwards.

While it is true that you can, in theory, create a buy down quite easily, the level of sophistication of the average retail loan officer or mortgage broker is not up to the task without a little coaching or marketing-department packaging. In most cases during early 1995, the investor assistance was sorely lacking, and an opportunity was lost.

Fixed-Rate Mortgages Return

Before most companies could build steam behind the buydown concept, buy prices launched skyward in February 1995 and vaulted back to levels not seen since the previous September. Suddenly, the fixed-rate mortgage was back, with popularly advertised two point rates in the middle to lower 8% range.

As you can see from Figure 6-6, the peak lasted for a week and then reversed in early March 1995 amidst the defeat of the balanced budget amendment in the U.S. Senate.

Summary

To review, there were three product choices during the period: short-term ARMs, buydowns and fixed-rate mortgages. One could have offered longer-term adjustables or 11th District Cost of Funds programs, but when carefully analyzed by a potential customer, these often would not have had the maximum

FIGURE 6-6

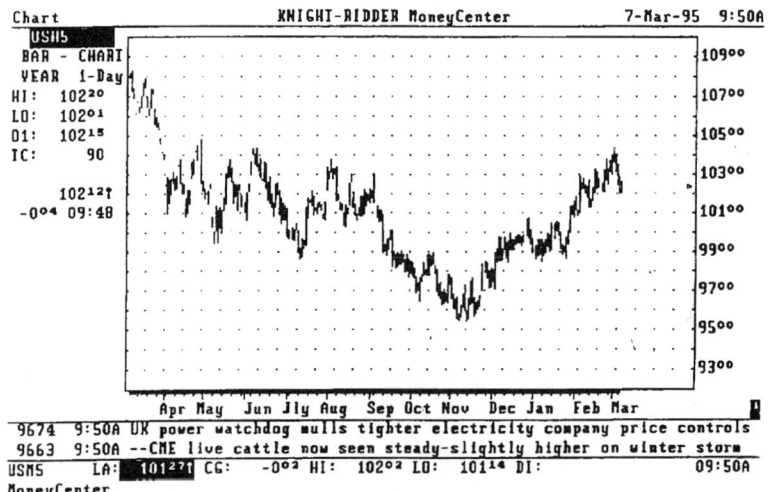

Reprinted with Permission,© Bridge, 30 South Wacker Drive, Suite 1810, Chicago, IL 60606
You may have stared at a chart such as this one many times, wondering if there was a way to divine what would occur next. Your suspicion that there was a person who could make sense out of the apparent chaos was correct. See Figure 6-7, it is another chart of this same March 1994– March 1995 time period

benefits from the borrower's perspective because of their higher rate and/or point combinations than the standard products.

The successful lenders during the fast-paced highly volatile 1994-1995 period were usually just plain lucky. In the case of ARMs, the winners were often subsidiaries of banks or thrifts with plenty of portfolio power. buydowns were most easily accomplished if the mortgage banker was accustomed to offering high premium pricing on fixed-rate products. Just about everybody else lost money, according to published reports.

Now, we come to the hard part — how to discern market moves in advance — so that you will be ready with the right

Analyzing Interest-Rate Trends 143

program and pipeline hedging strategy before the next marketing opportunity is missed.

Technical Analysis

To accomplish this task, it is important to know how to read charts. If you look at Figure 6-6, you will see what appears to the untrained eye to be a random pattern. However, when lines are drawn on that chart, as in Figure 6-7, a different picture emerges.

FIGURE 6-7

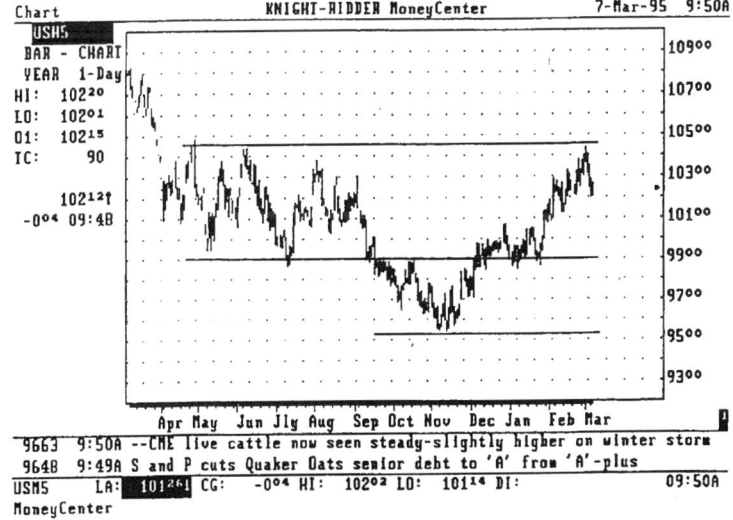

Reprinted with Permission, Bridge, 30 South Wacker Drive, Suite 1810, Chicago, IL 60606
Prices tend to move in ranges. When they hit the top or bottom of the trading channel, they bounce. It's when they do not bounce that a longer term buy/sell signal is given. The line near the 105 level is called resistance. The barrier near the price of the 95 is termed support. The middle line at 99 is both, depending on which side the market is trading.

For purposes of illustration, we will discuss the CBOT's March 1995 T-bond futures contract for the period under analysis. You could use the Fannie Mae 30-year 8.5% security chart to accomplish roughly the same goal, but as you will see later, the T-bond futures usually provide a more efficient timing mechanism.

Trading Ranges

Figure 6-7 clearly shows that from the start of April through the beginning of September, futures traded in a strict 5.5-point trading band with only three isolated violations lasting no more than two days at a time.

Resistance and *support* are terms which describe the ceiling and floor, respectively, defining a particular trading range in prices or yields. After the market makes a major move, it tends to stabilize into a horizontal pattern with discernible peaks and valleys. These may be viewed either on short-term charts spanning weeks and months or longer-term charts covering years.

For example, Figure 6-2 of the 10-year T-note yield shows a sideways trading pattern lasting from 1987 through 1991. A shorter term chart of January-June 1991 would have shown flatness as well. Technically, resistance is the price point at which most traders will automatically sell, and support is the spot where they will buy, unless volume on the move is very strong. In that case, they will follow the fresh trend which develops on a new price level.

Often, market players will set up automatic buy orders a few ticks above a resistance barrier and set sell orders a few ticks below a support line. If the border is crossed, these trades are triggered, thus exacerbating the move and causing more transactions in the same direction. Often such price activity is sudden and dramatic, hence the need for automatic orders to ensure profit-making or loss-limiting outcomes are not missed. The result is a "break" of resistance or support. If prices suddenly rise, old resistance becomes the new support line. If they fall, old support turns into new resistance.

Turning back to Figure 6-7, notice how on each occasion when prices approached *resistance* at the upper line near 104.5, they pulled back. The first three times that prices challenged *support* at 99, they rallied higher once again. However, when support was broken in early September 1994, the market was unable to recover immediately or on a second try in mid-October; finally, it was forced to seek a new price bottom in the first part of November.

After successfully holding above 95, the market quickly moved back up. Once the new resistance line was breached at the old support level of 99, prices were poised to move higher, and they did so starting in late January 1995. However, the old resistance level from the previous summer (slightly above 104) was too tough to breach, and sure enough, prices fell back again.

Keep in mind that the seeds of the rally germinated in late November 1994. That was well before most analysts were actively discussing the possibility of an impending economic slowdown. In fact, the Federal Reserve had just tightened monetary policy and would do so again on February 1, 1995.

The divergence is explained in part by the fact that the futures market is, in and of itself, a leading economic indicator. You may recall that on October 15, 1993, prices started to collapse on the heels of a government report that the Consumer Price Index was indicating that inflation was under control, which normally is a piece of good news. At the time, many wondered how the bond market could be selling off when all appeared to be well. The answer came in the last week of January 1994, when the flash reading on fourth quarter gross domestic product showed a stunning 7% annualized rate of growth. Somehow, the bond market had forecast the event only 15 days into the survey's time period.

Relative Strength Index

What's not on Figure 6-7 is one of the technician's "secret" weapons — the Relative Strength Index (RSI). RSI is a mathematical computation of the *oversold* or *overbought* status of the market. Oversold and overbought mean that too many people are on one side of the fence. In other words, an imbalance has been created between buyers and sellers.

Figure 6-8 shows that each time the price action causes the 25 or 75 line to be touched, prices move back the other way. This gauge is particularly useful in conjunction with the support/resistance line chart, because it tells you when to look for a change in direction. However, the mere fact that the 25 or 75 lines have been crossed does not automatically imply an immediate correction to neutral territory. In particularly dramatic market moves, such as

FIGURE 6-8

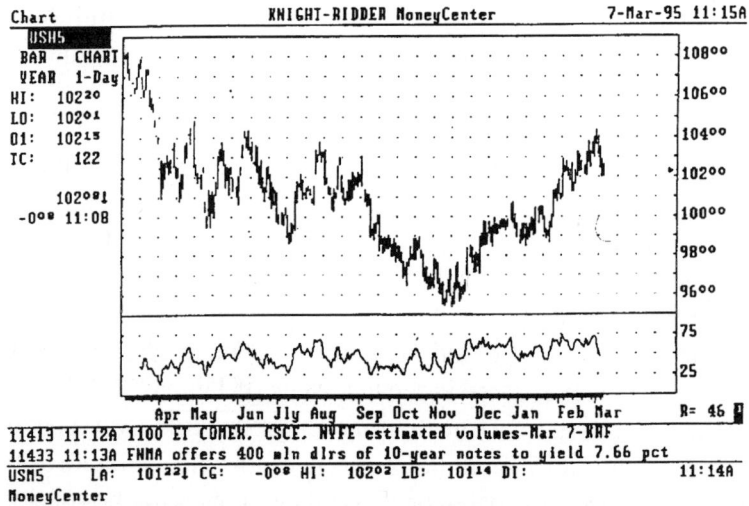

Reprinted with Permission, © Bridge, 30 South Wacker Drive, Suite 1810, Chicago, IL 60606
This chart is identical to the previous two, but includes the RSI displayed along the bottom. The RSI is an overbought/oversold indicator. When it reaches 75, the market is said to be overbought; when it touches 25, prices are considered oversold. Notice how the two barriers provide excellent short term buy/sell signals.

Analyzing Interest-Rate Trends 147

those seen in February/March 1994 (an oversold down move), and May/June 1995 (an overbought up move), RSI may transition into the single digits or remain above 90 before cooling off.

The 20-Day Moving Average
Another terrific trend indicator has been the 20-day Moving Average (M/A), which is an exponentially smoothed look at prices. As shown in Figure 6-9, the 20-day M/A line has been operating as an excellent support/resistance barometer; you can see how the market walked along either side of it all the way back to September 1994. The significance of the 20-day M/A is that it may provide important clues to direction when used in combination with the other charts.

FIGURE 6-9

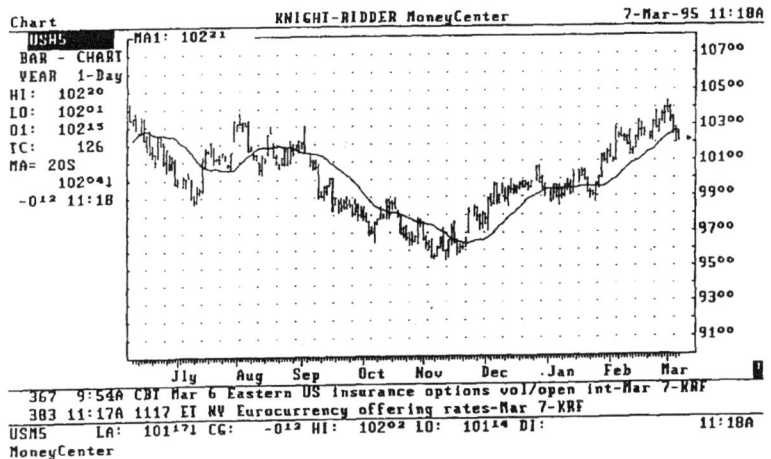

Reprinted with Permission, © Bridge, 30 South Wacker Drive, Suite 1810, Chicago, IL 60606
There are many ways to guage market condition. You can plug in any time measure to see what's happening. However, the 20-day M/A of prices proved accurate in this look at price action in March 1995 T-bond futures for the period from June 1994 to early March 1995.

148   Handbook of Secondary Marketing

Recap

In summary, the RSI and the 20-day M/A can offer good buy/sell signals that will sharpen your ability to anticipate directional changes. But for the purpose of identifying major trend shifts, the longer term support/resistance lines that separate the trading channels may be your best indicator. The longer a support or resistance line contains the price action, the more important it becomes. As prices approach these barriers, it is time to dust off the next battle plan. When prices breach these lines, it is time to implement a new marketing strategy.

The Head & Shoulders Pattern

Another excellent predicting tool is the Head & Shoulders (H&S) pattern. It is relatively easy to comprehend and has a high rate of reliability.

One of the best examples of an H&S pattern occurred during the summer of 1995. Figure 6-10 depicts on the yield chart of the

FIGURE 6-10

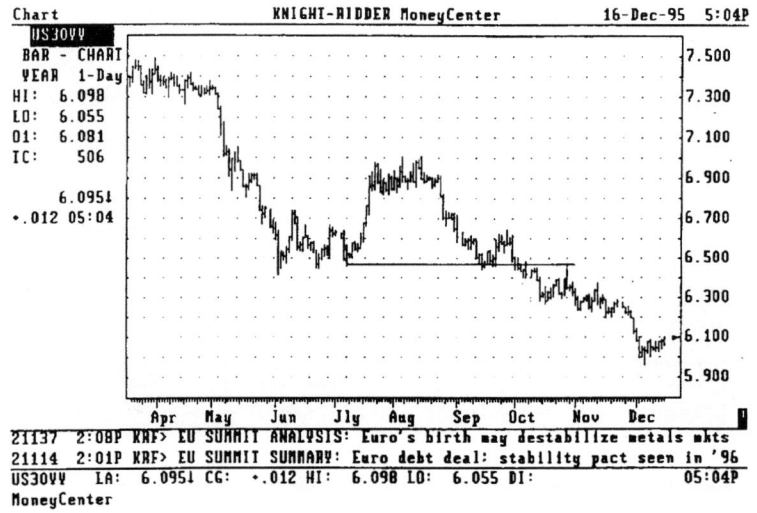

Reprinted with Permission, © *Bridge, 30 South Wacker Drive, Suite 1810, Chicago, IL 60606*

30-year Cash Treasury Bond. Notice that the left shoulder, which formed in June, was followed by a head formation in July-August and a right shoulder in September.

The way to read the pattern is to calculate the distance from the neckline near 6.50% to the top of the head near 7.00%, and then measure downward from the neckline by the same amount, in this case one half of one percent. The result is 6.00%, which constitutes the minimum downside target defined by the pattern. Sure enough, in December 1995, the predictions of the pattern were realized. In fact, the H&S was so perfect that it even included a classic return move in late October, which failed as expected, further confirming the authenticity of the formation.

The Yield Curve

There is another pattern that is not found on any single price or yield chart, yet is critically important to technicians. It defines the shape of the yield curve. The yield curve is the spread between short- and long-term rates, depicted on a graph.

When 1-year T-bill rates are low and 30-year T-bond rates are high, the curve is said to be steep. When the rates are the same, you have rate compression, and the curve is flat. When the 1-year yield is higher than the 30-year yield (as was the case in the late 1980s), the curve is inverted and usually predicts a recession resulting from a tight monetary policy on the part of the Fed.

Figure 6-11 depicts the pattern as it appeared in December 1995. With the Fed Funds Rate at 5.75%, all securities, with the exception of the 10-year and 30-year Treasury obligations, were below the overnight target. In fact, the 1-year T-bill and the 2-year T-note sported yields lower than the 3-month T-bill. The spread between the 3-month and 30-year securities was slightly less than three-quarters of one percent. Considering that, in February 1994, the distance from the 3-month T-bill at 3% to the 30-year bond

FIGURE 6-11

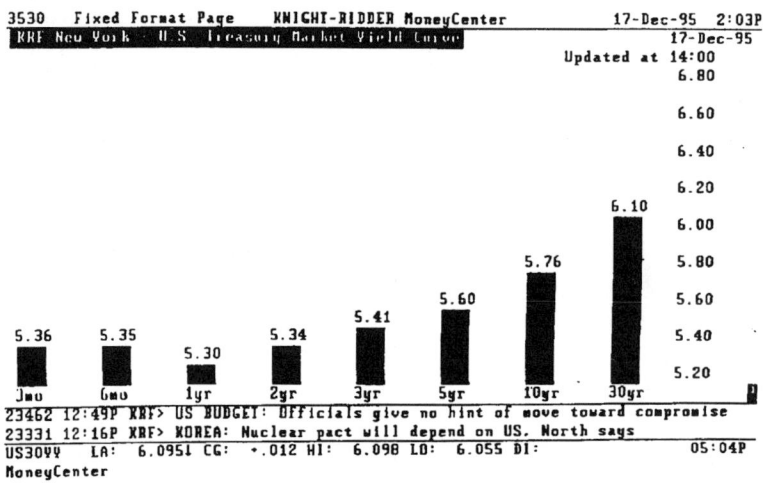

Reprinted with Permission, ⓒ *Bridge, 30 South Wacker Drive, Suite 1810, Chicago, IL 60606*
All three curves are represented on this December 15, 1995 yield chart. There is the inverted curve from the 3 Month T-bill to the 1-year T-bill, the flat curve from the 3 Month T-bill to the 2-year T-bill, and a midly rising curve from the 2-year T-note out to the 30-year Bond.

at 6% was a full 3% — a steep yield curve — you can quickly discern that the curve was much flatter two years later.

When the curve is steep, as represented by a quickly rising slope on a graph, the implications are that the market considers Fed policy to be too accommodative. In other words, rates are too low. Therefore, the bond vigilantes must boost long end yields to stave off inflation in the absence of Fed discipline. The Fed nearly always follows a steepening trend by boosting short term rates to catch up with the market.

When the curve is flat, or nearly so, the indications are that the Fed is approaching a point where it should consider the desirability of a rate cut to avoid a restrictive monetary policy which could choke off growth.

Analyzing Interest-Rate Trends   151

When an inversion takes place, as in the late 1980s, it is clear that quick action is necessary to avoid a recession. But in that particular era, policy makers were more concerned with the return of hyperinflation and therefore permitted a downturn to further inhibit the potential for a resurgence of price pressures.

Calendar Buys

It is important to consider the role of the market timers, who use the calendar to make technical buy/sell decisions. A 15-year study of the T-bond futures charts makes one point very clear: There are two times to buy the market each year. Because the signals are so reliable, action may be taken without regard to outside considerations, with a strong likelihood of success.

As depicted on the Moore Research Center chart in Figure 6-12, the buying opportunities are near Memorial Day in late May

FIGURE 6-12

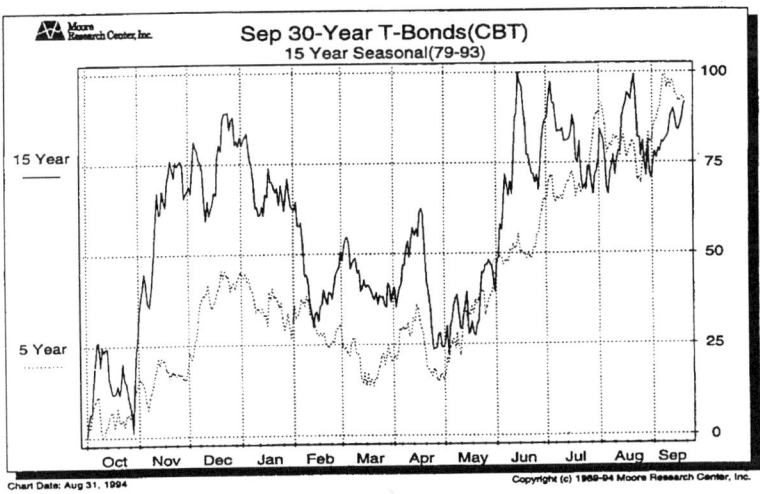

Reprinted with Permission, © *1989-1996 Moore Research center, Inc., 85180 Lorane Highway, Eugene, OR 97405*

When people say they have seen it all before, it is probably because they are T-bond futures traders. As this 15-year study dating from 1979 through 1993 demonstrates, seasonal patterns tend to be repetitive. The strongest predictable move takes place in May and June on a regular basis. It is the Memorial Day Rally, so named because with uncanny precision, prices usually improve significantly near the May 30th holiday.

and during the early part of November. During both 1994 and 1995, strong market advances, with resultant lower yields, were seen during these periods. Why? Because T-bond futures are closely related to the KR-CRB index. The KR-CRB index is heavily influenced by agricultural prices, which tend to rise and fall with the seasons due to planting and harvesting considerations. So, if you see the market suddenly doing the unexpected, it may be because the calendar has just hit a critical date, and it is buying time based on this methodology.

Mortgage Prices
So far, we have focused on T-bond futures. What about mortgages? Figure 6-13 shows that mortgages tend to follow Treasuries.

FIGURE 6-13

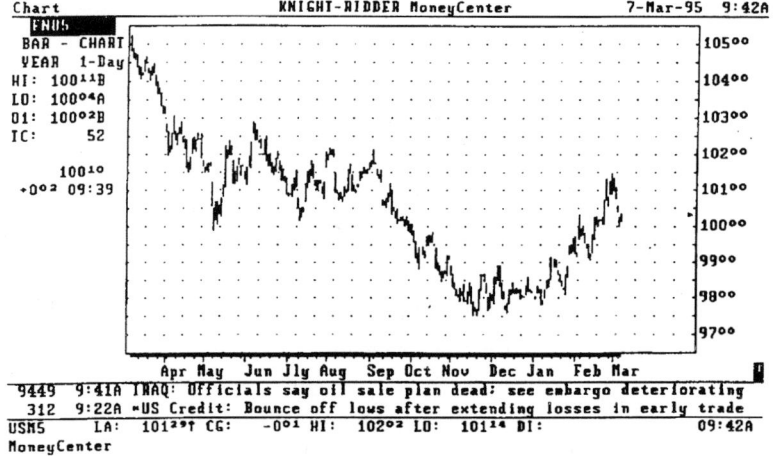

Reprinted with Permission, © 1989-1996 Moore Research center, Inc., 85180 Lorane Highway, Eugene, OR 97405
While it is true that mortgage prices trade in the world of fixed-income instruments, a precise daily correlation between US Treasury futures and mortgages is not possible. Cash treasuries are largely noncallable instruments whereas mortgages are subject to prepayment. However, T-bond futures have a powerful influence on mortgage price direction, as demonstrated in this chart of the Fannie Mae 8.5% front month security from March 1994 to March 1995. You can see how the most recent mortgage rally failed before major resistance was reached, because T-bonds had touched the top of their trading range and were heading the other way.

However, a careful study of the mortgage chart would not have alerted you to the sudden change in direction that occurred in early March 1995, which was so clearly seen in T-bonds. If you have to make a decision about which predictor is more reliable, you may wish to opt for the T-bonds for two reasons: The trading volume is much higher, and there are more technical analysts watching the price movements. Therefore, there is a greater chance that a technical buy or sell signal will be acted upon.

Gaps

One technique that is easier to use on the mortgage chart involves the "rule of gaps." Simply stated, technicians often follow prices by using a bar chart, such as the one shown in Figure 6-13. Each bar represents one day of price action, including the complete range from the high to the low. A gap forms from one day to the next when the low of the previous session is followed by a much steeper overnight drop. It can also happen the other way around. Prices may open on a new trading day substantially higher than they closed on the last one. These conditions create a price gap in the bar chart.

Over the years, traders have noticed that gaps are usually filled, either immediately or in the not-too-distant future. In other words, the price eventually declines or rises so that a new bar covers the area of the gap during subsequent sessions. So, when you see a lot of gaps, there is a greater than 50% chance that prices will reverse.

Technical Conclusions

Now that you have additional insight into the predictability of price movement, you know enough to be dangerous. Remember: just as beauty is in the eye of the beholder, interpretations of the same chart may vary. There is no substitute for experience. If you have analysts or outside hedgers who are paid to stare at price screens all day long, consult them for additional insights.

Implications for Pipeline Hedging

Support and resistance lines, RSI, moving averages and the other indicators discussed in this chapter can be used to fine-tune pipeline coverage levels. For example, as buyprices approach support, coverage could be increased in anticipation of increasing rates; as buyprices approach resistance, coverage levels could be pared back. The greater the number of indicators that signal a change in interest rates, the greater confidence the technical analyst has in the prediction.

Considerable experience is required to successfully employ any of the analytical techniques for pipeline hedging described in this chapter. For example, if prices should break through support, this could signal the onset of a new bearish interest rate trend. The secondary marketing manager who had earlier reduced coverage in anticipation of an upward bounce in MBS prices would then have to re-establish and perhaps increase coverage. If the signal were to turn out to be false and prices subsequently increase, the additional coverage might have to be paired off at a loss. The phenomenon of false signals resulting in a series of pair-off losses is known as whipsaw.

Fundamental Analysis

Fundamental analysis is the practice of basing tactical decisions on news and data rather than on chart patterns.

The Unemployment Factor

If the monthly payroll jobs report indicates that more Americans than expected are finding employment, the development is

Analyzing Interest-Rate Trends 155

said to be negative for the bond market because more jobs means more cash in the hands of consumers. Additional money will result in more spending, thus creating greater demand and lower supply of finished products. Eventually, higher consumer prices come along, translating into a loss of value for fixed-income instruments due to the ravages of inflation.

Figure 6-14 shows the inverse relationship between the unemployment rate and T-bond yields over the past 16 years. During the period from 1983-1984, the jobless rate declined from nearly 11% to just above 7 percent. At the same time, the cash bond yield rose from near 8% to almost 10 percent. The pattern was reversed during the recession of the early 1990s, when unemployment grew from 4% to 9.5% while rates fell from 9% to 7.5 percent. However, the relationship is not quite as strong as that between the KR-CRB index and T-bond futures discussed earlier.

FIGURE 6-14

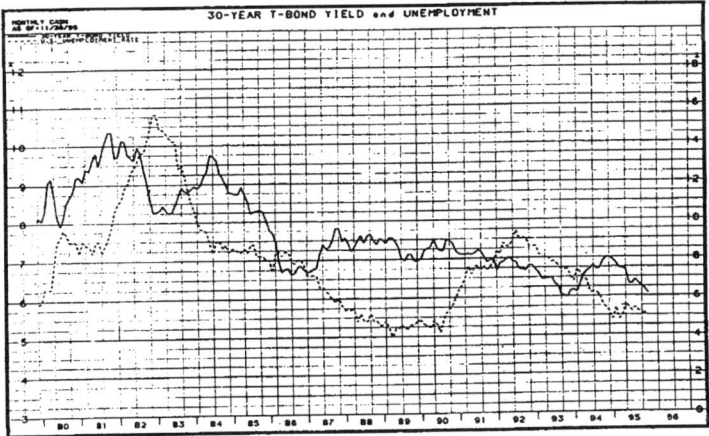

Reprinted with Permission, ©*1989-1996 Moore Research Center, Inc., 85180 Lorane Highway, Eugene, OR 97405*

Federal Reserve Policy

The problem is that fundamental analysis in isolation does not work well, because a myriad of conclusions may be drawn. Aside from the earlier example of the CPI giving a false buy signal in October 1993, one only need look at the reaction of the market to the first Federal Reserve rate hike of the 1994-1995 series on February 4, 1994. Within 90 minutes of the announcement, the bond market changed direction four times before deciding that the news was bad! To understand why that happened, an anecdote is in order.

The story comes from the 1987 medieval adventure/comedy film, *The Princess Bride*. The hero and the villain are having a battle of wits to decide who will gain custody of the princess. In the scene, the hero appears to have placed poison in one of two wine goblets, and then challenges the villain to determine which cup contains the fatal concoction. It is a deadly game, because the proof will be in who dies when they both drink, after the decision is made.

The villain begins the discussion by pointing out that a clever hero would put the poison in his own goblet, figuring that only a foolish opponent would accept what was initially placed in front of him. But since the villain declares that he is not a fool, he cannot take the wine in front of the hero. However, the villain knows that the hero knows that the villain is not a fool, so the villain cannot chose the wine that has been offered to him either. How does it end? Sorry, you will have to rent the movie!

However, this scene does provide some insight into the four direction changes. At 11:15 a.m. EST on that aforementioned Friday, the bond market rallied shortly after the tightening was announced. The theory was that a tougher Federal Reserve monetary policy would prevent inflation from increasing — the Fed's stated goal. However, within minutes, prices started heading sharply lower for two reasons: First, technical traders noticed that the upside momentum was fading. And, second, fundamental players realized that the Fed might have to engage in a series of tightenings, which would force all rates higher. Then, the thought was that if interest rates initially headed higher, that would slow the economy substantially, which meant rates would then come down again. So, there was no need to take long-term rates higher now, because they would simply resume their downward trajectory shortly. By 1 p.m., that theory had been tossed onto the trash heap, and the market started selling off in earnest, with help from a bearish technical formation known as a negative outside day. (An *outside day* is a chart pattern in which a higher high and a lower low in price is achieved within the same trading day. It is considered a positive technical indicator when the closing price is higher than at the start of trading. It becomes a bad omen when the final price is below that of the previous day.)

Unfortunately, a number of Wall Street firms placed too much faith in fundamental analysis and clung to the hope that the market would correct. As a result, some companies failed; others were forced to severely cut back trading staffs. Even Fed Chair Alan Greenspan and other voting members of the FOMC were surprised by the magnitude of the bond market sell-off.

Predicting Reactions

Regardless of where the markets are at any given point in an economic cycle, the debate rages about whether the Fed will ease or tighten policy, when it will do so and what the event will mean for interest rates. As far as technicians are concerned, the question is irrelevant. The only thing that matters is the chart pattern, which has already taken into account all of the available technical and fundamental considerations. If the market trades above resistance for a few days, these traders will be buyers. If the market fails to move up, they will be sellers until initial support levels are reached.

Fundamentalists have a bigger problem. If the Fed tightens monetary policy, does that mean the economy will be thrown into recession from over zealous action? If so, long-term interest rates may begin to fall further. Such was the case after the tightenings of November 1994 and February 1995.

Or, traders may begin to worry (as was the case in February 1994) that the Fed knows more than they do. Perhaps inflation is making a comeback, which means that interest rates have sunk too far too fast and need to be brought back to higher levels.

If the FOMC does not tighten, the fear might be that the FOMC is no longer vigilant in the battle against inflation. This would mean that the markets must act to protect investor value by raising rates to ensure that the economy slows further.

On the other hand, the markets may have already figured the Fed would not make another move, so traders will follow the technique of buying the rumor (of no tightening) and selling the fact (when there is no tightening), thus sending rates higher anyway.

Combining Technical and Fundamental Analysis
To solve the dilemma facing fundamentalists, many use a mixed strategy. They take a long-term position in the marketplace based on the fundamentals, such as falling gross domestic product, and then make buy/sell adjustments by watching technical support and resistance levels.

Note: Although carefully verified, data are not guaranteed as to accuracy or completeness. BestRates, Inc. cannot be held responsible for any direct or incidental loss or liability incurred by applying any of the information or opinions in this chapter.

7

EDI: Applications for Lenders in the Secondary Market

Scott Cooley, President
Contour Software, Inc.

Technology has become a key difference between lenders. The use of technology, and more specifically, Electronic Data Interchange (EDI), has had a profound impact on efficiency and service levels for all lenders. Those lending institutions that embrace the new era of electronic communications are quickly becoming the market leaders of tomorrow. This chapter addresses the direction in which the industry is moving and how lenders can use EDI to leap ahead of the competition.

The Four Methods of Communications

It is important to understand the basic infrastructure available to lenders for EDI. There are four primary methods of communications available for all parties involved in a loan transaction. Each has its own advantages and disadvantages. The methods used by a lender can play a critical role in the success of any EDI program. In general, the most open and nonproprietary methods tend to be the most successful. However, proprietary systems are often developed when alternative solutions are not available. Lenders are likely to use at least three different communication methods to meet the different transaction requirements.

Direct Dial

Direct dial phone calls are often used by vendors who have dedicated systems for modem communications with their clients. The best examples are credit reporting companies. Over 95% of all communications to credit reporting companies are carried out through direct dial methods. Toll-free 1-800 numbers often are set up to reduce a lender's communications costs. Direct dial works best when proprietary software is installed by the vendor into a lender's office. The advantages are that it is usually free, it provides instant communications, transactions are secure, and it offers push-button simplicity within the vendor's software program. When available, this is usually the preferred choice of communications.

E-mail

Electronic mail (e-mail) is quickly becoming a standard business tool, much like the FAX machine became standard in the late 1980s. Already, lenders are beginning to place e-mail addresses on business cards, stationery and advertisements. The mortgage industry provides the perfect environment for e-mail because of the vast amount of communication required among the involved parties. E-mail is a vital business tool that every lender should adopt. Ideally, each employee in a company should have his or her own e-mail address to increase productivity.

The advantages of e-mail include that it is inexpensive and uses existing communications infrastructures. Also, data files can be attached to e-mail messages. The disadvantages are that most e-mail messages travel through the Internet, which is not very secure, and e-mail is not "real time," as it can take from 30 minutes to several hours to arrive. E-mail provides one-way communication, which is impractical for transactions such as sending borrower information to a credit reporting company (with the exception of an immediate return of the "merged infile" report).

E-mail is the best communication medium to use when transactions are not time critical. Consider e-mail a new business staple whose role will continue to escalate within the industry.

Value Added Networks

Value Added Networks (VANs) are used to carry EDI transactions between agencies, investors, servicers and others. Both Fannie Mae and Freddie Mac offer VAN capabilities for communicating with third parties. In addition, both companies use these networks for much of their reporting requirements. Servicing reporting and loan delivery details must flow to the agencies in an electronic format. Expect further developments in these areas for generating new business opportunities with investors, servicers and secondary marketing agencies.

VANs are providing the electronic means to deliver solutions for rate distribution, rate lock-ins, conditions postings and so on. However, it is unlikely that VANs will become the communication medium of choice between wholesalers, brokers and third parties. In general, VANs are more expensive, more complicated and less integrated than other communication alternatives. VANs will likely become the primary method of communication with the vendors that offer them, but will do little to serve other industry communication needs.

The Internet

By the time you read this, the Internet may have dramatically changed. Because it is expanding at a phenomenal rate, trying to write current information about the Internet is an exercise in futility. It is clear that the Internet will have a major impact on the secondary market. Its most important impact will be carrying the vast majority of e-mail throughout the industry. However, the Internet's potential vastly expands past its e-mail capabilities.

Soon, every wholesaler and industry participant will have its own home page — an address on the Internet, where it can list all offerings, products and services, as well s important phone numbers, e-mail addresses and frequently asked questions (FAQs). Wholesalers can post rate information, product details, underwriting guidelines and industry news.

The Internet is a tremendous information resource that goes beyond text and graphics retrieval and serves as the perfect medium for client/server applications. Examples are rate locking and confirmation systems. It can also be used for real time data feeds for hedging purposes. Eventually, web sites will be integrated into desktop applications so that information from every business you work with will be instantly accessible. Loan origination systems that can perform a rate lock, check the loan against underwriting requirements and retrieve policy requirements from a given wholesaler are the next generation of streamlined origination products.

File Formats and MBA's X.12 Initiative

The format in which data is stored is not of great importance. There is a long list of pros and cons for using each of the different data formats.

The MBA has initiated the development of ANSI X.12 standard data formats for most industry transactions. For larger

EDI: Applications for Lenders in the Secondary Market 163

lenders with proprietary in-house systems, using the X.12 formats provides them with the greatest level of industry connectivity.

Lenders must rely on software vendors to develop appropriate EDI interfaces. These interfaces are often programmed in the most desired methods by the suppliers to the mortgage industry. If using a third-party software developer, make sure that it is aggressive in ensuring industry EDI connectivity. The ability to communicate quickly and efficiently is increasingly becoming a key competitive weapon.

Natural market forces will determine the most frequently used data formats. However, each transaction will likely have its own set of parameters to determine which data structures to use. While one type of transaction may find its way through a VAN, stored in an X.12 format, others may be completely text based and embodied in an e-mail.

Automated Underwriting and Its Impact on Communications

Automated Underwriting Systems (AUSs) are the single most important driving force towards EDI in the mortgage industry. Underwriting remains the core of the mortgage loan business. In the past, this function was always completed through the review of paper forms, including roll after roll of calculator tape. Because everything was paper based, there was little need to use a digital format. However, with the introduction of AUSs, this is changing. The industry is faced with new requirements for collecting data. In some cases, reps and warrants are being waived if the data submitted is accurate. The new objective is to capture the data as quickly and accurately as possible.

In the case of broker-to-wholesaler communication, the wholesaler can provide significantly improved services and faster underwriting decisions by receiving electronic loan data. Most major lenders are planning to implement or have already implemented methods to capture borrower details electronically from the brokers. This usually requires an interface from the broker's loan origination system.

On a longer term basis, AUSs will eventually evolve to the point where each loan will be priced differently in the secondary markets. Loans are currently slotted into categories to determine the points and interest rates. Manual underwriting required the use of such tactics, but technology heralds a new methodology. Eventually, every loan will be priced individually. Sophisticated artificial intelligence and modeling systems will weigh all of the characteristics about the borrower, loan type and property. Categories will be eliminated, and each loan will be given its own interest rate and points based upon the determined risk characteristics. This is what Wall Street ultimately wants, but today's technology does not offer this capability. This will be a natural outgrowth as complete information is collected and underwritten and the time of application.

Communication with Third Party Originators

EDI and other industry changes will drive a powerful electronic communications capability between wholesalers and third party originators (TPOs). Wholesalers must begin to map out strategies for communicating with TPOs, including e-mail, rate locks, rate distribution, condition listings and loan product posting. To start, wholesalers should implement a company-wide e-mail application so that every employee can receive e-mail through an Internet address. The second stage is providing a means for other communications mediums.

The selected system should provide two fundamental features. First, it must not be highly proprietary; in other words, it should not involve developing your own software. Most TPOs prize their independence, work with many wholesalers and have little interest in installing and learning software that only works with one wholesaler. Second, you must have the ability to expand and enhance the electronic interface with your clients on a continuous basis. Look for systems that incorporate both of these capabilities.

Improving Communication and Enhancing Service Levels
The most important aspect in developing your EDI strategy is to clearly understand the objectives. Look at the calls you currently receive from TPOs. What kind of information requests would be better handled by EDI? The possibilities are endless, as most communications are fairly homogenous and they lend themselves well to automation. The obvious answer includes rate distribution, product information dissemination, rate locking, loan submission and underwriting communication. However, there are many other types of faxes and phone calls that are routine. Status information, condition issues, product questions and logistic details can all be handled through basic e-mail and automated response systems. Internal systems should be highly automated for distributing every piece of information possible.

Rate Distribution
Perhaps the most sought after objective is that of "Wholesaler to Retailer Electronic Rate Distribution," the Holy Grail of the mortgage industry. Over my 14 years in the industry, I have met with no less than 20 vendors who have tried to capture this Holy Grail. In all these years and with all their valiant efforts, not a single company can be described as successful in this endeavor. In fact, all but a few are out of business. Those remaining have achieved only a presence in small geographic areas.

Today, the lure of this marketplace is still attractive to some of the largest names in the industry. Fannie Mae and AllTell (CPI), for example, have invested significant resources to build the information superhighway for electronic wholesaler-to-mortgage broker rate and loan product distribution. Neither has been successful to date. While these systems may ultimately become successful, I would like to challenge the current trend and propose a radical new system in a different direction from today's current thinking.

Virtually every system tried, to date, has the same basic premise. Rate and product information is gathered from wholesalers and placed into a central data repository which is then distributed electronically to mortgage brokers. The mortgage brokers have the capability to sort and review this product information and, in most cases, prequalify potential loan applicants using this database. The technology to accomplish this has been available for at least 10 years. While such a system might be a little faster and easier with today's technology, there has not been any recent technological development which would make a huge difference.

On the surface, this appears to be not only a perfectly acceptable form of distribution but also one which every mortgage broker will agree is in great demand. Everybody wants it, feels it's viable, and is willing to pay for it. This creates the perfect trap for entrepreneurs seeking a lucrative, wide-open market. Many entrepreneurs have tried to fill this need and so far, all have failed. But why?

The reasons are many and varied. Here are nine reasons why Wholesaler-To-Retailer Electronic Rate Distribution has not worked:

1. Relationships between mortgage brokers and wholesalers are dynamic. Wholesalers will tell you that not all of their brokers get the same deal. Quality of loan sub-

EDI: Applications for Lenders in the Secondary Market 167

missions, quantity of loan submissions, broker commitments and other factors can all affect the price that a broker obtains for a particular loan. It is virtually impossible for an independent third party to fully grasp this environment and turn it into a single database for all brokers to access. Wholesalers find pricing perhaps their most difficult area, requiring constant attention and change based upon market demands.

2. Different geographic locations require pricing variations that are difficult to define. Wholesalers may use regions, states or even counties.

3. Many wholesalers do not wish to compete on rate and points alone. They will often resist participating in such rate distribution systems, especially if such systems included added costs.

4. Wholesalers tend to specialize in certain niches. Rate distribution systems cannot distinguish between the preferences of each wholesaler to the degree desired by the wholesaler. The independent vendor is in charge of stratifying the product database for its needs. Ideally, a different system would exist to allow the wholesaler to select the most desirable loan types on an hour-by-hour basis. This would allow the wholesaler to better fill commitments made to investors and agencies.

5. Wholesalers cannot control pricing to individuals. Often, wholesalers offer special pricing to get a sweet deal (such as 50% LTV) from a favored broker. Wholesalers are not given the ability to review the broker's "in hand" deal.

6. Each product price can have a huge number of tradeoffs between the rate and points. This makes the searching process much more difficult since one product can only be compared to another when the points are the sam-3Xe.

7. Current systems do not allow the mortgage broker to compare service levels. Everyone in the industry knows that the lowest rate is not always the best deal.
8. Mortgage brokers are used to receiving their rate pricing for free. While brokers will claim there is significant value to having them delivered electronically, the average broker is not willing to pay what a rate service would have to charge in order for its system to be viable.
9. When a broker wishes to sort and select loans electronically, all of its wholesalers should be included. This is a catch-22 situation. Brokers will not use a distribution service if less than 90% of their wholesalers are on the system, and wholesalers will not participate if the majority of their brokers are not using it. The end result is that neither party actively participates.

It came to me one day that perhaps the entire process is backwards! When looking at many other wholesale-to-retail industries where the product is highly complex, the retailer often submits a bid request from a wholesaler for a consumer application in hand. Why should our industry be any different? Why not take the loan application and send the borrower details to the wholesaler for a rate and product quote? With today's applications being taken on laptops, systems are currently in place that will allow brokers to send basic borrower details to any of their desired wholesalers.

Imagine that a broker gathers information about a borrower and a given loan — enough to provide about a dozen data elements such as LTV, ratios, assets, property type, property address, desired loan programs, broker names and even desired broker markup. This information could be sent directly to the wholesaler via dial-up lines, and an immediate response could be provided and printed on a portable printer or sent back by FAX.

This response is a "qualified rate sheet." The wholesaler would not underwrite the loan, pull a credit report or do any other time-consuming or cost-incurring procedure. The wholesaler would simply take basic borrower information, sort its product database and return a printed response. This response would simply be a advertisement that could be given to the potential borrower. The quoted rates and APR would already be included in the broker markup.

On the surface, this may not seem like a superior method. However, it does have some advantages:

1. There is no cost to the broker, no third-party vendor fees, and the only cost to the wholesaler would be a one minute phone call on their 800 number (about 15 cents). With such a low cost, the wholesaler could encourage frequent use, and the broker would not hesitate to use the service since there would be no sign-up charges and no monthly fees.

2. It provides a fantastic service from the wholesaler to the broker. The broker receives a customized advertisement which is complete with multiple products, amortization graphs and product details. This allows the broker to more easily sell the wholesaler's products.

3. The wholesaler could fine-tune pricing and product mix exactly as desired with up-to-the-minute accuracy. Rates and products are no longer a day old or made to fit into certain categories. Each wholesaler could modify its system to the exact degree desired. For example, a wholesaler could determine the specific broker, geographic location, consumer preferences, expected loan risk and much more. The wholesaler could require any amount of information wanted about the deal in hand. This allows the wholesaler to be selective, based upon

its strengths in the marketplace and the desires of its secondary marketing departments.
4. Brokers could submit to as many of their wholesalers as desired and only to those desired. Existing systems might match wholesalers with brokers whose business is not desired and vice versa. Brokers could choose to submit information to only those wholesalers who meet their service needs and who might accept the deal in hand. The broker must remain in control of the loan placement; a computer is not qualified to make that decision.
5. Brokers often make mistakes in quoting rates from a wholesaler and they sometimes mistakenly believe that a given wholesaler might accept a particular deal. This is always a problem and creates constant fear in the broker's heart. How often have you seen a given product and rate quoted by a loan officer when such a loan could not be made? This often happens on nonowner occupied prospects. The proposed system would give a reasonable (but not complete) assurance that the wholesaler is interested in the deal in hand, and the broker would receive a solid rate quote direct from the source with little chance of error. Issues, such as not accepting condominium loans near an earthquake fault, could be handled easily, and mistakes would be reduced significantly.
6. The system would be totally automated. Wholesalers could stop spending untold hours on the phone with brokers looking to place a deal. One-minute turnaround would solve these issues and reduce the work load tremendously for both parties.
7. Wholesalers could use off-the-shelf software products that would integrate with their existing product databases. Application suites, such as Microsoft Office, could be a perfect platform to receive a call, search the

EDI: Applications for Lenders in the Secondary Market 171

database, pull together marketing materials, graph the loans and send back a professional presentation either online or by FAX.

8. Wholesalers would not have to re-enter their entire product matrix into another system or accept constant errors when a rate service chooses to rely on a faxed rate sheet.
9. To get started, this service would not require significant participation from both wholesalers and brokers. It would not have the catch-22 of existing systems. One wholesaler can start offering it to their brokers, and the first one to do so has a significant marketing advantage over their competition.
10. Both Wall Street experts and Former Fed chair Alan Greenspan have been quoted as saying that mortgage pricing will eventually get down to the borrower level based upon the risk of each loan. This will be the natural course that technology is beginning to allow. Qualified rate sheets fit perfectly with this theory of individual pricing.
11. The wholesaler's representatives see the deal in hand, allowing them to contact the brokers if they want to "chase the deal," which is often the case.

The only downside to the proposed system is that brokers would have to make multiple calls with the computer, which might require a few more minutes. However, this system would eliminate the need to search products, review product information, create presentations and explain all of the details of each loan to each borrower. The materials from each wholesaler would do all of this much more accurately. Brokers would not need to learn complex sorting software, yet would receive better presentations than they could put together themselves. The wholesalers have a strong incentive to detail their offerings in a professional and comprehensive presentation.

The proposed system could be implemented easily with point-of-sale software applications currently on the market. It would require only simple communications and transmission of basic information already present in most existing mortgage software applications.

Should current efforts to develop a wholesaler-to-retailer distribution system be scrapped? It is difficult to say. The best solution is not always the one most sought after in the marketplace. Many years ago, the R&D department at Xerox found a way to build a copier to make paper copies. The marketing department decided that such a machine would not sell because using carbon paper in typewriters was still the best solution for creating duplicates at far less cost. Xerox almost scraped the whole idea. Their market research determined that carbon paper used in typewriters was still the best solution for creating duplicates at a far less cost. Today, copiers are an indispensable business tool. Sometimes it makes sense to forge a new paradigm rather than trying to improve an existing method.

Eliminating the Paper Loan Package

We are headed toward paperless loan packages. Although a majority of the underwriting process can be completed electronically, lenders still require paperwork be submitted prior to funding. Eventually, the underwriting process will become completely electronic as faster modems and better technology allow for the development of a truly paperless loan. Because the mortgage industry requires communication with such a large group of industry suppliers, this will be a very difficult and complicated feat to accomplish. With each vendor, details must be worked out and communication systems must be linked.

EDI: Applications for Lenders in the Secondary Market 173

Communications with Vendors

As previously noted, the methods used for EDI with each vendor will vary based on the requirements of the vendor, lender and transaction. A relatively new trend in the industry is for mortgage software vendors to build EDI capabilities into their applications. These capabilities include order screens for each vendor, communication capabilities and "seamless EDI" so information can automatically flow to and from lenders' systems. Figure 7-1 provides an example of a point-and-click EDI screen. Behind each icon is a list of transactions available from each participating vendor. Vendors who have significant data requirements can have

FIGURE 7-1

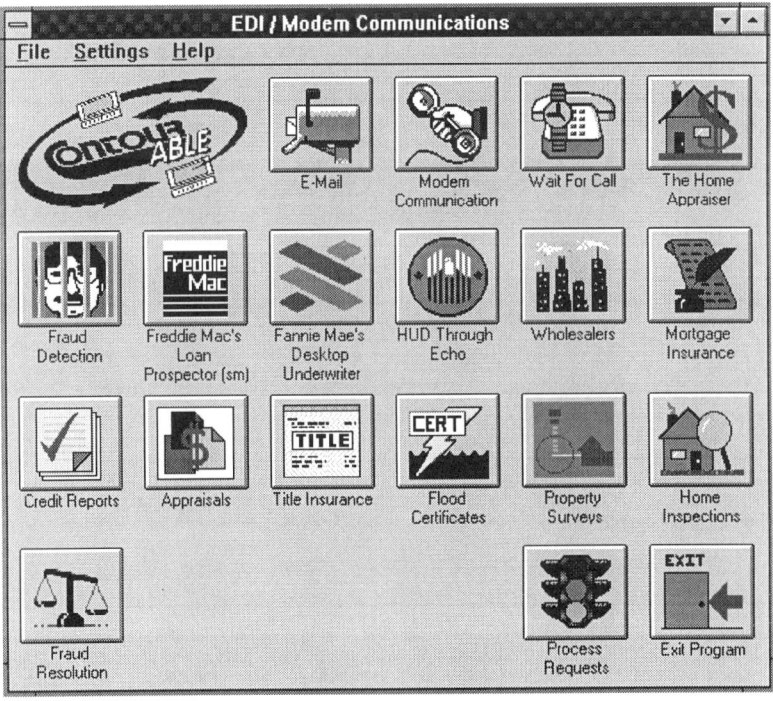

174 Handbook of Secondary Marketing

FIGURE 7-2

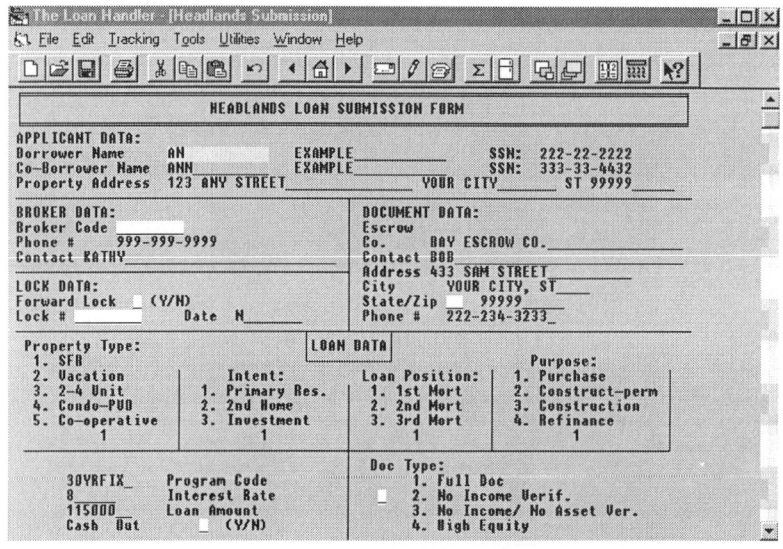

their own data entry screens built into a lender's software. Figure 7-2 is an example of a wholesaler's loan submission screen that TPOs can complete prior to electronically sending a loan. Figure 7-3 is an example of a screen for ordering private mortgage insurance. Each vendor or transaction type can have its own screen. Other examples include appraisal ordering, wholesaler rate lock, flood certification and receipt, ordering and automated underwriting data entry screens.

Appraisals

Appraisals are perhaps the most difficult EDI transactions because pictures are required to support an appraisal. Mortgage software companies are working with major appraisal software providers to allow lenders to receive electronic appraisals with

FIGURE 7-3

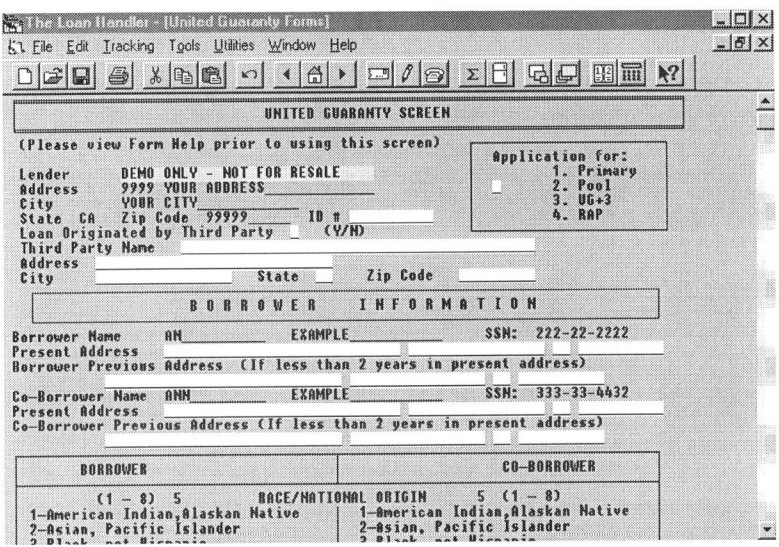

digital pictures and then access the data for an AUS, review the forms on screen and/or print the documents. The ability to receive the appraisal electronically will allow wholesalers to be more efficient and to provide faster service, while eliminating many sources of fraud. It is likely that the X.12 format will play a significant role in the development of this transaction. Specific plans are being made to allow wholesalers and mortgage insurance companies to receive the entire appraisal package, including pictures, as well.

Credit Reporting Companies

This data-exchange interface is the highest in demand and is the most mature interface. Currently, the direct dial method is used to order and receive reports. It is expected that this access method will continue to use e-mail systems for providing status information and for general correspondence. Employing e-mail will enhance communication among the different parties involved.

RMCR companies are the most advanced at developing interfaces with origination and secondary marketing systems. One recently added feature allows TPOs to order and pay for reports that then may be requested by wholesalers for no additional cost. When the wholesaler receives an electronic loan submission, the RMCR vendor and the report ID# is passed in the data file. This allows wholesalers to order duplicate reports from the vendor.

Flood Services

The ordering of flood certification and receipt is perhaps the easiest of all transactions. Simple e-mail messages can be used for ordering, status information, general correspondence, and receiving the certificates. Using e-mail for flood certifications makes good sense because of its ease and wide acceptance. Another viable option is MBA's X.12 format sent through a direct dial method.

Private Mortgage Insurance Companies

Recently, software vendors have finished developing interfaces with most of the major mortgage insurance companies. The transactions are often direct dial in nature and allow the lender to order and receive mortgage insurance. While X.12 formats are available, many mortgage insurance companies have chosen to use different formats. EDI from the mortgage insurance companies includes both delegated and nondelegated underwriting. Planned enhancements include allowing brokers to order mortgage insurance and providing electronic certificates to wholesalers and brokers.

Loan Servicers
Many lenders have already developed EDI capabilities between their secondary marketing and product systems and their servicing systems. Such interfaces, due to their complexity, can be costly to develop.

Closing Documents Providers
Already, closing companies are well developed for EDI. In many cases, they use a direct dial approach in a proprietary format. They have excelled in developing interfaces with major mortgage software suppliers. You can expect these vendors to adapt to your systems and needs.

Title Companies and Settlement Service Providers
While the transaction is a simple one, the title industry pales in comparison to others in terms of automation. Few title companies offer any sort of EDI, and there is no national electronic network of title companies, which limits the feasibility of real EDI capabilities. Title transfer may be one of the last transactions to become EDI capable.

Fannie Mae and Freddie Mac
Both of these agencies are leaders fully equipped with EDI capabilities. The MORNET and MIDANET systems have been around for years communicating with secondary market transactions. Both have implemented VANs for other types of transactions, including most of those noted earlier in the chapter. It is clear that all transactions with these two agencies will continue to be EDI capable. What is not clear is if the agencies will become key players in EDI for other vendors in the industry.

HUD

While HUD is not considered to be on the leading edge of EDI, it has made significant progress. In connection with a VAN called ECHO, lenders can now perform many HUD transactions electronically. To date, ECHO is the only VAN that allows this, but others are expected to follow. HUD is also allowing direct dial communications for those willing to make the efforts. These transactions are non-X.12 and somewhat complicated to develop.

8

Working with a Wall Street Dealer: Advanced Tools for Pipeline and Servicing Portfolio Risk Management

Stephen S. Harris, Vice President, Mortgage
Banking Group
Goldman, Sachs & Co.

Mortgage-Backed Securities

The most common method of hedging or selling conforming loan production is through the MBS market. This market has become the choice for most originators because of its tremendous liquidity and ease of execution. What is not often so clear to risk managers, though, is the number of different opportunities the market presents beyond the traditional and very easy sale of their production into a security that has a coupon 50 bp below the note rate of the loans it contains. Most risk managers overlook the occasional opportunities to hedge their production by selling a coupon that, in dealer parlance, has become very rich, or by effecting a coupon-spread trade that will provide them incremental income should the market move in one direction and serve as a production sales vehicle should the market move the other direction.

For example, suppose that the Treasury market has just experienced a significant rally. While some discount mortgages have performed in line with the Treasury market, other premium coupon prices have remained relatively unchanged. Here is an opportunity for the originator to sell its production into a lower coupon than that in which it generally sells — that is, into a coupon more than 50 bp lower than the note rate — and thereby sell a coupon that has become "rich" or "expensive." While this strategy requires the creation of some amount of excess servicing, it would typically be booked at a multiple in excess of what is implied by the coupon spread of the MBS market, which is obviously in a state of flux.

Another popular hedge for aggressive risk managers is to execute a coupon swap that is market-directional in character. Often, following a modest move in the market, originators will have good intuition into how their pipelines are likely to respond should the move continue. If the market is rallying and the risk manager is bullish, he may want to complement his hedge position by executing a bullish coupon swap through the forward sale of a premium coupon MBS and the purchase of an equal amount of a discount coupon MBS. In the event the market does continue to rally, the discount MBS that the risk manager is long will typically outperform the premium that he is short, thereby generating a profit to offset the expected loss of loans as a result of fallout. If, however, the market deteriorates, the risk manager could simply deliver loans against the premium MBS and sell back the long position at a loss. The reverse of this trade, buying a forward premium MBS and selling a discount MBS, is often a rewarding trade in a negatively trending market. In the deteriorating market, the discount coupon that is sold short will decline in value faster than the premium coupon that is held long, thereby resulting in a profit that can be used to offset the loss associated with any loans that close in excess of expectations.

Treasury Securities

Treasury securities have become a popular alternative to simply selling mortgages and have been particularly effective for hedging ARMs. The underlying principle in using Treasury securities to hedge mortgages is that most mortgages are either priced at a spread over a particular Treasury security or they are packaged into another security that will ultimately be priced at some spread over the Treasury market. The mortgage/Treasury spread is a volatile variable that has its own risk profile and complexities. However, if the originators are willing to accept some basis risk (the difference between the price action of the hedge and the price action of the mortgage being hedged), the Treasury market can be an effective hedge for specific products at appropriate times. Further, Treasury securities generally have a narrower bid/ask spread than do MBSs and can effectively serve as a generic hedge for a pipeline of mortgages with diverse characteristics. The difficult part in using Treasury securities for hedging mortgage pipelines is determining which Treasury to use and at what period of time. This is where the Wall Street dealer can be very helpful.

Generally, Wall Street dealers look at the multitude of fixed-income instruments as simply alternatives to one another, with each instrument providing a little more or less yield in exchange for specific characteristics of maturity, credit quality, liquidity and cash flow certainty, among others. As such, dealers are constantly measuring the performance of each type of security against others. Consequently, dealers have a good idea about how to hedge one security with another, which can be very useful for originators who want to use Treasuries to hedge their mortgage pipeline. Dealers will determine the market-based duration of a mortgage or, through the application of some proprietary prepayment model, determine a theoretically based duration for the security. Consequently, we can replicate the duration of that mortgage through the application of specific Treasury securities. It should be no surprise that most current coupon fixed-rate mortgages have durations similar to five- or seven-year Treasury securities. Therefore, once we determine a duration for a specific mortgage, the risk manager can short a weighted amount of the appropriate Treasury security as a proxy for, and a hedge of, the mortgage. In practice, we typically see sophisticated risk managers utilizing Treasury securities as pipeline hedges when there is an unusual product type present or less than a critical mass of production rate locks to justify selling any one type of mortgage security forward.

ARM Hedging and Treasuries

It seems that most risk managers are burdened by ARM products that have odd characteristics, limited liquidity and significant market risk. However, using sophisticated modeling, we can determine a theoretical duration for these loans and consequently construct a Treasury-based hedge for them. Typically, the Treasury hedge is based on two specific securities: the 2-year T-note and the 10-year T-note. A blended hedge using the two Treasury securities attempts to replicate the assumed duration of the loan, usually something around two years, while incorporating the extension risk and cap components of the loan. It is the caps and their influence upon the extension of the loan's average life that require a longer-duration security such as a 10-year T-note to effectively hedge in a deteriorating market. Table 8-1 details the recommended 2-year/10-year Treasury blend for some generic Ginnie Mae ARM securities on a recent day:

TABLE 8-1
ARM Hedging Analysis
Two-Year & 10-Year Hedge Analysis

ARM Product	Price	Duration	% 2-year	% 10-year
Ginnie Mae 4.5%	98.28	3.59	0.61	0.32
Ginnie Mae 5.0%	99.63	3.21	0.59	0.28
Ginnie Mae 5.5%	100.76	2.80	0.54	0.24
Ginnie Mae 6.0%	101.72	2.50	0.51	0.20
Ginnie Mae 6.5%	102.58	2.36	0.52	0.18
cofi tba	101.76	1.20	0.27	0.09

To specify an example of ARM hedging, we can look at the recommended 2-year/10-year combination for the Ginnie Mae 5% with a January reset. In Table 8-1, our model has determined that the optimal Treasury hedge requires a short of 59% of the loan amount in 2-year T-notes and 28% of the loan amount in 10-year T-notes. The specific ratios of this Treasury hedge would, of course, need to be adjusted with significant changes in the ARM or Treasury market.

Basic Strategies for Trading Volatility

In this section, we will focus specifically on strategies to effectively hedge the volatility position an institution incurs through writing options to mortgagors, shorting volatility, in the form of a rate lock or mortgage commitment.

Straddles

Straddle trades (see Figure 8-1) are generally executed as a combination of both a call and a put option, where both options have the same strike price. Typically, originators execute straddle trades with both options struck at the money. An institution is said to be *long a straddle* when both options are purchased, and the institution is said to be *short the straddle* when both options are sold. Either way, long or short, when the straddle is struck at the money, the trade is effectively market-neutral because any move in the underlying securities will not affect the value of the combined options. This is simply the result of a gain in value of

FIGURE 8-1
The Value of a Long Straddle at Expiration

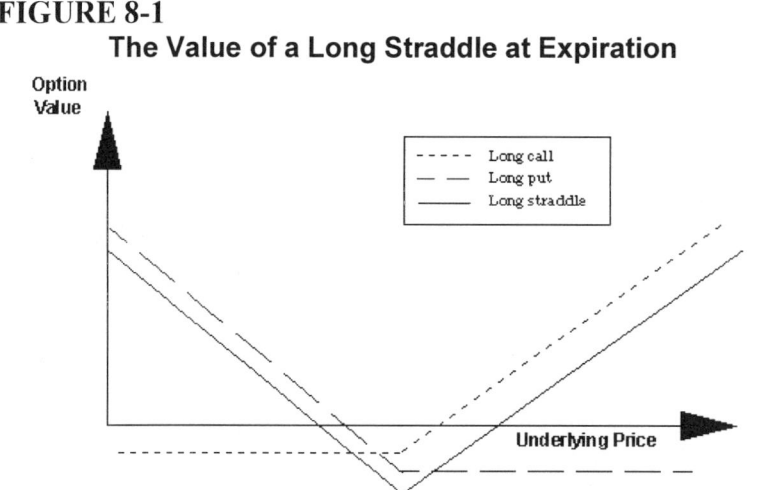

Working with a Wall Street Dealer   185

one leg of the trade offsetting an equal loss in value from the other leg of the trade. Consequently, a straddle is primarily a hedge on the volatility of the underlying security.

The buyer of a straddle is taking the position that volatility will increase over the term of the option, and a seller of a straddle is taking the opposite position that volatility will decrease over the term of the option. Risk managers will ordinarily use a long straddle trade to hedge themselves against an increase in volatility, which generally creates greater fallout in the pipeline. Increased fallout commonly occurs during periods of high volatility when the market is gyrating higher and lower, thereby providing mortgagors with a greater number of opportunities to capture better rate locks from competing lenders.

Strangles

Strangle trades (see Figure 8-2) are similar to straddle trades except that in a strangle, the put and the call options each have

FIGURE 8-2
The Value of a Long Strangle at Expiration

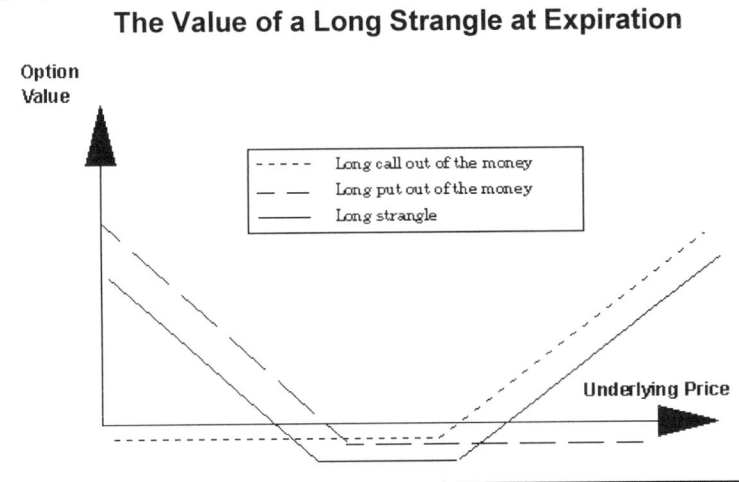

different strikes. Originators typically purchase strangles one or two points out of the money, as a mechanism to hedge themselves against movements in volatility outside of a wider range than if they had purchased a straddle. Further, in comparing strangle trades with straddle trades, we note that the strangle is a lower-cost alternative but one that will benefit only from big movements in volatility.

Fence Trades

Fence trades (see Figure 8-3) have become popular recently, particularly with institutions that use option-inclusive delta-hedging strategies for their pipelines and have a good handle on the processing status of each loan in their pipeline. Effectively, a *fence* is a synthetic short position in the underlying security. Typically, originators execute fences in two steps. First is the sale of an at-the-money call that is expected to be covered by their anticipated closed loans. This leg of the trade also serves to provide some premium income for purchase of the second part

FIGURE 8-3

Payoff Chart for Fence Trade

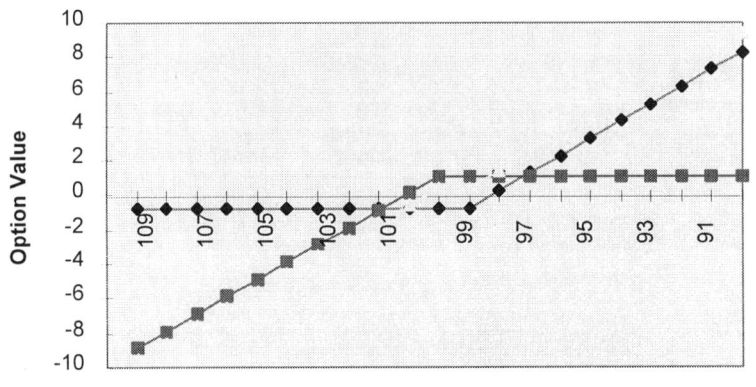

of the trade: an out-of-the-money put. The put is customarily purchased one point out of the money and is generally intended to hedge the portion of the pipeline that is most sensitive to changes in the market — for example, wholesale refinances.

There are many derivations of this trade where the originator may sell out-of-the-money calls to buy at-the-money puts or some other combination of strikes. The underlying principle of this trade is that in a rallying market, the securities will be called away at the strike price. From the risk managers' perspective this is a positive event, because they have effectively sold their securities at a level that is better than what they would have received if they had simply sold an MBS forward. It is a better level because they also received the premium up front. This premium is additional income supplementing the price at which the securities are called away.

On the other hand, in a sinking market, the securities are not called away. However, there is downside protection, albeit at a lower level than what they could have received if they had simply sold MBSs. The lower level of execution results from the out-of-the-money strike of the put and the fact that there was a premium paid for the purchase of the option. Many risk managers think of this trade as a mechanism to sell off their closed inventory while purchasing coverage for the part of the pipeline that is of an uncertain status. In essence, it is a synthetic short position where an institution's potential market upside is sold in exchange for incremental market downside protection.

Servicing Hedging and Wall Street Dealer Products

Given the promulgation of SFAS 122 and its requirement for the periodic valuation and impairment of mortgage servicing rights (MSRs), many secondary marketing risk managers have become responsible for developing the hedging strategies required to help their institutions eliminate the impairment risk imbedded in their MSRs.

Servicing: Another Mortgagor Option

Risk managers who are well versed in option modeling and pricing for pipeline hedging purposes are now applying many of the same techniques to analyzing and hedging their servicing portfolios. The migration of pipeline hedging technology to servicing hedging occurs because the originators/servicers/investors effectively give the mortgagors a call option when they close or invest in a mortgage. This call option literally gives the mortgagors the right to call away the mortgage through a curtailment, prepayment or default. In effect, the mortgagors have a valuable, long-dated option.

The issue risk managers face is how to hedge this option, typically referred to as the prepayment option, without spending so much on the hedge that the value of the MSR is consumed. Wall Street dealers offer many products risk managers can use for hedging servicing. A few of the most popular strategies are introduced below.

OTC Mortgage Options

In early 1996, many servicers were taking advantage of the historically low implied volatilities prevailing in the OTC options market by purchasing long-dated call options on discount mortgages. Typically, the options that servicers purchase are written on the current coupon or next lower discount coupon and have a term to expiration of six to nine months. While this strategy may be an efficient method of purchasing a servicing hedge that is directly correlated to the mortgage market and its performance, the troubling concept of buying a call on a negatively convex instrument does turn an equally large number of risk managers away from this strategy.

Further, these mortgage options are generally too limited in term to efficiently hedge a servicing portfolio over its expected life without the need to regularly roll the options. The rolling of such positions can create high transaction expenses because of the typical OTC option's bid/ask spread. Consequently, long calls on discount mortgages tend to be only a small component of a typical servicers portfolio of servicing hedges.

Treasury Market and Option-Inclusive Delta Hedging
The Treasury futures market has been used by a limited number of servicers who believe that they are able to determine the delta of their portfolio, like their pipeline, and effectively replicate that delta through the purchase of long puts or the creation of synthetic puts on the Chicago Board of Trade. The application of this strategy requires much intervention on behalf of the risk manager because the hedges must be rolled forward with the expiration of each futures contract, and the volatility on interest rate futures is relatively greater than that of mortgages. This volatility difference affects the strategy by requiring the execution of significant amounts of rebalancing trades as the delta of the hedges fluctuates with the volatility of the underlying contract. Consequently, the transaction costs, in concert with the bid/ask spread on the underlying futures and options, tend to reduce the total efficacy of this strategy. Returns from this strategy may fall short of those realized through the purchase of a series of long-dated call options in the form of Treasury floors.

Treasury Floors and Swaptions
Treasury floors have become far and away the most popular financial instrument for hedging mortgage servicing rights. Much of the popularity stems from their flexibility and tremendous liquidity. Treasury floors are commonly purchased by servicers with a 5-year term using the 10-year CMT index with a strike

some distance in yield terms out of the money. For those not familiar with Treasury floors, the easiest way to conceptualize a floor is as a series of long-dated call options on Treasury bonds or long-dated puts on interest rates. The floor contract specifies a monthly payment that is called away from the floor writer on every reset date that the market is below, in yield terms, the strike yield. In practice, most servicers choose the 10-year CMT index because there is a strong positive correlation between the movement of the index and the yields of current coupon mortgages.

Another appealing attribute of Treasury floors that helps make them the hedging instrument of choice is their ability to function as both a capital hedge and an income hedge for mortgage servicing. The floor is structured to provide income to the servicer when the market rallies and penetrates the yield strike of the floor. This income can be used to offset the loss of current-period cash flow resulting from MSRs prepaying and, by extension, the attendant loss of future income. Further, Treasury floors can perform effectively as capital hedges. For example, when the market rallies, and yields move either through the strike of the floor or closer to the strike, the floor itself becomes more valuable, just as a standard call option increases in value as the market rallies. The added feature of the floor is that it, or any fraction thereof, may be sold back to the floor writer or any other interested party, at any time during the term of the floor. Following 1995's market rally, many servicers have chosen to sell their in-the-money floors and recognize the associated gain to offset the current period charge that occurs from the contemporaneous impairment of their servicing portfolios.

Currently, however, there are two concerns regarding Treasury floors that mortgage servicers seem to be focused on. First, there is basis risk between the Treasury index used for the floors and the mortgage-based portfolio they own. Second, implied volatility is now considered high, and therefore Treasury floors are expensive. Consequently, servicers are beginning to investigate other more complex and less traditional instruments to hedge their mortgage servicing portfolios.

Mortgage Derivatives and Swaps

Many mortgage servicers whose regular monthly income is limited to the principal payment from a large pool of mortgages, have sought principal-only securities (POs) to hedge their servicing portfolios. Unfortunately, though, there are not many individual POs available, because few new POs have been issued recently and also because the past two refinance booms have significantly prepaid outstanding issues. In addition, POs owned outright by an institution will not generally be afforded hedge accounting because they are clearly securities and are therefore excluded under SFAS 52 & 80.

Wall Street dealers have, however, found a mechanism to circumvent this accounting treatment for servicers wanting to own PO cash flows. Instead of purchasing the PO outright, the servicer enters into a swap agreement where the dealer pays the monthly income that is generated by a particular PO or group of POs while the servicer pays on a monthly basis some negotiated spread over the London Interbank Offering Rate (LIBOR). In effect, the servicer is receiving the income benefits associated with owning a particular PO while actually only financing the issue rather than taking the security onto its balance sheet.

Bullish Fixed/Floating Swaps

Over the past several years, many risk managers have entered into bullish fixed/floating swaps in order to hedge their servicing portfolios. The logistics of this strategy are that the servicer enters into a swap contract whereby it agrees to receive fixed payments and pay a floating rate, typically three-month LIBOR, over the term of the swap. The principle of this strategy is that in a positively sloped rallying market, the servicer will continue to receive a fixed payment and pay a declining floating payment, which has the net effect of yielding the servicer incremental income to offset the impairment of its servicing. Conversely, when the positively sloped market deteriorates, the servicer will pay an increasing floating rate while receiving the fixed payment. This has the net effect of costing the servicer incremental income that should be available, as its servicing portfolio is not likely to be running off.

Mortgage Price Spread Hedge

Another servicing hedge that has recently gained some attention from risk managers is purchasing a put option on the price spread of two mortgage securities. For example, a servicer will commonly purchase a put on the spread between the price of Fannie Mae 7.5% and Fannie Mae 6.5% securities for settlement six to nine months forward. Since the servicer owns a put, if the market rallied and the lower coupon outperformed the higher coupon, then the spread would compress and the put would increase in value. The underlying principle of this trade is that when the market rallies, the money earned on the coupon spread put will offset some of the current period charges associated with the impairment of mortgage servicing rights.

Concluding Thoughts: A Complementary Relationship

In this extremely competitive origination environment, the Wall Street dealer and the secondary marketing risk manager have complementary goals. Risk managers are attempting to limit the exposure of their firms to the vagaries of the interest rate market and the resultant negative impact on their enterprises. Concurrently, Wall Street dealers are developing markets and products that help risk managers accomplish these goals. The motivation to profit from the origination business is absolutely paramount

Working with a Wall Street Dealer   193

for both institutions. However, what ultimately drives the two institutions to work together are the traditional market forces of supply and demand: demand from the dealers' customers for the mortgage supply that the originators produce.

Further compelling the two sides to work together is the nature of the information that each institution provides the other. For dealers, the information about potential supply of new securities and the prospects of the mortgage market are key issues that originators can certainly influence and often can determine. For originators, the information concerning investor demand and specific mortgage investment interests, relative to the larger fixed income market, can strongly affect the environment in which the mortgage origination industry operates and prospers.

9

Managing Mortgage Optionality: An Innovative Approach to Protecting Pipelines with Futures and Options

Mark R. Turner, Assistant Treasurer
Federal Home Loan Bank of Chicago

Keith Schap, Product Manager
Chicago Board of Trade

The challenge of hedging a mortgage pipeline arises from the homeowners' prepayment options. That right generates the phenomena summarized in the term "negative convexity" which makes mortgages behave so differently from other kinds of fixed-income securities, especially Treasury issues, when interest rates rise and fall. Yet, as this discussion will show, risk management tactics crafted from Treasury futures and options can provide effective, low-cost solutions to the classic pipeline hedging problem.

That may seem a strong claim, as hedging with futures and options has seemed less than straightforward to many participants who cite basis risk as the source of their trouble. Without denying the presence of basis risk, this discussion will suggest another source of hedging.

Of course, deploying exchange-traded futures and options in this cross-hedging application requires careful thought about the nature and sources of pipeline risk and about what configuration of hedging tools promises to generate optimal hedging results. Accordingly, this chapter will discuss the nature of the risk that pipeline managers face, develop the intuition that informs the current approach, comment briefly on earlier approaches to pipeline hedging, and finally, show more formally what goes into the design of effective pipeline hedges. This approach provides useful and robust hedges yet remains easily within the reach, in terms both of technology and cost, of pipeline managers operating on any scale.

The Nature of the Risk

Mortgage hedging discussions often distinguish between pipeline and warehouse, and among fallout, prepayment and interest rate risks. For the purpose of this discussion, the term "pipeline" subsumes "warehouse." "Pipeline" as used here extends from rate-lock to sale into the secondary market — typically a period of 60 to 90 days. Similarly, the fallout and prepayment risks are considered only special cases of interest rate risk.

To understand the motive for those simplifications, consider the following example. Before the mortgage closes, falling interest rates can result in applicants withdrawing applications — that is, fallout. Theoretically, at least, falling interest rates after the closing can result in refinancing. From that perspective, there is no reason to distinguish between pipeline and warehouse, and fallout risk can be viewed as a special case of prepayment risk. Both result from falling interest rates, and both lead to a reduction in the size of the pipeline or pool of mortgages, even though the individual mortgage may be worth more than its par value.

Similarly, if interest rates rise before or after closing, the applicant or mortgage holder will be more likely to stay the course. In that case, the number of mortgages in the pipeline will remain the same, but each mortgage will be worth less than par. As a result, the lender cannot realize full value from the sale of the paper. Equally bad, if the paper were sold forward, the lender would now have more loans than were sold forward.

Clearly, all the negative possibilities that accompany pipeline management reduce to interest rate risk, and rising and falling interest rates each have their own negative implications.

Locating the Intuition

Logical as it may be to identify pipeline risk in terms of interest rate risk, that by itself fails to account for what secondary marketing managers need to know in order to design effective hedges. If it did, a simple duration-neutral futures hedge would provide satisfying results — as, in fact, it does not. A simple contrast of profit and loss diagrams shows why so many secondary marketers express skepticism concerning futures hedges.

A hedge involves designing an opposite position to neutralize a risk. Accordingly, a hedger who holds a 10-year T-note position can offset that long cash market holding with a short 10-year futures position. The result should be a flat payout line, as Figure 9-1 shows, such that the hedged position will remain impervious to interest rate changes across a broad range.

But contrast a similar mortgage hedge, such as the one shown in Figure 9-2. Here the hedger holds a Fannie Mae 7% current coupon issue and uses 10-year Treasury note futures to

FIGURE 9-1
10-Year Treasury: Long Cash, Short Futures

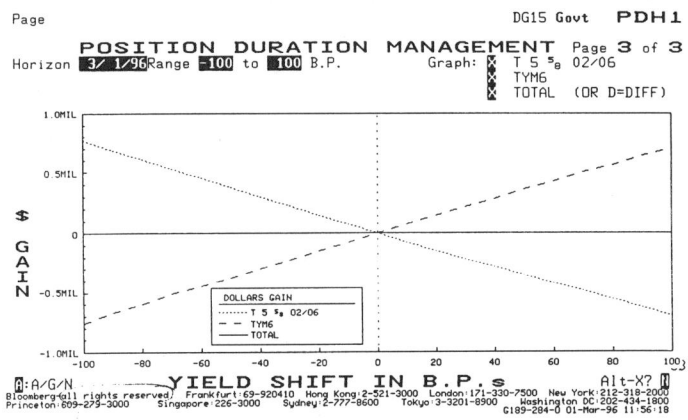

FIGURE 9-2
Long Fannie Mae 7%, Short 10-Year Futures

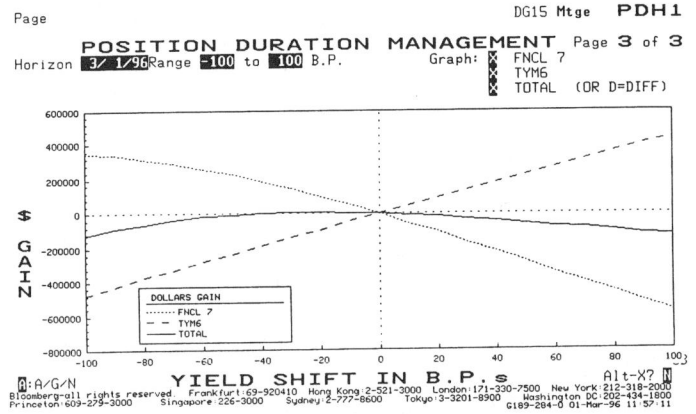

Managing Mortgage Optionality 199

hedge. At almost no point on the profit and loss chart is the hedged position neutral. Rather, the hedged position slopes downward. The hedge generates losses whether interest rates rise or fall.

Clearly, pipeline hedgers must not only recognize the interest rate source of the risk, but they must also give thought to what mortgage features cause the pronounced differences in response to the interest rate changes highlighted in Figures 9-1 and 9-2. Indeed, effective hedge design requires attention to two sets of details: the sources of risk and the factors that shape the way the hedged instrument responds to market forces.

Basis Risk Considered

To large numbers of secondary marketers, basis risk encapsulates the primary force that causes trouble with pipeline cross hedges. Treasury futures, those people say, simply do not track mortgages well. This view requires further examination.

The "basis" refers to the difference between cash and futures prices. The 10-year T-note futures contract and the cheapest-to-deliver 10-year T-note trade in a relationship shaped by financing costs, coupon payments and time to futures expiration. Arbitrage forces along the way, and especially at delivery when the two prices should converge to zero, enforce that relationship. As a result, the Treasury basis is far more well behaved and predictable than either prices or interest rates.

Any time that risk managers design a cross hedge, as between cash mortgages and Treasury futures, that relationship becomes harder to control with arbitrage activity because mortgages cannot be delivered into the Treasury futures contracts. So the mortgage basis is less well defined and less predictable. But that is a matter of degree and not at all the same as saying that the mortgage basis is unpredictable. The basis can still cause malfunctioning hedges, but such problems arise far less often than common wisdom holds to be the case. It is more useful to look elsewhere for the factors that have led to disappointing pipeline hedging results in order to develop ideas that will prove more satisfying.

A More Fruitful Line of Inquiry

The payout diagrams themselves suggest a more fruitful line of inquiry. Absent the cash and futures lines from the earlier charts, the Treasury hedge payout diagram in Figure 9-3 exhibits a U-shaped line. The hedged position is really neutral only at the entry point (at the entry interest rate level). It outperforms the market at either interest rate extreme.

In contrast, the mortgage hedge payout shown in Figure 9-4 exhibits a sharply downward sloping line — much as in the earlier chart only more so.

Risk managers have long noticed a similarity between the hedged Treasury position and the option strategy known as a long

FIGURE 9-3
Treasury Hedge Payout

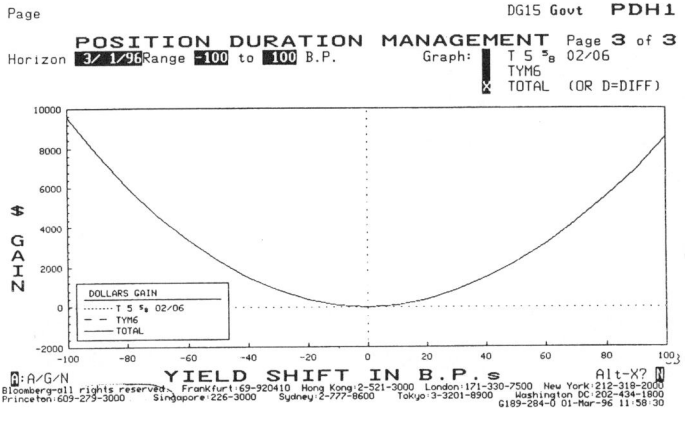

Managing Mortgage Optionality 201

straddle, which consists of long at-the-money calls and puts with the same expiration. Such an option position benefits whether interest rates go up or down but suffers when interest rates do nothing. Figure 9-5 is the payout diagram for the long straddle at

FIGURE 9-4
Mortgage Hedge Payout

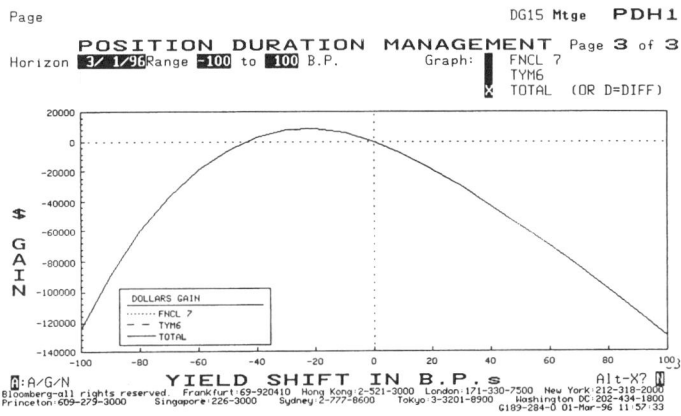

FIGURE 9-5
Long Straddle Payout

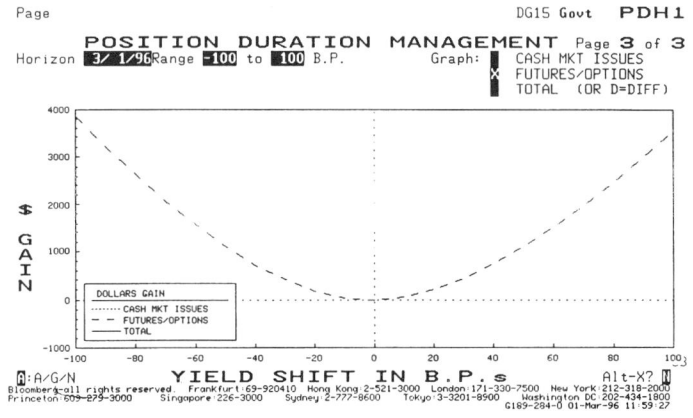

FIGURE 9-6
Short Straddle Payout

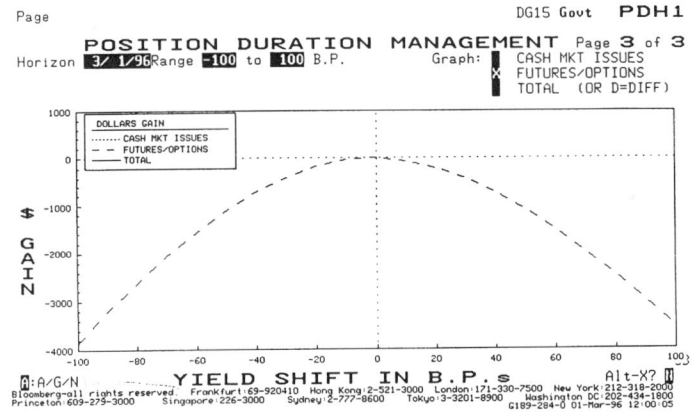

any time before expiration. It has roughly the same U-shape as the hedged Treasury position.

Not surprisingly, the inverse short straddle payout in Figure 9-6, which results from using short at-the-money puts and calls with the same expiration, looks very much like the mortgage hedge payout in Figure 9-4.

Defining an Intuition

That observation leads to a useful intuition concerning what factors shape mortgage response to interest rate change. In general, for pipeline risk management purposes, the collection of rate locks and mortgages in a pipeline behaves more like a portfolio of options than like a portfolio of bonds.

This should not come as a surprise. The familiar bending back, or price compression, of the mortgage price-yield diagram in Figure 9-7 results from the borrowers' prepayment rights. As

FIGURE 9-7
Mortgage Price Compression

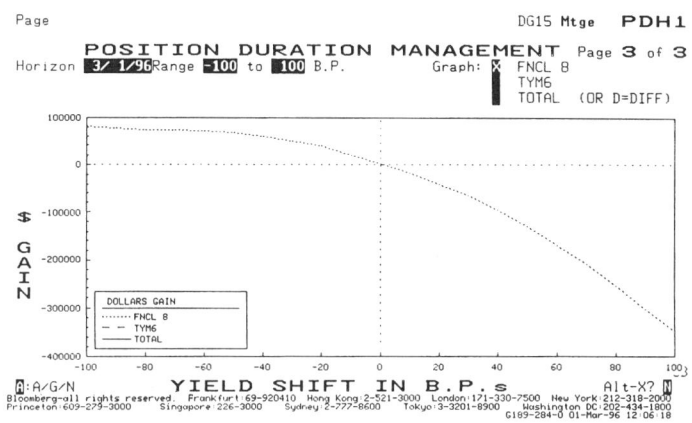

interest rates fall, increasing numbers of borrowers prepay, and that reshapes that end of the line.

The prepayment right amounts to a call option that the borrowers hold and that the lenders are short. A short-call payout diagram curves down, just as the left half of the hedge diagram does. This piece of the mortgage pipeline puzzle is discussed frequently and should seem obvious.

The right half of the hedged mortgage curve may at first glance seem intuitively obvious. But a moment's thought should make possible a satisfying account for that segment of the hedge diagram as well. Consider that as interest rates rise, borrowers will prepay at increasingly slower rates. At the same time, the amortization schedule will shift, and successive cash flows will be discounted at higher and higher interest rates. Accordingly, these mortgages have successively lower present values, which explains the downward sloping right half of the curve. That amortization shift has the same effect as a short put option position.

The reasoning behind the approach presented here, then, is that a mortgage behaves differently from a Treasury instrument because of its optionality. Lenders and MBS holders have positions that more nearly resemble collections of short options than long bond holdings.

Relating Bonds and Options

Fixed-income theorists isolate three basic bond properties in their discussions: level, slope and curve. The interest rate sets the level. Duration defines the slope of the payout line. Convexity adds the curvature. Mortgages have the same properties with the exception that the convexity changes sign — mortgages exhibit negative convexity.

In option terms, delta equates to duration, and gamma equates to convexity. Delta and duration define linear relationships between price and underlying factors that shape prices. Gamma and convexity define the curvatures seen in the various figures discussed here.

From this it should be clear that options alone could provide an effective pipeline hedge. But the correspondence of the relevant bond and option properties suggests that a combination of futures, to neutralize duration, and options, to neutralize convexity, should produce satisfying results as well — and at a lower cost.

To put it more simply, mortgage pipeline managers suffer from being short options, whether consciously or unconsciously. The way to neutralize a short option exposure is to use long offsetting options.

Reviewing Prior Approaches

Interest rate change plays a crucial role in the management of any mortgage investment — whether it takes the form of a pool of pipeline originations or an institutional investor's portfolio of MBSs — because the interest rate level drives the prepayment speed, including the fallout phenomenon.

Regional and individual experience varies markedly with regard to prepayment levels. For the purpose of illustration, assume that for every 100 commitments, or rate locks, 5 will not make the credit cut, 70 will respond to interest rates and may fall out, and 25 will close pretty much no matter what. We will ignore the 5% that are eliminated for credit, and will assume it is safe to sell the 25% that always close forward to the secondary market. The pipeline therefore consists of the 70 commitments that remain. Those numbers must be adjusted to reflect local experience.

Further, assume for the sake of example that across a range of interest rate scenarios, the fallout experience for those 70 commitments will be as shown in Table 9-1. These fallout estimates indicate that, even if interest rates remain stable, 30%, or 21, of the remaining 70 commitments will fall out of the pipeline.

This observation has guided earlier pipeline hedging recommendations, many of which suggest a three-pronged approach to pipeline hedge design. On the surface, that three-pronged approach, using forwards, futures and options, may not seem to differ greatly from the one presented here. Those hedgers focus

TABLE 9-1
Fallout Assumptions

Rate Change	Percent fallout
-100	75
-25	40
-10	35
stable	30
+10	30
+25	20
+100	10

on the 25 that will close no matter what interest rates do, the 49 that will most likely close if interest rates remain stable and the 21 most subject to fallout. They sell the first group forward, hedge the second group with futures and hedge the third group with options.

The primary weakness of such an approach lies in its inattention to the bond and option characteristics that shape the prices of the securities involved in the construction of the hedge — the convexity and gamma, or curvature. Granted, the curvature results from prepayment speed or fallout. However, the entire pipeline exhibits this curvature, not just the most problematic segment. As a result, this kind of hedge fails to address the real pipeline issues and thus has failed to satisfy numerous pipeline managers who have tried to hedge.

Pipeline Hedging in a New Key

Grasping the underlying intuition that mortgage pipelines resemble options causes a pipeline manager to focus on the problem of convexity, rather than basis risk. But putting that intuition to work in an effective hedging strategy is quite another thing. Still, pipeline hedgers can meet the challenge, and even make the hedging dynamics work for them, if they approach hedging from a slightly different angle.

Typically, financial hedgers design hedges in terms of price sensitivity measures — delta for options, duration for fixed-income securities. Hedge design, in those terms, requires finding a ratio between the sensitivities of the hedged position and the hedge vehicle that will make the mortgages and the hedging tools react equally to changes in underlying prices or interest rates. Unfortunately, such a design serves mortgage pipeline hedges poorly because the pipeline and the hedge vehicle exhibit different convexity and volatility structures. Crucially, prepayment speeds drive mortgage volatility structures but not the volatility structures of other fixed-income instruments. As a result, mortgage delta contrasts strongly with conventional option delta — a contrast illustrated by the payout diagrams discussed earlier.

Accordingly, the relevant hedge goal for pipelines involves matching the potential dollar loss in the pipeline with an offsetting dollar gain in the hedge vehicle. Estimating the pipeline dollar loss requires hedgers to evaluate the price elasticity of the mortgage pipeline. Matching the loss with a gain requires similar elasticity evaluations for the futures and options used in the hedge. Here, "elasticity" refers to the expected price moves across a wide range of interest rate scenarios. This discussion considers seven interest rate possibilities: no change, up 10 bp, down 10 bp, up 25 bp, down 25 bp, up 100 bp and down 100 bp.

To determine the price elasticity of the mortgage pipeline across that range, the hedger must reprice the mortgage pipeline for those scenarios in terms of the relevant fallout estimates and measure the expected price changes in dollar terms.

Table 9-2 shows the results of such an analysis.

Among other things, Table 9-2 shows how expected changes in prepayment speeds (PSAΔ) interact with changing interest rates to alter mortgage prices and durations. Notice that if PSA holds constant, a 100 bp drop in yield drives the price to 105.40625 and the duration to 5.29 years. But the changing prepayment speed — or the negative convexity factor in the mortgage make-up — shortens the average life of the mortgage and reduces the price to 103.25. That means the cost of convexity is 2.15625 or $21,562.50 for each $1 million in mortgages if interest rates fall 100 bp.

Table 9-2 incorporates the assumption that PSA will remain constant for the 0, +/- 10 bp and +/- 25 bp change scenarios. In fact, a 25 bp change is likely to alter PSA estimates, but the complexity that it introduces seems unnecessary for the purposes

TABLE 9-2
Typical Mortgage Performance

Basis Point Move	Expected Market Yield	Resulting Price	Price Change	Basis Point Value	Modified Duration	Expected Fallout
-100*	5.84%	103.25000	3.25000	.0379	3.64	75%
-100	5.84%	105.40625	5.40625	.0563	5.29	75%
-25	6.59%	101.31250	1.31250	.0524	5.11	40%
-10	6.74%	100.53125	0.53125	.0516	5.08	35%
none	6.84%	100.00000	0.00000	.0511	5.06	30%
+10	6.94%	99.50000	-0.50000	.0507	5.04	30%
+25	7.09%	98.75000	-1.25000	.0499	5.00	20%
+100	7.84%	95.093752	-5.18750	.0466	4.84	10%
+100*	7.84%	94.50000	-5.43750	.0536	5.61	10%

*PSA∆

of this discussion. Also, fallout assumptions vary markedly from region to region and even from lender to lender. Here, the method is what matters most. Given local assumptions, this approach adapts easily and provides relevant data and hedge structures.

Pay particular attention to the numbers in the price change column. These are what the pipeline manager is trying to hedge. The key question concerns the acceptable loss level. A -5.4375 price change (if interest rates rise 100 bp and PSA changes) implies a $54,375.00 loss for every $1 million in the pipeline.

TABLE 9-3
Futures Hedging Alternatives

Basis Point Move	2-year T-note	Price Change	5-year T-note	Price Change	10-year T-note	Price Change	Hedge Value
-100	107.0313	1.7500	115.2188	4.2500	121.2813	6.5938	8,407.03
-25	105.7188	0.4375	112.0313	1.0625	116.2813	1.5938	2,032.03
-10	105.4275	0.1563	111.4063	0.4375	115.3125	0.6250	796.88
0	105.2813	0.0000	110.9688	0.0000	114.6875	0.0000	0.00

Table 9-3 shows a similar set of price changes for CBOT® 2-, 5- and 10-year T-note futures.

In the case of futures and options, PSA change loses relevance. Interestingly, the "hedge value" column shows the gain or loss from a hedge position using 1.2570 10-year T-note contracts for every $100,000 of par mortgages. If the interest rate drops 100 bp, one 10-year T-note contract gains 6.5988 or $6,593.80, and 1.2750 contracts gain $8,407.03 (6,593.80 x 1.275, rounded).

Recall that a hedge which simply shorts futures will exhibit massively short convexity, for it will add the negative futures convexity to the already negative mortgage convexity. As the earlier discussion suggests, the way to combat this problem is to buy options. Hedgers could use options alone to hedge a pipeline, but cost factors rule against that. Rather, for reasons of both effectiveness and cost, the recommended way to hedge a pipeline involves a combination of futures and options.

The choice of options depends partly on the hedger's interest rate view. If contemplating a 25 bp move, at-the-money options seem preferable. However, if contemplating a 100 bp move, out-of-the-money options provide the most robust hedging solutions.

To evaluate the option possibilities, hedgers can use data such as that displayed in Table 9-4.

Here, at the money refers to an option with a strike price that matches the price of the underlying futures contract. In the money and out of the money identify options with strike prices set to yield +50 bp from the at-the-money strike price. Thus, with at the money based on a 114-22 futures price, the in-the-money put has a 117-30 (118) strike price. Notice, also, that these examples assume 6% volatility throughout.

TABLE 9-4
Option Sensitivity

Basis Point Move	At-the-money-options				Out-of-the-money-options				In-the-money-options			
	Call Price	Price Change	Put Price	Price Change	Call Price	Price Change	Put Price	Price Change	Call Price	Price Change	Put Price	Price Change
-100	6.205	4.819	0.048	-1.341	3.267	2.930	0.385	-3.237	8.938	5.671	0.004	-0.381
-25	2.316	0.927	0.737	-0.652	0.705	0.368	2.408	-1.214	4.534	1.267	0.161	-0.224
-10	1.714	0.352	1.091	0.298	0.461	0.124	3.093	-0.529	3.773	0.506	0.272	-0.113
0	1.389	0.000	1.389	0.000	0.337	0.000	3.622	0.000	3.267	0.000	0.385	0.000
+10	1.113	-0.267	1.732	0.343	0.241	-0.096	4.148	0.526	2.816	-0.451	0.524	0.139
+25	0.755	-0.634	2.334	0.945	0.139	-0.198	5.012	1.390	2.189	-1.078	0.796	0.411
+100	0.049	-1.340	6.611	5.222	0.004	-0.333	9.938	6.316	0.337	-2.930	3.622	3.237

Designing the Hedge

Once hedgers have defined the various price elasticities, they can formulate an effective pipeline hedge. Because the focus here is on hedging the pipeline dollar value change, the hedge must satisfy an equation of the form:

(mortgage price change x expected fallout) =
(hedge price change x notional contract value)

For example, assume a forward sale of $1 million of mortgages and a 10 bp drop in interest rates. The mortgage price will move from 100.8750 to 101.40625, a change of 53.125 bp (0.0053125). If only 65% of the original mortgages close, the loss will be $1,859.38.

price change x expected fallout
1,000,000 (1.00875 - 1.0140625) x 0.35 = -1,859.38

That means that, for a 10 bp interest rate change, the hedge value should change $1,859.38 for each $1 million in the pipeline.

Table 9-5 shows the results of similar calculations for the entire range of interest rate and PSA changes.

Once hedgers have identified the "hedging gain needed" and assembled the relevant futures and options price elasticities, they can locate the quantity of futures and options that will generate enough aggregate price change to offset the expected mortgage loss. For that purpose, they can refer to an accumulation of price change data such as that in Table 9-6.

Hedgers with sufficient computer resources can use a linear programming device to run an optimization routine that will determine the best possible hedge. Yet, by simply using the tables and a calculator, and making some trial and error calculations, hedgers can quite readily discover that a combination of four 10-year T-note futures and six out-of-the money 10-year puts will

TABLE 9-5
Required Hedging Gains

Basis Point Move	Price of Mortgage	Price Change	Dollar Change	Expected Fallout	Hedging Gain Needed
-100, PSA	103.25000	3.25000	32,500.00	75%	24,375.00
-100	105.40625	5.40625	54,062.50	75%	40,546.88
-25	101.31250	1.31250	13,125.50	40%	5,250.00
-10	100.53125	0.53125	5,312.50	35%	1,859.38
0	100.00000	0.00000	0.00	30%	0.00
+10	99.50000	-0.50000	-5,000.00	30%	-1,500.00
+25	98.75000	-1.25000	-12,500.00	20%	-2,500.00
+100	95.09375	-4.90625	-49,062.50	10%	-4,906.25
+100, PSA	94.50000	-5.50000	-55,000.00	10%	-5,500.00

TABLE 9-6
Expected Price Changes

Basis Point Move	2-yr Price Change	5-yr Price Change	10-yr Price Change	ATM Call Change	ATM Put Change	OTM Call Change	ITM Put Change	ITM Call Change	OTM Put Change
-100	1.75	4.25	6.59	4.82	-1.34	2.93	-3.24	5.67	-0.38
-25	0.44	1.06	1.59	0.93	-0.65	0.37	-1.21	1.27	-0.22
-10	0.16	0.44	0.63	0.35	-0.30	0.12	-0.53	0.51	-0.11
0	0.00	0.00	0.00	0.00	0.00	0.00	0.00	0.00	0.00
+10	-0.19	-0.41	-0.66	-0.28	0.34	-0.10	0.53	-0.45	0.14
+25	-0.44	-1.03	-1.59	-0.63	0.95	-0.20	1.39	-1.08	0.41
+100	-1.72	-4.06	-6.19	-1.34	5.22	-0.33	6.32	-2.93	3.24

TABLE 9-7
Discovering Total Hedge Value
(The hedge position consists of short 4 10-year T-note futures and long 6 OTM puts.)

Quantity Basis Point Move	0 2-yr Price Change	0 5-yr Price Change	4 10-yr Price Change	0 ATM Call Change	0 ATM Put Change	0 OTM Call Change	0 ITM Put Change	0 ITM Call Change	6 OTM Put Change	Total Hedge Value
-100	0	0	26,375	0	0	0	0	0	-2,286	24,089
-25	0	0	6,375	0	0	0	0	0	-1,344	5,031
-10	0	0	2,500	0	0	0	0	0	-678	1,822
0	0	0	0	0	0	0	0	0	0	0
+10	0	0	-2,625	0	0	0	0	0	834	-1,791
+25	0	0	-6,375	0	0	0	0	0	2,466	-3,909
+100	0	0	-24,750	0	0	0	0	0	19,422	-5,328

provide a useful hedge. Table 9-7 shows the findings of such an exercise.

The results are straightforward. The use of 10-year T-note futures and options follows from their similarity in duration to conventional 30-year mortgages. The use of the out-of-the-money put reflects the desire to protect against large interest rate moves. The numbers in the price-change columns are simply the dollar amounts of the price changes for that number of futures or options, and the final column reflects the sum of those two values for each interest rate scenario.

Evaluating the Hedge

Table 9-8 provides an overview of how the hedge will perform over the full range of interest rate scenarios.

TABLE 9-8
Hedging Results

Basis Point Move	Resulting Price	Price Change	Dollar Change	Expected Fallout	Needed Hedge Gain	Hedge Value	Hedge Position	% of Loss Original Value
-100	103.25000	3.25000	32,500.00	75%	24,375.00	24,089.00	-286.00	-0.03
-25	101.31250	1.31250	13,125.00	40%	5,250.00	5,031.00	-219.00	-0.02
-10	100.53125	0.53125	5,312.50	35%	1,859.38	1,822.00	-37.37	0.00
0	100.00000	0.00000	0.00	30%	0.00	0.00	0.00	-0.03
+10	99.50000	-0.50000	5000.00	30%	-1,500.00	-1,791.00	-291.00	-0.08
+25	98.75000	-1.25000	-12,500.00	25%	-3,125.00	-3,909.00	-784.00	0.02
+100	94.50000	-5.50000	-55,000.00	10%	-5,500.00	-5,328.00	172.00	0

Table 9-8 pulls together selected data from the previous tables and shows the net of the "needed hedge gain" and "total hedge value" columns in the "hedged position" column.

Interestingly, those amounts represent tiny percentages of the original $1 million mortgage pipeline value, as the final column shows. The worst result for any of these scenarios shows a loss of 8 bp on the hedged position — $800 for every $1 million hedged. The next largest losses amount to only $300 for every $1 million.

Risk management specialists favor "robust" hedges — positions that afford good protection across a broad range of interest rate changes with little or no adjustment to the hedge position. Certainly our example qualifies as a remarkably robust hedge.

Two Caveats

Of course, the example assumes a stable mortgage position. In reality, a mortgage pipeline incurs losses throughout the rate-lock period. And the pipeline ebbs and flows constantly. Because of this, a process of dynamic hedging — periodic revaluation and hedge adjustment — is required.

Also, any strategy involving options must confront the problem of time decay. Even if underlying prices and volatilities stay the same, options lose value as they approach expiration. The relevant time decay period equals the rate lock period — 60 days in this example. Table 9-9 shows what can happen to the at-the-money options considered in the earlier tables during such a 60-day period.

TABLE 9-9
Option Time Decay

Basis Point Move	ATM Call Prices	60-day Call Decay	Call Px After 60 Days	ATM Put Prices	60-Day Put Decay	Put Px After 60-Days
-100	6.205	0.086	6.119	0.048	0.043	0.005
-25	2.316	0.411	1.905	0.737	0.403	0.334
-10	1.741	0.437	1.304	1.091	0.429	0.662
0	1.389	0.429	0.960	1.389	0.429	0.960
+10	1.113	0.429	0.684	1.732	0.437	1.295
+25	0.755	0.394	0.361	2.334	0.403	1.931
+100	0.049	0.043	0.006	6.611	0.077	6.534

Hedgers can deal with time decay in two ways. Because time decay becomes most pronounced in the last 30 days before expiration, hedgers can select longer-lived options. The options used here have 96 days to expiration and so avoid the worst decay period. Of course, the longer the time in the option, the greater the time value and the higher the cost.

Even in the case of these longer options, hedgers will need to buy additional options to compensate for lost value. Again, the focus should be on the dollar change in option value, not on more conventional sensitivity measures.

Important as those caveats are, hedgers can easily monitor positions and make the necessary adjustments by using the analytical tools illustrated in this discussion. Further, numerous data and software vendors supply the needed information and analytical tools. Alternatively, hedgers can use ordinary spreadsheet software to generate the analyses used in this discussion.

Turning the Process Around

Pipeline managers can use the process illustrated here for more than hedging. Having plugged in the locally relevant data, managers may discover that the coupon rate the bank is using produces little more than a break-even result. That hardly seems sufficient reward for all the effort of originating mortgages and managing the pipeline.

Such managers may decide that an adequate return would be 25 bp (or some other figure). Profit goal in hand, they can enter that amount in the "hedged position" column of the "Hedging Results" table. Refer to Table 9-8. Then they can work backwards to arrive at the coupon rate necessary to produce that result. They can also use the hedging model to calculate the interest rate they must charge for the mortgage in order to generate the level of profits required in their business plans.

The idea that a hedging tool can be more than merely defensive should have great intuitive appeal. Most secondary marketing managers will agree with Sir Winston Churchill: "It is a socialist idea that making profits is a vice. I consider that the real vice is making losses."

10

State-of-the-Art Systems for Risk Management

Stephen R. Rigsbee
Sirri S. Ayaydin
Charles A. Richard III
Quantitative Risk Management Group

The authors would like to thank Joel Brown for his assistance in producing this chapter.

Effectively managing pipeline interest rate risk while maintaining profitability has become a formidable task. Unstable origination volumes, irrational pricing, high interest rate volatility, rapidly changing systems technology, the proliferation of new mortgage products and the complexity of new financial instruments have dramatically increased the challenges faced by risk managers.

Clearly, one of the keys to success in mortgage banking is a strong secondary marketing operation. Accurate loan pricing and efficient risk management are prerequisites to consistent profitability. Success requires mastery of finance, trading, logistics, computer systems, data management and accounting, all coordinated by highly skilled individuals equipped with the proper analytical tools.

Recently, there has been a great deal of progress in the systems technology arena, including improvements in areas such as loan data management (front-end loan tracking systems), automated loan underwriting and loan shipping. Traders can now click a button and automatically execute a trade with the Fannie Mae and Freddie Mac. Another click provides access to a wide range of real time market prices. These prices can be downloaded directly into internally developed spreadsheets that are used for producing daily rate sheets, performing simple position mark-to-markets and best execution analyses. Several commercially available secondary marketing systems also accept price downloads. Many institutions are looking to new technology to help them reduce costs and stay competitive in the current environment where automation and economies of scale rule.

However, while the days of running secondary marketing calculations on the back of an envelope may be long gone, most mortgage banks still have a long way to go in meeting the major challenges of the secondary marketing department. This is especially true in the areas of position analysis and reporting. The challenge is to quickly transform a mountain of raw data into informed analysis that can be used in the critical area of interest rate risk management. This analysis must be easily understood by secondary marketing personnel as well as less initiated senior management.

This chapter will review the common obstacles in meeting this information challenge. It will expose the pitfalls of several commonly used methods and short cuts and offer some potential solutions. The review is divided into six somewhat overlapping areas related to the secondary marketing function:

State-of-the-Art Systems for Risk Management   221

- Loan tracking
- Position analysis
- Position reporting
- Hedge position management
- Trading analytics
- Mark-to-market procedures
- Loan pricing/profitability

We will start with an overview of the problems we typically find in these areas and will follow that with a detailed discussion of each.

Current State of the Industry

Loan Tracking
Most mortgage banks have loan tracking systems capable of providing the data needed to manage interest rate risk. However, this data is rarely used to the fullest extent possible. In addition, few mortgage banks have adequate controls over the flow of information between their loan tracking systems, trade management systems, exposure management systems, delivery/settlement systems, and market information sources. Far too many mortgage banking operations inappropriately use their loan tracking or "secondary marketing" systems as a substitute for a true risk management system that contains the approach models for accurately measuring and managing risk.

Position Analysis
The majority of risk managers have a good understanding of interest rate risk associated with managing a mortgage pipeline. However, individuals charged with running the secondary

marketing function at institutions of all sizes, rarely, if ever, have the time, resources or background to develop the models and systems needed to optimize the interest rate risk management of a mortgage pipeline. Secondary marketing's main function is to price, sell and deliver loans, while squeezing every penny out of each stage of the process. This cannot be accomplished when risk managers become systems developers, spreadsheet maintainers and programming managers.

Both internally developed and commercially available systems currently being used for managing interest rate risk are inadequate when it comes to analyzing the complex mortgage products originated, the various hedge instruments used and especially the option or option-like positions. There is considerable confusion about what options are worth (particularly implicit options embedded in rate locks), when options are needed in a hedge position and how they should be incorporated.

Position Reporting

Accurate, timely risk management reports are an essential part of any successful secondary marketing operation. Although virtually every organization produces position reports on a daily basis, there is a great deal of confusion, inaccuracy and inefficiency in this process. Two major factors contribute to this problem: poor systems integration and modeling complexity. Reports are typically constructed from a patchwork of multiple systems, and analysis is performed on customized spreadsheet and database programs that leave much room for error and often necessitate duplication of effort. This inefficient process frequently requires hours of processing time, making it difficult to obtain updated reports throughout the trading day. Many institutions become overreliant on one or two individuals who understand the reporting process and the contents of the reports. This

State-of-the-Art Systems for Risk Management 223

overreliance opens them up to a potential disaster if key individuals leave.

Once the reports are produced, they typically do not contain concise, accurate, action-oriented summaries of interest rate risk exposure that can be understood by senior management without further explanation. Reports are often either too brief to be useful or so detailed that trading decisions cannot be made easily. Mark-to-market reports typically show only an open position profit and loss and do not accurately show month-to-date and historical performance. Most secondary marketing departments cannot judge their performance prior to obtaining data from their accounting systems after the completion of month end.

Hedge Position Management

Hedge positions are typically arrived at on an ad hoc basis, through trial and error or rule of thumb. There is particular confusion concerning how to define and measure fallout, and how different fallout patterns affect the cost of hedging and the optimal hedge strategy. Many risk managers have difficulty understanding the relative risks and rewards of two commonly used risk management strategies — delta hedging and global hedging. While most risk managers have abandoned "calling the market" as a risk management strategy, many still don't realize that their risk management strategies may contain hidden biases and may be, in effect, trading strategies.

Few, if any, secondary marketing departments have the combined statistical and financial algorithms needed to optimize the placement of hedge coverage between forward programs, between optional and mandatory delivery positions, between mortgage and Treasury products and between settlement months. The main obstacle is confusion as to how to integrate rate locks on the exposure side and options on the coverage side, given the uncertainties in their closing or being in the money on the option expiration date.

Further complicating the process is the daunting number of variables involved in the hedge and delivery processes. These variables include the position to hedge, the hedge instruments, the hedge target, the global clean up instrument, transaction type limitations, total option premium limits, basis risk limits and the maximum number of desired transactions.

Trading Analytics

Most secondary marketing operations could benefit from having more sophisticated tools for making trading decisions, particularly in the areas of best execution analysis and MBS and Treasury option evaluation. In addition, we find that risk managers continue to use crude statistical models or to rely on analysis provided by a broker or a "black box" quotation machine for determining the relations between different MBS types (for example, jumbo versus conventional), coupons and Treasury futures contracts. Far more precise results could be obtained by using state-of-the-art OAS models and other complex option models favored by sophisticated money managers.

Mark-to-Market

Typically, mark-to-market reports are based on subjective fallout estimates. They do not properly incorporate option values and are not produced in a timely manner. Yet, it is important that senior management get regular and timely feedback to warn them of any potential problems. In accounting for servicing values created, mark-to-market reports are typically "fuzzy" or arbitrary. They show only the open position profit and loss and do not accurately account for activity in prior periods.

Pricing/Profitability

Most mortgage bankers continue to use old rules of thumb or play "follow the leader" in pricing. Instead, pricing should be guided by careful, daily profitability analyses. Rate-lock pricing should be better differentiated according to differences in hedge costs and values of servicing. Mortgage bankers often ignore these and other important variables, such as interest spreads from expected closing dates to expected forward settlement dates, in pricing rate locks.

Loan Tracking

Loan records must contain information relevant to fallout behavior. To make good secondary marketing decisions, it is essential that current closed-loan warehouse and rate-lock inventory data always be available. Some tracking systems have the ability to show pipeline activity in real time. However, this information is rarely fed into risk management systems. Typically, the data is collected and processed overnight, making it impossible to incorporate into risk management reports. To develop an accurate profile of the interest rate risk of a given pipeline, rate-lock loan commitments in the pipeline must be categorized according to attributes that are known to affect fallout behavior. At a minimum, these attributes include mortgage purpose (for example, refinance versus purchase), source of business (for example, wholesale versus retail), geographical location, processing status (for example, application stage versus approved stage) and spread between rate-lock commitment price and underlying mortgage price. In addition to the above, wholesale originators should track their rate locks and fallout by branch code. This would be useful for hedging and profitability analysis, as behavior can vary dramatically by broker.

Relocks must be tracked, currently and historically. Another important capability in a loan tracking system is the ability to monitor renegotiated interest rates or points on rate locks. Many mortgage bankers have tracking systems that make it difficult or impossible to determine whether a repricing has occurred. Renegotiated rates must be tracked not only to control current profitability, but also to sharpen understanding of fallout sensitivity to interest rate movements. This is because a partial or full rate concession is equivalent to a partial or full fallout. It is not possible to formulate an efficient hedge position or strategy without a good understanding of how fallout relates to interest rate movements. Effective risk management requires that this relationship be monitored on a continuing basis. Relocked loans should contain an audit trail in the tracking system making it possible to later perform historical analysis.

Do not expect your loan tracking system to take the place of an expert interest rate risk management system. Loan tracking systems are superb for sorting, searching, and matching items. Some front-end systems contain secondary marketing modules that among other things, can produce simple exposure and mark-to-market reports and can provide the ability to automatically deliver loans to the agencies. These systems, however, do not contain the financial models required to manage the interest rate risk of the rate-lock agreement or the other instruments that comprise the exposure and coverage of a mortgage bank. One example of a such a model is the option-adjusted-spread (OAS) model. Risk exposure analysis, option trading analytics, hedge position management, optimization of the forward sale and delivery process, pricing and mark-to-market of option and option-like positions are beyond the ability of these systems. Considering the availability of more advanced systems and models, it is difficult to explain the heavy reliance on loan tracking and secondary marketing systems for interest rate risk management. For this reason, it is important that it be easy to export data from your loan tracking system; otherwise, you will be at the mercy of the loan tracking system for desired analyses and reports.

Position Analysis

Rate-lock modeling is a complex science, not an art. The interest rate risk of a mortgage pipeline is difficult to model, particularly because of the inefficient way in which borrowers exercise their option to "walk away" when rates fall. This complexity is compounded by the fact that the underlying mortgage is also a complex financial instrument. Ad hoc rules and seat-of-the-pants methods for risk management that might be successful under one set of circumstances will not work universally since different types of rate locks and underlying mortgages exhibit significantly different risk characteristics. For example, consider fixed-rate mortgages versus ARMs, retail versus wholesale rate locks, exotic rate locks (such as float-down and floating subject to a cap) and short-term rate locks versus long-term builder commitments. Properly measuring rate-lock fallout levels and elasticities and integrating these assumptions into a valid, option-based risk model is a prerequisite to establishing optimal hedging strategies. Quantitative techniques can be used to eliminate the "black art" that is sometimes associated with rate-lock modeling. Quantifying the risk in all meaningful dimensions effectively exposes the mystery and leaves only unhedgeable residual risk.

Fallout behavior should be expressed as a function of interest rate changes; point estimates should not be used. A well designed risk management system contains predefined fallout functions (not point estimates) for each category of rate lock. Then, as market movements take place, the system should automatically determine the impact of price changes on risk profiles. A system which requires entry of new fallout projections each time there is a market movement is bound to fail, because risk profiles and hedge positions should analyze how fallout ratios would change if rates were to change before rates do change. It is common in most secondary marketing systems and internally developed spreadsheets to require the user to enter the expected spot fallout prediction. Since fallout is correlated to market move, this is tantamount to calling the market.

Fallout can occur even when a loan closes. Fallout occurs when a loan does not close or when a loan closes at a lower rate or with fewer discount points in a falling interest rate (rising price) market scenario. In the case of a change in rate or price, a rate lock is said to have fallen out to the extent that the market improvement was passed through to the borrower.

Include rate-lock rate concessions as fallout. There should be a mechanism to automatically include rate concessions and, alternatively, rate increases. For example, the amount of loans that close at the original rate and points should be tracked as well as the amount of loans that close at a new rate and points. This relationship will vary, based on the magnitude of the market move. Correct application of this concept will result in the creation of better hedge positions for all market scenarios.

If you do not know your fallout, it is easy to formulate a conservative estimate until you have more data and experience. Assume the highest closing ratio you have ever experienced will occur for any down market and the lowest closing ratio you have ever experienced will occur for any up market. Then begin to relax this assumption as you compile more information. Generic fallout data may be made available by consultants that perform this type of analysis for their clients. In any case, you should use any third party information in conjunction with your own data and experience as a starting point.

Fallout can occur before you know it. Often times, loans remain in your pipeline even though they have already fallen out and are no longer at risk. This occurs in pipelines of all types but is particularly prevalent in wholesale operations where the risk manager has imperfect knowledge of the processing status of the loan. A typical wholesale operation knows when the loan is locked, but may not receive any additional information until the loan closes or falls out. The path of interest rates during the life of the lock has a significant bearing on the likelihood of the loan actually being at risk.

For example, if the loan was originally locked at market for 60 days, then rates drop significantly shortly thereafter only to return to the original lock rate, the loan may have already been pulled and placed with another lender. After borrowers submit the lock, they have no incentive to cancel the lock with the lender if they pull the lock. They will play their option with the original lender until the last possible moment in the unlikely event that they may still need to use the original lock. This phenomenon creates a unique valuation and hedging problem, adding even greater complexity to the difficult task of rate-lock modeling and pipeline management. It is often described by risk managers but few if any have been able to correctly implement a solution. The proper solution requires an application of a complex option model, such as the look-back option model, that can handle these characteristics.

Do not confuse rate-lock delta and closing ratio. We have seen many articles written and speeches given by risk managers who describe their method for calculating their position delta as follows: They estimate the amount of product that is expected to close for the static scenario and alter this estimate for several different market scenarios. Typically, closing estimates are reduced for price increases and increased for price declines. Some institutions vary expected closing ratio estimates by type of rate lock, source, status and time until expiration. Their strategy is to sell the base expected closing amount forward and to then make subsequent adjustments to their coverage as the market moves.

This strategy is by far the most serious error committed by secondary marketing professionals. The error seems to arise from a misplaced concern about having the right amount of coverage on the day the loan closes, instead of a proper concern for hedging profits and losses. Profits are a function of positions held throughout the life of the hedge, not a function of arriving on the loan closing date with the same amount of coverage as closed loans. It is surprising that so many practitioners believe that this approach yields the optimal hedge ratio, considering that this approach is not equivalent to hedging the profit/loss resulting from changes in underlying mortgage prices.

At the heart of this error is a confusion between marginal and average. Holding a short position equal to the closing ratio will work only if this size position is held throughout the life of the rate lock; however, this would happen only if the risk manager were able to predict the interest rate at the end of the hedge period, since the actual closing ratio is a function of the ultimate market interest rate.

Consider an example of a sustained period of falling interest rates (rising prices). During such a period, the expected closing ratio will be repeatedly revised downward, reflecting constantly increasing fallout expectations. As a result, the average position held will be larger than the position held at the end of the hedge period. In this example, risk managers who continuously maintain positions equal in size to the current expected closing ratio will inevitably lose more on their hedge positions than they make on the loans that close.

However, now consider the results if these hedgers had calculated the marginal profit/loss from a small additional change in the market price (that is, the position delta) and set the size of their positions based on the marginal effects of changes in price on their total profit/loss. Using this approach, they would have been consistently holding positions smaller than the expected closing ratio, resulting in cumulative losses that would not exceed profits on the volume of loans that actually closed at the end of the period.

The two approaches differ because there are two distinct effects on rate-lock profits when mortgage prices change: The first is the change in profit or loss on rate locks whose closing status is unaffected by the marginal price change; the second comes from the elimination or addition of all previous unrealized profits or losses on rate locks that fall out or close as a result of the marginal price change.

In summary, risk managers who use the expected closing ratio method build a predictable bias into their hedging strategy. The bias results in losses when the market moves in either direction. Expected closing ratios are typically greater than actual delta when market prices rise and lower than actual delta when market prices fall.

A rate lock, while containing elements of a put option, is not a standard put option. Recognize that, in principle, a rate-lock commitment is a sort of put option, since borrowers have the right, but not the obligation, to take down the rate-lock loan commitment. Some practitioners attempt to solve the option problem by simply assuming that the rate lock is a standard put option equivalent in substance to those traded on exchanges or over the counter. This approach is sometimes referred to as hedging against "the worst case borrower." The problem with this approach is that standard option models assume efficient exercise; that is, upon expiration, an in-the-money option will be fully exercised (all loans close) and an out-of-the-money option will not be exercised at all (no loans close). It follows that a standard put option model will accurately evaluate the delta of a rate lock only when fallout behavior is such that all rate locks close for any rise in rates, and all rate locks fall out for any drop in rates.

Most risk managers realize that this is a dramatic oversimplification of their borrower behavior. This method cannot be used to create optimal hedge positions or to accurately estimate hedge costs. The main reason for the popularity of this strategy, especially in the 1980s, was due to its easy implementation. The appealing simplicity of this approach led (and still leads) many institutions to pay excessive option premiums (rate locks have significantly lower hedge costs than standard put options) and to build bias into their hedging strategy. Since more complex models were not widely available, risk managers rationalized that results obtained using this method were close enough. Their hope was that actual borrower inefficiency would somehow work itself out.

Nowadays, standard option models are available in many forms, from market data providers, Wall Street firms, consultants and software companies that provide spreadsheet add-ins.

Figure 10-1 and Table 10-1 provide a comparison of expected closing ratio, rate-lock delta and option delta.

A rate lock is, in fact, a variable quantity option. The variable-quantity option model differs from the standard option model in that it allows for different degrees of option exercise depending on the relation between the market price of the underlying asset and the option strike price. Thus, it is ideally suited for evaluating rate locks, since it captures the optional nature of rate locks, while also allowing for any degree in exercise efficiency the hedger wishes to assume. It thereby overcomes the problems inherent in the static closing ratio approaches and the standard option models. As a result, it is the only approach that can provide the correct rate-lock delta. It provides the same delta as would be obtained by evaluating a portfolio of put options, call options and mandatory forward delivery positions, which collectively provide a profit/loss profile exactly equal to but opposite of the rate-lock commitment profit/loss profile.

The Black-Scholes model was not designed for evaluating MBS options, much less rate locks. Just as using a put option model to evaluate the risk of a rate lock leads to the efficiency problem discussed earlier, using the Black Scholes model to evaluate an option on a mortgage introduces another problem. The Black-Scholes model assumes that the asset on which an option exists has a symmetric return distribution — that is,

State-of-the-Art Systems for Risk Management 233

FIGURE 10-1

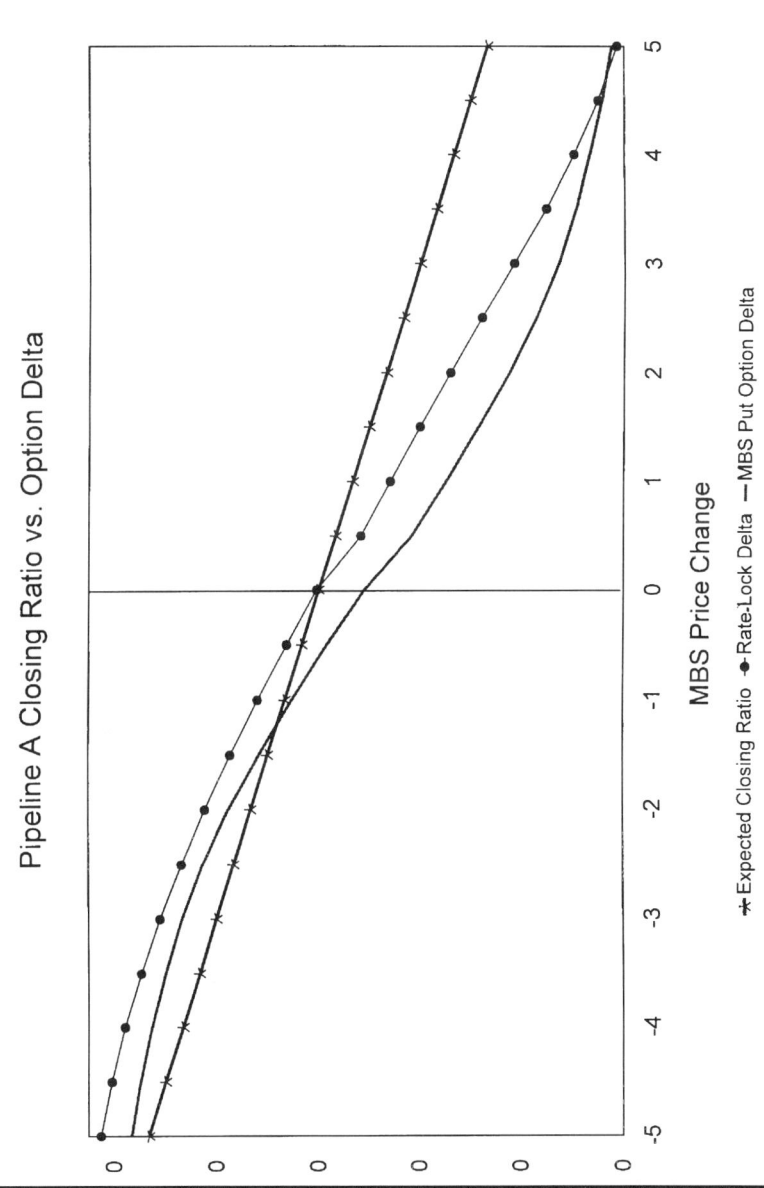

TABLE 10-1

Expected Closing Ratio vs. Option Delta

MBS Price Change	Expected Closing Ratio	Rate Lock Delta	MBS Put Option Delta	Black-Scholes Put Option Delta
-5.00	0.93	1.02	0.96	0.86
-4.00	0.86	0.98	0.92	0.82
-3.00	0.80	0.91	0.86	0.78
-2.00	0.73	0.82	0.77	0.70
-1.00	0.66	0.72	0.65	0.61
0.00	0.60	0.60	0.51	0.50
1.00	0.53	0.45	0.34	0.37
2.00	0.46	0.34	0.22	0.28
3.00	0.40	0.21	0.12	0.21
4.00	0.33	0.09	0.06	0.16
5.00	0.26	0.01	0.02	0.13

State-of-the-Art Systems for Risk Management 235

percentage increases of a given magnitude are equally likely as percentage decreases of the same magnitude. This is clearly not the case with a mortgage asset. Because of the embedded prepayment option, a mortgage has a very limited upside compared to its downside.

Figure 10-2 compares the delta of a put option on a mortgage measured with the Black-Scholes model versus the delta of the same option measured with a model that uses an accurate assumption with respect to the underlying asset return distribution. The bias of the Black-Scholes model can be characterized as follows: When the put option is out of the money, the Black-Scholes model overestimates the delta by implicitly overestimating the likelihood that the option will be in the money by the expiration date; when the put option is in the money, the Black-Scholes model underestimates the delta by implicitly underestimating the likelihood that the option will remain in the money on the expiration date.

These biases arise because the Black-Scholes model assumptions are not consistent with the compression (falling volatility) in the price of a given mortgage that occurs in rising markets or the decompression (rising volatility) in the price of a given mortgage that occurs in falling markets. When unable to implement the proper model, some practitioners deal with these Black-Scholes biases by manually assigning a different volatility to each strike price. For a put option, higher volatilities are assigned to lower strike prices and lower volatilities are assigned to higher strike prices.

Position Reporting

Exposure management reports often cover too narrow a range of interest rate movements. Many organizations do not produce shock reports of any kind. Reports focus on static "net position" analysis simply showing the net of long positions minus short

FIGURE 10-2

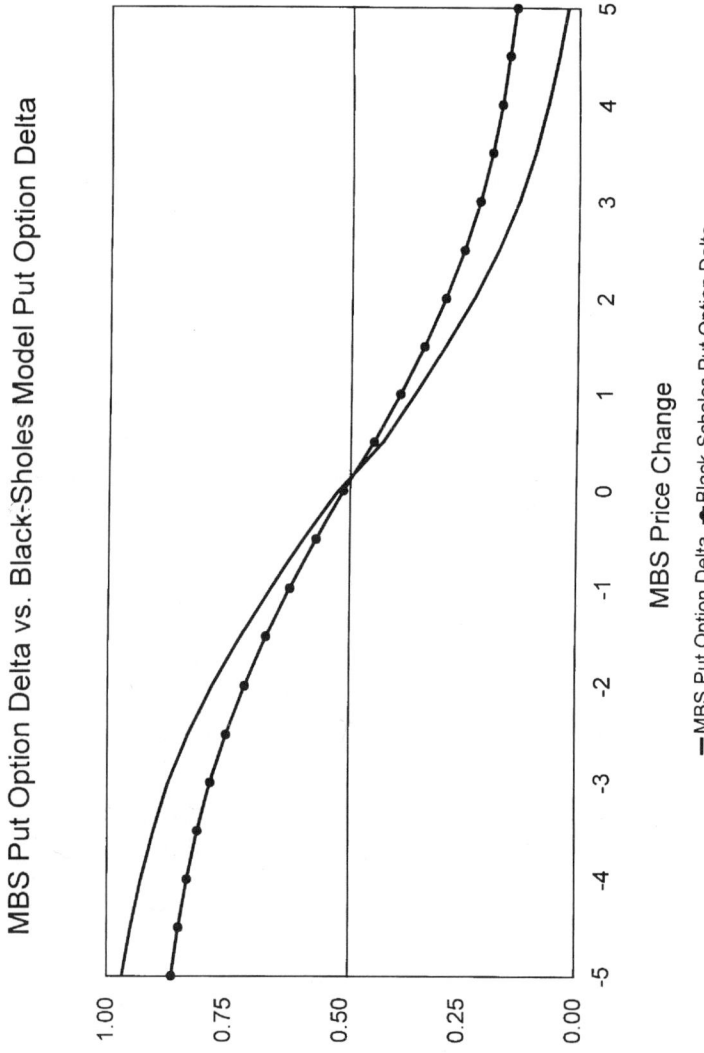

positions. We recommend projecting value changes for all exposure and coverage items for a range of MBS price changes of at least 5 points up or down, relating to 100 basis points up or down in the Treasury yield curve. Moves of these magnitudes have occurred several times in the last decade, during the 1987 stock market crash and more recently on March 8, 1996. There is no reason to believe that they will not experience such moves again in the future. This type of report effectively boils your risk down to a single curve and lends itself well to graphic analysis, thus making it easily understandable by management.

Reports 10-1 and 10-2 are examples of shock reports. Report 10-1 shows position value change and Report 10-2 shows position value level.

The impact of out-of-the-money options is often left out of position reports. Out-of-the-money options are often not included in basic reports that purport to measure overall longness or shortness of the mortgage banker's position. However, they may afford a substantial degree of protection or risk, particularly if they are near the money, if they have a long remaining life or if bond market implied volatility is high. Practitioners have tried to deal with this issue in several ways, including assuming that out-of-the money options offer no coverage and in-the-money options are equivalent to forwards which offer full coverage.

Others have applied different coverage percentages to options depending on how close they think these options are to the money. In a net position report, option positions should be included on the basis of a delta weighting. (Remember: Delta is the expected change in the market value of the option with respect to a change in the underlying asset price). Exposure reports that exclude the current effects of out-of-the-money options may indicate substantially long positions, when positions actually may be net short, or vice versa.

Report 10-3 is an example of a global net position report that correctly incorporates the effect of options.

Report 10-1

Value Change vs. MBS Price Shock Summary

(000s)

7.00% FANNIE MAE VALUE CHANGE

QRM SYSTEM

EXPOSURE:	Face Amt	97-24 -3-00	98-24 -2-00	99-24 -1-00	100-00 -0-24	100-08 -0-16	100-16 -0-08	100-24 -0-00	101-00 0-08	101-08 0-16	101-16 0-24	101-24 1-00	102-24 2-00	103-24 3-00
Fixed Rate:														
Closed Loans	865,135	-24,808	-16,538	-8,266	-6,198	-4,131	-2,065	0	2,064	4,127	6,193	8,261	16,570	24,753
Rate Locks	677,574	-14,188	-9,059	-4,257	-3,130	-2,042	-997	0	945	1,836	2,674	3,457	6,024	7,697
Not-at-Risk Loans	690,748	0	0	0	0	0	0	0	0	0	0	0	0	0
Total Fixed Rate	2,233,457	-38,996	-25,597	-12,523	-9,328	-6,173	-3,062	0	3,009	5,963	8,867	11,718	22,594	32,450
Adjustable Rate:														
Closed Loans	166,132	-2,279	-1,539	-777	-578	-381	-187	0	179	350	517	682	1,362	2,050
Rate Locks	98,932	-969	-624	-300	-221	-144	-70	0	66	128	188	244	461	650
Not-at-Risk Loans	28,743	0	0	0	0	0	0	0	0	0	0	0	0	0
Total Adjustable	293,807	-3,248	-2,163	-1,077	-799	-525	-257	0	245	478	705	926	1,823	2,700
TOTAL EXPOSURE	2,527,264	-42,244	-27,760	-13,600	-10,127	-6,698	-3,319	0	3,254	6,441	9,572	12,644	24,417	35,150
COVERAGE:														
Mortgage Forwards	-1,064,197	32,008	21,382	10,709	8,034	5,358	2,679	0	-2,681	-5,365	-8,053	-10,749	-21,610	-32,367
Mortgage Call Options	15,000	-179	-138	-79	-61	-42	-22	0	23	48	73	101	223	361
Mortgage Put Options	-360,000	7,375	4,302	1,789	1,271	799	375	0	-327	-608	-849	-1,055	-1,606	-1,868
ARM Forwards	-220,585	3,116	2,094	1,050	780	513	252	0	-240	-470	-694	-915	-1,827	-2,750
Treasury Futures	-3,000	96	65	33	25	17	8	0	-8	-17	-26	-34	-71	-109
Treasury Put Options	-20,000	288	172	76	55	35	17	0	-16	-30	-43	-55	-94	-118
TOTAL COVERAGE	-1,652,782	42,704	27,877	13,578	10,104	6,680	3,309	0	-3,249	-6,442	-9,592	-12,707	-24,985	-36,851
NET EXPOSURE	874,482	460	117	-22	-23	-18	-10	0	5	-1	-20	-63	-568	-1,701

State-of-the-Art Systems for Risk Management 239

Report 10-2

Value Level vs. MBS Price Shock Summary

QRM SYSTEM

(000s)

EXPOSURE:	Face Amt	97-24 -3-00	98-24 -2-00	99-24 -1-00	100-00 0-24	100-08 0-16	100-16 0-08	100-24 0-00	101-00 0-08	101-08 0-16	101-16 0-24	101-24 1-00	102-24 2-00	103-24 3-00
Fixed Rate:														
Closed Loans	865,135	-16,218	-7,948	325	2,392	4,459	6,525	8,590	10,654	12,717	14,783	16,851	25,160	33,343
Rate Locks	677,574	-12,576	-7,448	-2,645	-1,519	-430	615	1,611	2,556	3,447	4,285	5,068	7,636	9,309
Not-at-Risk Loans	690,748	0	0	0	0	0	0	0	0	0	0	0	0	0
Total Fixed Rate	2,233,457	-28,794	-15,396	-2,320	873	4,029	7,140	10,201	13,210	16,164	19,068	21,919	32,796	42,652
Adjustable Rate:														
Closed Loans	166,132	11	752	1,514	1,712	1,910	2,103	2,291	2,469	2,641	2,808	2,973	3,652	4,341
Rate Locks	98,932	-460	-116	209	288	364	438	508	574	637	696	753	969	1,158
Not-at-Risk Loans	28,743	0	0	0	0	0	0	0	0	0	0	0	0	0
Total Adjustable	293,807	-449	636	1,723	2,000	2,274	2,541	2,799	3,043	3,278	3,504	3,726	4,621	5,499
TOTAL EXPOSURE	**2,527,264**	**-29,243**	**-14,760**	**-597**	**2,873**	**6,303**	**9,681**	**13,000**	**16,253**	**19,442**	**22,572**	**25,645**	**37,417**	**48,151**
COVERAGE:														
Mortgage Forwards	-1,064,197	25,220	14,594	3,922	1,247	-1,430	-4,108	-6,788	-9,468	-12,152	-14,841	-17,537	-28,397	-39,155
Mortgage Call Options	15,000	-93	-53	8	24	44	65	86	108	134	159	186	308	447
Mortgage Put Options	-360,000	7,737	4,666	2,150	1,639	1,155	736	363	34	-247	-488	-693	-1,241	-1,505
ARM Forwards	-220,585	1,160	138	-907	-1,176	-1,443	-1,704	-1,956	-2,196	-2,427	-2,650	-2,871	-3,783	-4,706
Treasury Futures	-3,000	65	34	2	-6	-14	-23	-31	-39	-48	-56	-65	-102	-139
Treasury Put Options	-20,000	282	166	70	48	30	10	-6	-22	-36	-50	-62	-100	-124
TOTAL COVERAGE	**-1,652,782**	**34,371**	**19,545**	**5,245**	**1,776**	**-1,648**	**-5,024**	**-8,332**	**-11,583**	**-14,776**	**-17,926**	**-21,042**	**-33,315**	**-45,182**
NET EXPOSURE	**874,482**	**5,128**	**4,785**	**4,648**	**4,649**	**4,655**	**4,657**	**4,668**	**4,670**	**4,666**	**4,646**	**4,603**	**4,102**	**2,969**

POSITION VALUE vs FANNIE MAE 7.00% MBS PRICE CHANGE

Report 10-3

Interest Rate Explosure Derivitives Summary

QRM SYSTEM

EXPOSURE:	FACE AMOUNT (000s)	EQUIVALENT MBS* (000s)	TRSY BASIS PT VALUE (/100)	CONVEXITY (/100)	IMPLIED VOLATILITY (-0.01)	TIME DECAY (15 DAY)	AVERAGE DELTA (%)	EXPECTED CLOSE RATIO (%)
Fixed Rate:								
Closed Loans	865,135	827,061	46,753	-7,566	-350	100	100	
Rate Locks	677,574	390,169	22,056	-31,528	-192	528	56	63
Not-at-Risk Loans	690,748	0	0	0	0	0		
Total Fixed Rate	2,233,457	1,217,230	68,810	-39,094	-542	628	55	
Adjustable Rate:								
Closed Loans	166,132	72,889	4,120	-2,982	-92	11	100	
Rate Locks	98,932	27,583	1,559	-1,860	-39	19	62	67
Not-at-Risk Loans	28,743	0	0	0	0	0		
Total Adjustable Rate	293,809	100,473	5,679	-4,842	-131	31	77	
TOTAL EXPOSURE	**2,527,267**	**1,317,703**	**74,489**	**-43,936**	**-673**	**660**	**58**	
COVERAGE:								
Mortgage Forwards	-1,064,197	-1,073,431	-60,681	8,372	352	-96	-100	
Mortgage Call Options	15,000	8,963	506	555	6	-15	52	
Mortgage Put Options	-360,000	-139,291	-7,874	26,084	208	-499	-33	
ARM Forwards	-220,585	-98,201	-5,551	4,216	141	-16	-100	
Treasury Futures	-3,000	-3,373	-190	-13	0	0	-100	
Treasury Put Options	-20,000	-6,548	-370	698	41	-19	-29	
TOTAL COVERAGE	**-1,652,782**	**-1,311,882**	**-74,160**	**39,912**	**748**	**-647**	**-83**	
NET EXPOSURE	**874,484**	**5,821**	**329**	**-4,024**	**75**	**12**		

* 7.00% FANNIE MAE 30 Year

Prices of different mortgages do not move together point for point. A common error committed in the production of consolidated exposure reports is the assumption that all mortgage prices (Fannie Mae, Ginnie Mae, Jumbo, 8%, 9%) move together, point for point. However, MBS prices do not behave in this manner.

Some practitioners use regression analysis to establish a relationship. This too is incorrect, because the relation between two mortgage assets changes as interest rate levels change. Thus, the relation found in a regression is backward looking and will not hold for broad movements in rates, making it useless for a broadly scoped shock analysis. An OAS model that incorporates a sophisticated prepayment model is needed to accurately determine price elasticity relationships between different mortgage types and coupons, over a broad range of interest rate scenarios, so as to enable the construction of accurate consolidated exposure reports. Reports 10-1 and 10-2 are examples of shock reports that are constructed using the above method.

Proper hedge ratios should be used when producing consolidated net position reports. Because of the modeling complexity, we have found few risk managers who are able to produce an accurate, consolidated, net risk position report. Some institutions still have systems and reports that simply add up the face amount of their exposure and subtract the face amount of their coverage. Some institutions even set position risk limits based on this grossly simplified analysis.

More sophisticated institutions have used regression analysis to develop hedge ratios between different product types and coupons. This is an improvement over the face amount method, but is problematic due to the nonlinear relationship between mortgage prices and rate moves. Others have used published hedge ratios available from dealers and market quotations machines. The main problem with this method is that dealers do not publish hedge ratios that cover the entire universe of product types offered by a typical mortgage bank. Also, using these numbers is equivalent to relying on a "black box" in which you have no control over when and how the numbers are calculated or distributed.

Use of a standard benchmark, such as the Treasury yield curve makes it possible to produce a consolidated position report that can easily incorporate a diverse set of product types and hedge instruments, including exchange-traded futures and options.

By correctly applying the standard benchmark method, it becomes easy to express your net position in terms of any generic instrument. This greatly simplifies the expression of risk for senior management and risk managers alike. Unless the highest level risk management report consolidates the effects of all positions taken, it becomes very difficult to express the true net exposure of the institution.

Global position reports often do not include every instrument contained in the position. Institutions using such reports must produce separate reports showing nongeneric hedge and position data, which must somehow be mentally or manually integrated with the standard position reports. This is an inefficient and often ineffective process.

Report 10-3 is an example of a consolidated net position report constructed using the proper methodology.

Include your exposure to pending rate locks. An estimate of rate locks issued, but not yet reflected in computer files or reports available to the secondary marketing department, should be included in exposure management reports so that interest rate risk from those items can be reflected before hedge adjustment decisions are made. Not only do you have a current exposure to any rate locks that are likely to be issued prior to the next price resetting, but your exposure will be greater in falling price markets as borrowers rush to beat anticipated price changes as well. You should monitor pipeline velocity on a daily basis and place anticipatory hedges. The better your daily pipeline activity is understood, the more effective hedges you will be able to place.

Many institutions offer free overnight protection to their locks. The cost of offering overnight locks should be calculated and fully understood. Lags in receiving position data due to outdated loan tracking systems or generous lock policies could prove costly. This can be particularly true when the market deteriorates. Risk managers may not even see that their position is already under water. As data collection mechanisms improve, this lag phenomenon will surely become less of a factor. Systems technology already enables some risk managers to see new volume in real time. The availability of this technology, combined with risk management systems that can process and correctly analyze this data, will make real time interest rate risk management for a mortgage bank a reality.

Reports do not easily track multitrader or multiunit exposure and profitability. The consolidation of the industry has resulted in large trading operations with large positions. Many organizations have divided the risk management and trading responsibility. It is now common to see anywhere from two to five risk managers working side by side on separate positions. This scenario puts stress on the traditional reporting and processing function. The situation is made even more complex when mergers and regulations create the need to manage positions across multiple companies or legal entities. Traders need their own full complement of risk management and mark-to-market reports in order to perform their jobs effectively. Management needs the individual reports to measure the performance and the risk of each trader. Management also needs consolidated reports to make sure that the global position is being managed correctly. Few institutions have successfully implemented a flexible reporting mechanism that can accommodate the more complex reporting needs of the modern secondary marketing operation.

Executive summaries are ideal for communicating risk exposure. The three reports discussed above show ideal formats for communicating the interest rate exposure of a mortgage bank.

Reports like these should be produced daily and made available to top management. Report 10-1 shows the global position value change; Report 10-2 shows the global position mark-to-market level shock report and Report 10-3 shows the net equivalent position and the associated option characteristics also know as the "Greeks."

Hedge Position Management

Secondary marketing managers should not be forced to speculate on market direction. This often happens when unreasonable profit expectations exist. For example, some mortgage banks impose the arbitrary standard that secondary marketing "break even" with no credit given for the value of servicing created or interest income. Competition has, in many instances, driven average total origination profits, including the value of servicing, below the value of servicing. This of course does not mean that mortgage origination is no longer profitable on a net basis.

Secondary marketing managers should not be required to make secondary marketing profits (as defined above) if it is not possible to do so without assuming interest rate risk.

Assuming interest rate risk cannot improve profitability unless the mortgage banker is able to "call the market" on a consistent basis. The ultimate goal of risk management decisions should be to maximize long term average profits while minimizing the variability of profits from month to month.

Actual results should be measured against an objective performance benchmark based on quantifiable variables. This benchmark should be based on results that are attainable without taking on interest rate risk. What is attainable depends on the *marketing spread* (the difference between the commitment price and the forward price), servicing values, fees collected, operating costs and the determinants of hedge cost. Determinants of hedge cost include rate-lock period, fallout function elasticity and interest rate volatility. The greater the rate-lock period, elasticity of fallout and/or volatility of interest rates, the greater the hedge cost. Your risk management system should measure this expected "all-in, *ex ante* profitability" on a rate lock by rate lock basis. Since this performance benchmark includes the cost of hedging, it is by definition an amount that is attainable without taking on interest rate risk.

If interest rate risk is permitted, clearly articulated risk limits should exist. Management should establish limits on the amount of interest rate risk exposure that is allowable in terms of the amount of profit and loss that would be expected to result from shifts in interest rates of various magnitudes in either direction. For example, upper management might stipulate that expected losses not exceed $25,000 for a one-point move in the current coupon instrument or $50,000 for a two-point move.

Global and Delta Hedging

As far as the use of options is concerned, the two extreme approaches to risk management are global and delta hedging. Understanding the difference between global hedging and delta hedging is critical. Choosing which approach to take is particularly important for a mortgage banking operation that has fallout ratios which are highly sensitive to interest rate changes. Aside from whether or not to allow market calls, this is the most important risk management policy decision to be made.

Global hedging involves establishing a hedge position that has a return profile equal but opposite to the profit/loss profile of the exposure — for example, the profit/loss profile of the rate-lock pipeline. Global hedging is also called *static hedging* because a global hedge does not automatically require changes in response to market movements. The more sensitive fallout is to rate changes, the more asymmetric the profit/loss profile of the rate-lock pipeline will be, requiring a higher proportion of option purchases to forward sales in a hedge position designed to flatten the net profit/loss profile.

Delta hedging involves not the purchase, but rather the replication, of options. Actual market price volatility is what determines the cost of replicating options. If a mortgage bank does not actually purchase options, it must then replicate them, since it starts from a position of being short options (that is, from rate-lock commitments). Whether a strategy of avoiding options turns out to be cheaper than a strategy of purchasing options depends simply upon whether actual volatility over a given period is higher or lower than was the volatility implied by option prices at the beginning of the given hedge period. Delta hedging is sometimes referred to as *dynamic hedging* because a delta hedge automatically requires changes in response to market movements.

Global Hedging Advantages and Disadvantages

Global hedges do not require constant adjustment, since a global hedge is designed to self-adjust as interest rates and correlated fallout change. Thus, a global hedger avoids the well known portfolio insurance problem of not being able to adjust in time due to large sudden price movements. Global hedging allows you to know your hedge cost in advance. In short, global hedging provides more consistent, and more predictable, results.

Many risk managers mistakenly believe that it is too costly to purchase options to create a global hedge, the premise being that options are always overpriced. This is a common misconception. Options are at times overpriced relative to their replication value. When options are overpriced, they should not be used. In the case where MBS options are rich relative to Treasury options, Treasury options could be purchased to replicate the desired MBS option. If all options are overpriced, dynamic replication strategies

State-of-the-Art Systems for Risk Management 247

using forwards should be used. We have generally found that on-the-run, short-dated options have been closely approximating their replication value for quite some time. This does, of course, vary from day to day, but the variance seldom creates an opportunity for the typical mortgage banker to "arb" the market.

Another widely held misconception is that options are most expensive when you need them most. This confusion stems from the direct correlation between levels of market volatility and option premiums. When market volatility is high, option premiums are high. The reality is that when market volatility is high, all forms of hedging are more expensive, not just options. This, of course, includes forward selling. In fact, selling forward can have a much higher cost when there are significant gaps in the market; such a scenario could make forward selling at any level impossible. Market volatility increases the need for position adjustments and thus increases the transaction cost associated with delta hedging.

Delta Hedging Advantages and Disadvantages

In option theory, the option delta is the change in the value of the option with respect to a very small change in the value of the asset on which the option exists. It follows from this that exposure to an option may be offset, for very small changes in the underlying asset price, by taking a reverse fractional position — equal to the delta — in the underlying asset. Over time, however, slippage occurs in execution of this strategy since the delta changes after even very small changes in the market price of the underlying asset and the delta hedger is always at least slightly behind in adjusting his position to the theoretical delta of the option.

The delta hedger is, in essence, always chasing the market, buying high and selling low after the fact. In an efficient market, the cost of replicating an option through delta hedging (as a result of slippage) will be the same as the cost of buying the option outright — that is, the cumulative trading profits/losses and transaction costs will equal the premium cost of an outright purchase. Therefore, a delta hedger is simply betting that actual volatility will be lower than implied volatility.

The problem is that delta hedgers do not know in advance what actual volatility will be over the period of the option replication. A quick test of market efficiency is whether, on average, implied volatility equals actual volatility. Historically, on average, they have been close, except for the two-year period following the stock market crash (1988-1989) when implied volatilities on bond options were somewhat higher than actual volatility (ex post, premiums were 10% to 20% greater than fair value).

A common misconception held by delta hedgers is that they must aggressively follow their position delta when the market falls and that they must follow their position delta less aggressively when the market rises. In other words, delta hedgers believe they must increase their coverage percentages as the probability of loans closing increases and decrease their coverage percentages as the probability of loans closing decreases. The often-stated rationale for this strategy is that new loans will flow into the pipeline, enabling the delta hedger to fill trades that were previously taken. While this strategy may be valid in terms of balancing the interest rate risk of the net position (new loans added to the pipeline will offset loans that fall out), it does not eliminate mark-to-market losses incurred when lower note rate loans are delivered into higher coupon trades, or when the higher coupon trades are eventually paired-off.

For a mortgage originator with significant fallout risk, truly conservative risk management requires the purchase of options. Delta hedging involves several risks:

State-of-the-Art Systems for Risk Management 249

1. The cost of the hedge is not known in advance; it will be determined by the actual volatility experienced over the life of the hedge.
2. It introduces a human behavior risk, namely, that delta hedgers will freeze during a large market move and end up infusing a market view into their position, hoping the market will come back, instead of religiously following the delta.
3. The strategy involves frequent monitoring and recalculation of deltas to determine if an adjustment is needed.
4. Transaction costs can be significant; you pay the bid/ask spread each time you adjust your position.
5. Finally, there is the portfolio insurance problem.

When replicating option positions with non-option-like instruments (for example, forwards), option theory assumes that you can continuously adjust your forward position to match the change in the option delta. The success of the delta hedging strategy depends on hedgers' ability to adjust their positions for each market movement. This introduces execution risk. *Execution risk* is the risk that trades may be continuously executed as the market moves. If there are large gaps in market prices, adjustments are missed, and replication costs (that is, hedge losses) will be greater than expected. In extreme cases, such as the 1987 stock market crash, or more recently, on Friday, March 8, 1996, forward trades could not be executed at any level as the market moved dramatically. The purchase of options guarantees the buyer the right to sell or buy at the predetermined strike price, thereby avoiding the portfolio insurance problem.

Even in normal circumstances, few mortgage bankers have the combined trading expertise to consistently outperform the outright purchase of short-dated options from Wall Street. Successfully doing so would require constant monitoring of the position, very low transaction costs and enormous trading discipline.

Nonglobal hedgers should always have a contingency plan, such as the example provided by Report 10-4, in place. Secondary marketing department contingency plans, in the form of a standard report, should inform the head position manager what specific trades would be required to bring net exposure back into line in the event of significant market movements. Contingency reports should show how the net position should be altered for a wide range of possible market moves in terms of a current coupon equivalent. The reports should be denominated in increments of 1/8- or 1/4-point moves, depending on the nature of the position being managed. A typical delta hedger will need to reduce coverage when the market rallies and add coverage when the market falls. For global hedgers, by definition, this report would not be of great importance, since their hedge positions are designed to self-adjust to market movements. However, for followers of dynamic hedging strategies (delta hedgers), this report is critical.

Transactional efficiency should be considered each time position is adjusted. For each forward type, settlement month and coupon, the secondary marketing department should determine what the mortgage banker's net long or short position is, based on a loan-by-loan analysis of likely settlement month and market value sensitivity analysis. When hedge position adjustments are needed, they should be taken according to where the mortgage banker's current net long or short position is. Following this process will substantially reduce pair-off/roll costs. Report 10-5 is an example of a transactionally efficient risk management report.

Creation of optimal hedge positions requires the use of sophisticated optimization algorithms. Traditionally, hedge positions have been calculated on an ad hoc basis, through trail and error or rule of thumb. The large number of variables that require consideration make creating the optimal hedge almost impossible without using more sophisticated techniques. Once the global position has been properly analyzed using the techniques and

State-of-the-Art Systems for Risk Management 251

Report 10-4

Exposure Level vs. MBS Price Shock Summary

(000s)   QRM SYSTEM

FANNIE MAE 30 Year TBPV — 7.00% FANNIE MAE EQUIVALENT EXPOSURE

EXPOSURE:	Face Amt	97-24 / -3.00 / 6.06	98-24 / -2.00 / 5.94	99-24 / -1.00 / 5.8	100-00 / -0.24 / 5.77	100-08 / -0.16 / 5.73	100-16 / -0.08 / 5.69	100-24 / 0.00 / 5.65	101-00 / 0.08 / 5.61	101-08 / 0.16 / 5.57	101-16 / 0.24 / 5.52	101-24 / 1.00 / 5.47	102-24 / 2.00 / 5.25	103-24 / 3.00 / 5.05
Fixed Rate:														
Closed Loans	865,138	826,991	827,351	826,941	826,891	826,891	826,951	827,061	827,191	827,281	827,341	827,361	827,061	826,302
Rate Locks	677,574	525,674	500,714	458,788	444,425	428,249	410,191	390,169	368,985	347,441	325,446	302,921	210,404	131,439
Not-at-Risk Loans	690,748	0	0	0	0	0	0	0	0	0	0	0	0	0
Total Fixed Rate	2,233,460	1,352,665	1,328,065	1,285,729	1,271,316	1,255,140	1,237,142	1,217,230	1,196,176	1,174,722	1,152,787	1,130,282	1,037,465	957,741
Adjustable Rate:														
Closed Loans	166,133	76,255	72,939	78,738	78,847	77,944	75,967	72,889	69,672	67,318	65,868	65,372	69,304	68,122
Rate Locks	98,932	36,656	33,417	32,185	31,479	30,480	29,188	27,583	25,938	24,555	23,435	22,607	20,902	17,410
Not-at-Risk Loans	28,743	0	0	0	0	0	0	0	0	0	0	0	0	0
Total Adjustable	293,808	112,911	106,356	110,923	110,326	108,424	105,155	100,472	95,610	91,873	89,303	87,979	90,206	85,532
TOTAL EXPOSURE	2,527,268	1,465,576	1,434,421	1,396,652	1,381,642	1,363,564	1,342,297	1,317,702	1,291,786	1,266,595	1,242,090	1,218,261	1,127,671	1,043,273
COVERAGE:														
Mortgage Forwards	-1,064,197	-1,060,341	-1,064,764	-1,068,738	-1,069,816	-1,070,955	-1,072,153	-1,073,431	-1,074,719	-1,075,997	-1,077,245	-1,078,483	-1,083,516	-1,089,327
Mortgage Call Options	15,000	3,433	4,971	6,827	7,336	7,855	8,404	8,963	9,522	10,071	10,610	11,129	13,115	14,862
Mortgage Put Options	-360,000	-325,068	-280,711	-214,481	-196,273	-177,678	-158,688	-139,291	-120,538	-103,518	-88,260	-74,834	-37,456	-17,555
ARM Forwards	-220,585	-104,998	-100,898	-107,297	-107,088	-105,535	-102,590	-98,201	-93,673	-90,379	-88,379	-87,732	-93,414	-90,926
Treasury Futures	-3,000	-3,081	-3,202	-3,252	-3,272	-3,303	-3,333	-3,373	-3,413	-3,464	-3,504	-3,554	-3,756	-3,947
Treasury Put Options	-20,000	-12,596	-10,637	-8,627	-8,118	-7,598	-7,078	-6,548	-6,038	-5,538	-5,068	-4,629	-3,079	-1,889
TOTAL COVERAGE	-1,652,782	-1,502,651	-1,455,241	-1,395,568	-1,377,231	-1,357,214	-1,335,438	-1,311,881	-1,288,859	-1,268,825	-1,251,846	-1,238,103	-1,208,106	-1,188,782
NET EXPOSURE	874,486	-37,075	-20,820	1,084	4,411	6,350	6,859	5,821	2,927	-2,230	-9,756	-19,842	-80,435	-145,509

Exposure By Delivery Class/Coupon/Month

QRM SYSTEM

(Values Represent Convention of Millions)

	Feb-96					Mar-96					Apr-96					May-96					TOTAL				
COUPON	CLOSED LOAN	RATE LOCK	FWD	OPT	NET	CLOSED LOAN	RATE LOCK	FWD	OPT	NET	CLOSED LOAN	RATE LOCK	FWD	OPT	NET	CLOSED LOAN	RATE LOCK	FWD	OPT	NET	CLOSED LOAN	RATE LOCK	FWD	OPT	NET
30-Yr Conforming																									
5.50															0.1							0.1			0.1
6.00	4.0		-3.0		1.0	2.3	5.2	-7.0		0.5	9.3	-5.0			4.3	3.7				3.7	6.3	18.2	-15.0		9.6
6.50	94.4		-97.0		-2.6	25.6	21.6	-43.3	-5.3	-1.3	26.3	-5.0	-24.6		-3.2	7.0		-13.8	-6.8	120.0	55.0	-145.3	-43.7	-13.9
7.00	121.6		-127.3		-5.6	18.4	11.1	-28.0		1.5	13.5	-10.0			3.5	15.4			15.4	140.0	40.0	-165.3		14.7
7.50	27.8		-23.0		4.8	3.1	1.4	-14.3		-9.9	4.3				4.3	2.2			2.2	30.9	7.8	-37.3		1.4
8.00	6.5		-4.0		2.5	0.8	0.2	-3.0		-2.2	0.5				0.5	0.6			0.6	7.1	1.3	-7.0		1.4
8.50	0.1				0.1																0.1				0.1
	254.5		-254.3		0.2	50.0	39.4	-95.5	-5.3	-11.4	54.0	-20.0	-24.6		9.5	28.9		-13.8	15.1	304.5	122.4	-369.8	-43.7	13.4
15-Yr Conforming																									
5.50	3.1		-2.0		1.1	1.1	1.2	-3.0		-0.7	4.2	-4.0			0.2	1.0			1.0	4.2	6.4	-9.0		1.6
6.00	34.4		-25.6		8.8	6.0	7.1	-12.0		1.2	6.6	-10.0			-3.4	3.2	-3.0		0.2	40.4	17.0	-50.6		6.8
6.50	27.7		-26.0		1.7	4.8	4.5	-12.0		-2.7	4.7				4.7	2.5	-2.5			32.5	11.6	-40.5		3.6
7.00	8.3		-10.0		-1.7	0.8	0.9	-5.0		-3.3	1.1				1.1	0.4			0.4	9.1	2.5	-15.0		-3.4
7.50	1.5				1.5	0.1	0.2			0.3						0.1			0.1	1.6	0.3			1.9
8.00																									
	74.9		-63.6		11.3	12.6	13.9	-32.0		-5.2	16.7	-14.0			2.7	7.2	-5.5		1.7	87.8	37.8	-115.1		10.5
FHA/VA 30-Yr FR																									
6.0	3.8		-28.0		-22.4	1.8	1.3	-5.0		-2.1	4.3	-8.0			-3.7	1.2			1.2	5.3	6.8	-39.0		-26.9
6.5	46.2		-34.8	-7.1	6.4	12.6	16.0	-26.3	-2.4		22.1	-10.0	-20.1		-8.0	17.6		-14.5	3.1	60.8	55.8	-71.0	-44.1	1.5
7.0	125.4		-105.4	-7.1	15.8	18.3	16.2	-22.9	-8.8	5.8	27.8	-30.0			-2.2	15.7		7.8	23.5	146.7	82.8	-156.3	-8.1	43.2
7.5	60.6		-54.5		6.1	9.3	7.4	-36.3		-19.5	8.7	-10.0			-1.3	6.7			6.7	70.0	22.8	-100.5		-8.0
8.0	28.9		-2.7	-7.2	19.0	1.4	2.1	-6.0		-2.5	5.9				5.9	1.6			1.6	30.3	9.6	-8.7	-7.2	24.0
8.5	1.9		-1.5		0.4															1.9		-1.5		0.4
9.0	0.1				0.1															0.1				0.1
	271.7		-224.9	-21.4	25.4	43.3	45.9	-96.4	-11.2	-18.3	68.9	-58.0	-20.1		-9.3	42.9		-6.7	36.2	315.0	157.9	-379.2	-59.4	34.2
FHA/VA 15-Yr FR																									
5.50															0.2					0.3				0.5
6.00	2.9		-2.5		0.4	1.8	1.9	-5.0		-1.5	2.9	-1.0			1.9	2.7			2.7	4.5	7.5	-8.5		3.5
6.50	8.5		-8.5			3.7	1.9	-7.0		-1.4	3.0	-1.0			2.0	1.7			1.7	12.2	6.5	-15.5		2.3
7.00	5.4		-5.0		0.4	1.0	0.3	-1.5		-0.2	1.3	-1.0			0.3	0.7			0.7	6.4	2.3	-7.5		1.1
7.50	1.8				1.8	0.4	0.1	-1.5		-1.0	0.3				0.3					2.1	0.4	-1.5		1.1
8.00																									
	18.6		-16.0		2.6	6.7	4.1	-15.0		-4.2	7.8	-3.0			4.8	5.3			5.3	25.2	17.3	-34.0		6.5
7-Year Balloon																									
5.50	0.6		-0.5		0.1		0.1			0.1						0.2			0.2	0.6	0.3	-0.5		0.5
6.00	6.8		-4.0		2.8	0.5	1.9	-3.0		-0.6	0.9				0.9	0.7			0.7	7.4	3.5	-7.0		3.8
6.50	5.2		-4.0		1.2		1.0	-2.0		-1.0	0.7				0.7	1.1			1.1	5.2	2.8	-6.0		2.0
7.00	1.1		-2.0		-0.9		0.1	-1.0		-0.9						0.1			0.1	1.1	0.1	-3.0		-1.7
7.50	0.2				0.2															0.2				0.2
	13.9		-10.5		3.4	0.5	3.1	-6.0		-2.4	1.7				1.7	2.0			2.0	14.4	6.6	-16.5		4.7
5-Year Balloon																									
4.5	0.4				0.4															0.4				0.4
5.0	0.4				0.4															0.4				0.4
5.5	0.1				-0.4															0.1		-0.5		-0.4
6.0	1.7		-2.5		-0.8		0.3			0.3	0.4				0.4					1.7	0.7	-2.5		
6.5	0.8		-1.0		-0.2		0.1			0.1	0.1				0.1					0.8	0.1	-1.0		-0.1
7.0	0.3				0.3															0.3				0.3
	3.8		-4.0		-0.2		0.4			0.4	0.5				0.5					3.8	0.9	-4.0		0.7

* Note: This report does not contain entire position. It is intended to be a sample of the overall position.

methods described in this chapter, the following variables should be considered:

Global parameters. Hedgers must consider global parameters, such as allowable types of transactions (long/short forwards puts and calls), minimum and maximum transaction sizes, the maximum number of total transactions, the maximum amount of option premium outlay, the percentage of total coverage allocated to Treasury-related instruments and the proper global clean-up instrument. The global clean-up instrument will be used whenever other constraints are impossible or impractical to satisfy. It is typically defined as the on-the-run 30-year Fannie Mae or Freddie Mac security.

Coverage versus delivery preferences. Defining coverage versus delivery preferences involves choosing the preferred coverage vehicle for each type of product to be hedged. The preferred hedge instrument will vary, depending on whether a closed loan or a rate lock is being hedged. For example, many risk managers will cover closed loans with forwards or cash sales of identical product, but prefer to hedge rate locks with more liquid forwards or options.

Clean-up instruments. In addition to the global clean-up instrument, there should be clean-up instruments for each product type. These will be used when preferred instruments are not optimal choices and it would be more transactionally efficient to use an instrument of similar product type.

Tolerances for basis risk. Basis risk tolerances will dictate which hedge instruments are selected. These tolerances vary from very risk averse to risk neutral. Hedgers with low tolerance for basis risk will prefer to match loan products with hedge instruments of identical products, coupons and delivery months. Hedgers with high tolerance for basis risk are happy to cross-hedge products with liquidly traded clean-up instruments and Treasury-related instruments.

The type of hedge to create and the desired risk profile. This may include the creation of a delta hedge, a global hedge, or a combination of both. Target hedge positions that offset the risk of small movements in rates (delta hedges) or that match the position for larger movements in rates (global hedges) can be created. Other potential hedge targets include hedging volatility shocks and matching time decay.

The hedge instrument universe. Depending on the nature of the position and the desired type of hedge, this could vary from one instrument (delta hedging) to over 1000 possible combinations of product type, strike price, coupon, and settlement month. In practice, risk managers typically limit the hedge universe to forwards and options of on-the-run coupons and near-term delivery months of several major product types. Even with this limitation, the hedge instrument universe can easily include several hundred potential trades.

After all these variables are considered, it is time to perform the hedge optimization and present the results. A typical hedge objective would be to find the least number of transactions that satisfy the constraints and objectives defined by the variables discussed above. Producing recommended trade punch lists and new position reports that include the recommended trades will make it possible to decide on the feasibility of the recommended hedge. Report 10-6 is a recommended hedge adjustment report.

We have found that very few secondary marketing departments have the sophisticated financial algorithms needed to effectively create the optimal hedge positions just described. For mortgage bankers to remain competitive, they will need to enhance the hedge construction process by taking advantage of recent advances in modeling and optimization techniques.

State-of-the-Art Systems for Risk Management 255

REPORT 10-6

Hedge Recommendation Summary Report
By Mortgage Type, Gross Exposure,
Closed Loans + Rate Locks = Optimal Solution

(000s)

Adjusted Profile

	Current Position	Proposed Adjustment	Adjusted Net Position	Consider	Minimum	Maximum
CCE	1,317,713	-1,258,427	59,286	NO	0	0
TBPV	74,490	-71,138	3,352	NO	-100	100
CNVX	-43,945	38,585	-5,360	NO	-100	100
VEGA	-722	833	111	NO	0	0
TD	661	-788	-127	NO	0	0
-200	88,125	-93,125	-5,000	YES	-5,000	5,000
-100	55,576	-57,942	-2,366	YES	-2,500	2,500
-50	32,012	-31,761	251	YES	-1,000	1,000
-25	17,272	-16,744	528	YES	-750	750
+25	-19,816	19,066	-750	YES	-750	750
+50	-41,287	40,722	-565	YES	-1,000	1,000
+100	-87,425	88,684	1,259	YES	-2,500	2,500
+200	-183,000	188,000	5,000	YES	-5,000	5,000

Coverage Adjustment Punch List

Buy/Sell	Amount	Name	Type	Coupon	Settlement Date	Expiration Date	Strike Price	Option Total Cost	Option Premium	tal Option Premium	Delta	TBPV	Convexity
SELL	25,952,168	Fannie Mae 15 Yr	Forward	6.500	2/15/96						-1.0000	-4.328	0.560
SELL	87,990,653	Fannie Mae 30 Yr	Forward	6.500	2/13/96						-1.0000	-6.342	0.615
SELL	113,334,653	Fannie Mae 30 Yr	Forward	7.000	2/13/96						-1.0000	-5.653	0.927
BUY	104,237,456	Fannie Mae 30 Yr	Put	6.500	2/13/96	3/6/96	-1.50		0.240	250.170	-0.2306	-1.463	6.702
SELL	47,431,210	Ginnie Mae 30 Yr	Forward	6.500	2/20/96						-1.0000	-7.277	0.610
SELL	126,655,386	Ginnie Mae 30 Yr	Forward	7.000	2/20/96						-1.0000	-6.484	0.993
SELL	704,607,415	Ginnie Mae 30 Yr	Forward	7.500	2/20/96			805.562			-1.0000	-5.631	1.172
BUY	180,035,001	Ginnie Mae 30 Yr	Put	6.500	3/19/96	3/12/96	-1.50	132.780	0.397	714.739	-0.2821	-2.053	7.849
BUY	86,163,060	Ginnie Mae 30 Yr	Put	7.000	3/19/96	3/12/96	-1.50	10.693	0.316	272.275	-0.2628	-1.704	6.878
	1,476,407,002							949.035		1,237.184			

Rate Risk Profile

QRM SYSTEM

Trading Analytics

Select hedge instruments based on relative value. Management should be familiar with the different types of hedge instruments available, their risk/reward characteristics, their appropriateness within the context of their operations and the relative advantages and disadvantages of each. In general, specific hedge instruments should be chosen based on a joint consideration of the company's desired profit and loss profile and the current relative cost of the alternative instruments.

Choose option strike prices based on relative value. Options of various types/strike prices are often mispriced and should be chosen based on relative value. The same hedge objective can often be accomplished by mixing OTC and exchange-traded options on different, but similar, assets of different strike prices and expirations because they provide the same basic protection at a lower total cost. Table 10-2 shows a matrix of fair values for on-the-run MBS put options.

Treasury-based hedges should be used more when OASs on mortgages are high. Policy statements that permit varied usage of Treasury futures should require a prior examination of spreads between MBS and Treasuries, on an option-adjusted basis. In other words, it is important to consider the effect changing values have on embedded prepayment options. In general, it is best to use Treasury futures when OASs on MBSs are high, since high OASs indicate relative cheapness of mortgages and low OASs indicate relative richness.

Use OAS models to derive hedge ratios. Statistical models for determining the relations between and among different MBS types and coupons and Treasury futures contracts should be avoided. Far more precise results can be obtained by basing hedge ratios on option-adjusted durations derived from state-of-the-art OAS models which have been widely favored by money managers for several years.

TABLE 10-2

Option Calculator Report

OPTION TYPE	MORTGAGE TYPE	COUPON	EXPIRATION DATE	NOTICE PERIOD	STRIKE PRICE	OPTION VALUE	DELTA	GAMMA	VEGA	TBPV	OPTION COST	CONVEXITY	FORWARD VALUE	IMPLIED* VOLATILITY	-25BP	25BP
PUT	FNMA30	7.50	1	13-Mar-96	-2.50	0.0550	-0.0844	0.0999	0.0180	-0.4050	-0.0410	2.3960	102.2830	0.1819	-0.0500	0.2000
PUT	FNMA30	7.50	1	13-Mar-96	-2.00	0.0970	-0.1338	0.1406	0.0260	-0.6420	-0.0640	3.3890	102.2830	0.1819	-0.0850	0.2900
PUT	FNMA30	7.50	1	13-Mar-96	-1.50	0.1650	-0.2027	0.1858	0.0350	-0.9730	-0.0920	4.5050	102.2830	0.1819	-0.1370	0.4030
PUT	FNMA30	7.50	1	13-Mar-96	-1.00	0.2680	-0.2929	0.2289	0.0440	-1.4060	-0.1220	5.5960	102.2830	0.1819	-0.2130	0.5350
PUT	FNMA30	7.50	1	13-Mar-96	-0.50	0.4170	-0.4025	0.2607	0.0520	-1.9330	-0.1410	6.4500	102.2830	0.1819	-0.3150	0.6790
PUT	FNMA30	7.50	1	13-Mar-96	0.00	0.6220	-0.5252	0.2728	0.0590	-2.5220	-0.1470	6.8600	102.2830	0.1819	-0.4410	0.8220
PUT	FNMA30	7.50	1	13-Mar-96	0.50	0.8890	-0.6504	0.2599	0.0630	-3.1240	-0.1340	6.7000	102.2830	0.1819	-0.5660	0.9530
PUT	FNMA30	7.50	1	11-Apr-96	-2.50	0.1660	-0.1571	0.1141	0.0350	-0.7540	-0.0600	2.8030	102.1610	0.1819	-0.1210	0.2920
PUT	FNMA30	7.50	1	11-Apr-96	-2.00	0.2370	-0.2107	0.1393	0.0430	-1.0120	-0.0730	3.4400	102.1610	0.1819	-0.1680	0.3730
PUT	FNMA30	7.50	1	11-Apr-96	-1.50	0.3330	-0.2758	0.1537	0.0510	-1.3240	-0.0850	4.0750	102.1610	0.1819	-0.2280	0.4660
PUT	FNMA30	7.50	1	11-Apr-96	-1.00	0.4610	-0.3521	0.1845	0.0580	-1.6910	-0.0960	4.6370	102.1610	0.1819	-0.3020	0.5590
PUT	FNMA30	7.50	1	11-Apr-96	-0.50	0.6250	-0.4379	0.1991	0.0640	-2.1030	-0.1020	5.0660	102.1610	0.1819	-0.3900	0.6770
PUT	FNMA30	7.50	1	11-Apr-96	0.00	0.8320	-0.5303	0.2047	0.0690	-2.5470	-0.1020	5.2960	102.1610	0.1819	-0.4920	0.7860
PUT	FNMA30	7.50	1	11-Apr-96	0.50	1.0850	-0.6246	0.2200	0.0720	-2.9990	-0.0950	5.2890	102.1610	0.1819	-0.6020	0.8910
PUT	FNMA30	7.50	1	13-May-96	-2.50	0.2850	-0.2112	0.1215	0.0460	-1.0140	-0.0550	3.0310	102.0150	0.1819	-0.1820	0.3540
PUT	FNMA30	7.50	1	13-May-96	-2.00	0.3740	-0.2628	0.1376	0.0530	-1.2620	-0.0620	3.4580	102.0150	0.1819	-0.2320	0.4260
PUT	FNMA30	7.50	1	13-May-96	-1.50	0.4870	-0.3218	0.1522	0.0590	-1.5450	-0.0690	3.8580	102.0150	0.1819	-0.2910	0.5060
PUT	FNMA30	7.50	1	13-May-96	-1.00	0.6270	-0.3879	0.1639	0.0650	-1.8530	-0.0740	4.2200	102.0150	0.1819	-0.3590	0.5910
PUT	FNMA30	7.50	1	13-May-96	-0.50	0.7990	-0.4599	0.1717	0.0700	-2.2090	-0.0770	4.4580	102.0150	0.1819	-0.4370	0.6800
PUT	FNMA30	7.50	1	13-May-96	0.00	1.0050	-0.5360	0.1744	0.0740	-2.5740	-0.0770	4.6020	102.0150	0.1819	-0.5230	0.7710
PUT	FNMA30	7.50	1	13-May-96	0.50	1.2490	-0.6133	0.1711	0.0760	-2.9480	-0.0730	4.6100	102.0150	0.1819	-0.6150	0.8590

Mark-to-Market

The mark-to-market process should provide timely feedback. Marking a mortgage rate-lock pipeline to market can be an arduous task. Many mark-to-market systems are based on only the "intrinsic value" of options and rate locks, ignoring the uncertainty, or option "time value," element. This can lead to large errors and often opens the door to arbitrary accounting. For example, in the case of rate-lock commitments, most mark-to-market systems use expected closing percentages that can be arbitrarily changed from day-to-day, either ignoring completely or only loosely considering the impact of the relationship between market rate levels and existing rate-lock rates on fallout probabilities. Fallout ratios should be estimated based on processing status and the difference between commitment price and market price. A mark-to-market that is based on option evaluation techniques and a constant rate-lock fallout function provides an objective measure of daily profit and loss. Report 10-7 is an open position mark-to-market report by product type and delivery month.

Establish a reserve for future hedge costs. Although it is now well-recognized that rate-lock commitments issued to a borrower are short put options, marks-to-market invariably do not evaluate rate-lock commitments based on their option characteristics (such as implied volatility, time to expiration and dispersion of in/out of the money amounts). Many practitioners acknowledge that higher volatility results in higher hedging expense. This should be reflected by the establishment of fluctuating reserves for hedge costs. Your mark-to-market system should be able to compute and report this.

Secondary marketing departments should produce income statements that include the effects of closed positions. Secondary marketing departments should produce daily and month-to-date income statements that show the change in the value of inventories, plus the gain/loss on positions liquidated between marks.

State-of-the-Art Systems for Risk Management   259

REPORT 10-7

Profit/Loss Summary By Class/Month

(000s)

DELIVERY CLASS	Feb 96 CLOSED LOAN	RATE LOCK	FWD	OPT	NET	Mar 96 CLOSED LOAN	RATE LOCK	FWD	OPT	NET	Apr 96 CLOSED LOAN	RATE LOCK	FWD	OPT	NET	May 96+ CLOSED LOAN	RATE LOCK	FWD	OPT	NET	TOTAL CLOSED LOAN	RATE LOCK	FWD	OPT	NET	QRM SYSTEM NET
30-Yr Conforming	2,542		-2895		-353	220	260	-421	-98	-38		111	-6	144	308		-23		148	123	2763	409	-3322	191	41	
15-Yr Conforming	698		-544		-154	80	83	-80		73	37	-31		6			6			-9	759	138	-970		224	
FHA/VA 30-Yr FR	2951		-1798	-34	1093	235	304	-335	-76	129	269	-94	149	324	38			268	306	3239	612	-2255	257	1853	
FHA/VA 15-Yr FR	239		-147		92	39	31	-55		15	35	6		41		7			7	277	73	-196		154	
Non-Conf 30-Yr Fixed	247	53	-119		180		187			187	58	-40		18		3			3	247	298	-158		396	
Non-Conf 15-Yr Fixed	88	3	-13		77		20	-14		6	3	-11		-9						88	26	-38		75	
FHA/VA 1-Yr ARM	1951		-1568		383	261	124	-334		51	332	-54		277	52				52	2213	508	-1956		786	
7-Year Balloon	141		-80		61	5	28	-37		-4	13			13	-1				-1	145	40	-117		68	
5-Year Balloon	19		-31		-12		4			-4	3			3						19	7	-31		-5	
TOTAL P/L	8827	55	-7223	-34	1676	821	1052	-1276	-174	423	922	-230	293	984	98			414	495	9748	2131	-8744	449	3584	

Secondary marketing departments should receive credit for interest earned on mortgages while they are in the warehouse. As a result of not giving interest credit to the secondary marketing department, at least two distortions occur:

1. When placing forward coverage, there is an incentive to bet on the possibility of an early settlement because forward prices are generally higher the closer to the settlement date.
2. There will be pricing glitches once a month when the projected settlement month for new rate-lock commitments rolls back a month. This glitch could be avoided if the secondary marketing department factored in interest carried from the loan closing date to the forward settlement date — something they would be disinclined to do if they do not receive credit for interest accrued during the warehousing period.

Pricing

A profitability analysis should be performed each day on a loan-by-loan basis, taking into consideration hedging costs and the value of servicing. Relative pricing of different rate locks should consider differences in hedge costs and servicing values.

Forward drops should be calculated to the expected day of closing rather than to the settlement date following the expected closing date. This way, if the loan closes prior to the settlement date, an interest spread (*carry*) is earned or paid.

Mortgage banks should establish internal transfer prices for servicing that are equal to the economic value of the servicing to the mortgage bank, based on its cost of capital and cost of servicing. The effect of these variables, along with macroeconomic parameters such as prepayment functions and interest rate volatility, can be determined by periodically running OAS model evaluations. This would thereby discourage transfers of excess servicing to third parties for prices that are less than the economic value of the excess servicing to the mortgage bank.

Conclusion

The complexities and challenges faced by modern risk managers are clear. Today's rapidly changing and unforgiving marketplace will result in even greater challenges. To remain competitive, secondary marketing departments will need to quickly adjust to the new, more sophisticated risk management methodologies and to the technology required for these analyses. Organizations that take shortcuts, fail to improve and continue to rely on outdated methods and systems are sure to suffer.

11

Fannie Mae: Programs for Mortgage Bankers

Frank Demarais, Vice President for Product Development
Fannie Mae

This chapter introduces you to Fannie Mae and the basic steps in successfully doing business with Fannie Mae in the complex secondary mortgage market. Fannie Mae has committed all its resources to providing profitable partnership opportunities in meeting both lenders' objectives for efficient and flexible mortgage sales programs and its own commitment to increase home ownership opportunities among low-, moderate- and middle-income Americans.

Fannie Mae: The Company

Fannie Mae is a shareholder-owned, privately managed corporation. It is the largest corporation in the United States, based on assets, and the largest source of American home mortgage funds.

Fannie Mae's mission is to provide financial products and services that increase the availability and affordability of housing for low-, moderate- and middle-income Americans.

Fannie Mae's Products

Whether a lender needs a source of funds for new originations, a way to meet a changing market need, a tool for restructuring a portfolio or a source of fee-based income — whatever the financial goal — Fannie Mae offers ways to gain a competitive edge. In addition to the traditional services offered for loan sales, securitization, short-term funding and trading, Fannie Mae provides services and products to increase overall efficiency and connect the various mortgage functions through technology products. Fannie Mae's technology products serve to enhance origination, trading and servicing processes for its mortgage lending customers.

Mortgage Sales or Securitization

Fannie Mae will purchase for cash, or swap for MBSs, a wide variety of current-production or seasoned loans. Depending on the type of loan, lenders can sell or swap mortgages using Fannie Mae's standard terms, published in the Selling and Servicing Guides, or they can negotiate transactions according to their specific needs.

Fannie Mae purchases and swaps more than 50 types of mortgages on the basis of standard terms. All the requirements, procedures and legal documents for these standard types of mortgages are included in the Selling and Servicing Guides. Some of the specific types of mortgages for which Fannie Mae offers discrete pricing in its purchase program, or MBS pooling in its swap program, are:

- 10-, 15-, 20- and 30-year fixed-rate mortgages.

- 1-, 3- and 6-month and 1- and 3-year ARMS indexed to Treasury securities, LIBOR, Wall Street Journal and Cost of Fund indexes.
- 3-, 5-, 7- and 10-year fixed period ARMs, which adjust annually after the fixed period.
- FHA/VA fixed-rate and graduated-payment mortgages.
- 15- and 30-year biweekly payment mortgages.
- 5- and 7-year Two-Step® ARMs.
- 7-year balloon mortgages with refinance option.

Mortgages must meet certain standards to be eligible for sale or swapping. The most significant standard is the "conforming" loan limit. In 1996, Fannie Mae can only purchase or swap single-unit loans with original balances less than or equal to $207,000 (except for loans secured by properties in Alaska, Hawaii or the U.S. Virgin Islands, where the limit is 50% higher). The limit on maximum original loan balance is set annually based on a survey of changes in home sales prices.

Fannie Mae purchases and swaps first mortgages secured by one- to four-family residences, including units in approved condominiums, cooperatives and planned-unit developments. Fannie Mae also purchases conventional multifamily loans secured by income-producing residential properties of five or more units. The multifamily program has its own loan limits and guidelines included in separate guides.

Fannie Mae will purchase or swap mortgages on properties that are owner-occupied principal residences, second houses, or investment properties. The underwriting standards and requirements for each type of property and each type of mortgage are addressed in the Selling Guide. The maximum loan-to-value ratios depend on several factors but generally range from 70% to 95 percent. Mortgages with loan-to-values greater than 80% require mortgage insurance to reduce Fannie Mae's loss exposure to 75% of the property's value.

Cash Sales Program

The Cash Sales program offers the opportunity to sell single loans, or groups of loans, against flexible commitments which match the demands of origination processes. Cash transactions are available with a range of delivery dates and pricing options that match pipeline needs.

Decisions on the most appropriate use of the Cash Sales program are directed by the characteristics of the mortgage pipeline and the objectives of management — the valuation of cash proceeds versus servicing income and operational efficiencies. Managing a mortgage pipeline involves the price risk of matching commitments to borrowers with the setting of terms for the sale of those mortgages to a secondary market investor, as well as efficiently funding the mortgages between closing and sale. Fannie Mae's Cash Sales program offers the options of 5-, 10-, 15-, 30-, 45-, 60-, 75- and 90-day deliveries, with prices varying due to short-term carrying costs. These products and prices are posted on wire services, such as Telerate and Knight Ridder, and are distributed over Fannie Mae's computer-based MORNET® electronic mail system.

Fixed-rate mortgage commitments can be made at standard pricing — pricing all purchases at par (100%) for delivery of a net note rate equal to or greater than the posted required net note rate for that delivery period — or at a discount to par if the net note rate is below the posted rate. The premium/discount pricing options allow delivery of net note rates above or below the posted rate in exchange for prices at a premium above or discount below par. Lenders may also elect a "flex" commitment on fixed-rate mortgages, allowing delivery of a range of net note rates at predetermined prices against a specific commitment. These commitment options accommodate a pipeline of various note rates, which are subject to borrower and market fluctuations in closing timing and rates. ARM commitments offer options for selecting various combinations of levels of net note rate, net margin and life cap for each standard ARM loan type and each delivery period.

Managing a mortgage pipeline also requires the ability to react to movements in the capital markets in which the prices offered for mortgages change from minute to minute. Fannie Mae offers lenders an electronic commitment process known as Desktop Trader®, which allows the lenders to commit to sell loans at current prices directly from their personal computers.

A key feature of the Cash Sales program is its flexibility in meeting lenders' needs for nonstandard delivery or pricing options. Fannie Mae also offers a range of products on a negotiated price basis. Fannie Mae works with its customers through account teams assigned to each geographic area. The account management teams work with individual lenders to support each lender's business objectives.

Many of Fannie Mae's cash products are offered with a choice of remittance options for the monthly principal and interest cash flow. The most commonly used option — Actual/Actual (A/A) — requires next day remittance of principal and interest, but only for the amounts actually received. The Scheduled/Actual (S/A) remittance option requires monthly remittance of scheduled interest, whether received or not, and remittance of the actual principal received.

Deliveries against cash commitments can be made at any time during the delivery term and, after validation, can be funded the next business day. Deliveries must be completed by the expiration of the commitment, within the delivery tolerance of the commitment. Cash commitments require delivery of at least 95% of the commitment amount. If a lender cannot deliver the required amount, a portion of the commitment can be repurchased, or "paired-off." Fannie Mae will charge a fee representing market price movement for the amount paired off.

Fannie Mae offers delivery technology options to reduce errors and speed funding. The MORNET® electronic communications system incorporates a software application, the Cash Delivery system, that allows lenders to key in loan and commitment data by hand or by importing it directly from an origination system. The software edits and formats the data for electronic transmission to Fannie Mae. The lender must follow the transmission with the delivery documentation, including the original mortgage notes, assignments to Fannie Mae, and copies of loan schedule reports generated by the MORNET® Cash Delivery system.

MBS Swap Program

The MBS Swap program provides a process to efficiently swap a group, or pool, of loans for a Mortgage-Backed Security representing those loans. Fannie Mae issues the MBS and guarantees the timely payment of principal and interest to the investor. MBS swap transactions provide access to the trading and pipeline management flexibility of a market that is second only to the US Treasury market in liquidity.

Fannie Mae's MBS program has its own requirements, but provides flexibility in matching loan origination process requirements. Mortgages must be pooled separately by product, with 30-year fixed-rate separate from 15-year fixed-rate. The pass-through rates, or MBS coupons, generally trade best on the half percent (7.50%, 8.00%, 8.50%) and lenders pool their loans to take advantage of these coupons. The mortgage note rate in each pool must support the pass-through rate plus minimum servicing plus the guaranty fee required by Fannie Mae. Lenders negotiate the guaranty fee, generally 25 bp to 35 bp (0.25% to 0.35%), based upon the product type. For example, an 8.00% 30-year fixed-rate loan with a 0.25% guaranty fee and 0.25% minimum servicing can be pooled in a 7.50% MBS pass-through. The lender retains the 0.25% servicing fee each month as compensation for the collection and remittance of borrowers' monthly mortgage payments.

The MBS program allows pooling of as little as $1,000 in current production mortgages under a multi-lender pooling process known as Fannie Majors®. Fannie Mae establishes specific "Majors" pools for specific MBS coupons for each month, and lenders can submit multiple individual submissions against these pool numbers throughout the month. Lenders will service these separate submissions as a single pool. All lenders receive MBS equal to their submission amount, but the pool backing the loans represents all the loans submitted by all the lenders. Investors value pool size and therefore will price and trade the individual pieces as if they were larger pieces — avoiding the usual price penalties for trading small pieces.

In determining what loans to include in which specific pass-through rate, lenders have the opportunity to "buy down" or "buy up" the guaranty fee to reduce the spread required for the guaranty fee or to sell excess servicing spread to Fannie Mae. If a lender wanted to include a 7.875% mortgage in a 7.50% pass-through MBS, it can buy down the guaranty fee to 0.125% from 0.25% by paying Fannie Mae the present value equivalent of the 0.125% difference and maintaining the 0.25% minimum servicing. If a lender chose to include an 8.125% mortgage in that same 7.50%, instead of keeping 0.375% servicing, it can sell the excess 0.125% servicing to Fannie Mae in return for a present value equivalent of 0.125 percent. The buy down and buy up features allow lenders to maximize current period income.

Fannie Mae MBS can generally be traded for settlement as much as 120 days in the future with a wide range of securities dealers and investors. Fannie Mae offers the services of the Customer Service Trading Desk (CSTD) to approved lenders to facilitate those trades. The CSTD offers services in trading the MBS and in financing the MBS prior to sale through reverse repurchase agreements (repos) that enable lenders to borrow funds at short-term rates to carry the MBS until future settlement. If the MBS is traded through the CSTD, the As Soon As Pooled®

funding process can be used to fund a pool of loans two days after delivery — before the MBS is issued.

The MBS delivery process is efficient and fast. Lenders deliver their notes and assignments to a document custodian of their choice and must have the document custodian certify their schedule of mortgages. Fannie Mae provides a MORNET® software application known as MBS Pool Submission System® for editing and transmitting loan schedule data. Fannie Mae will issue the MBS in an electronic form to the lender's or the designated investor's account. The security delivery can occur as soon as four business days after transmission of the MORNET® data, as long as the certified schedule arrives the day following the MORNET® transmission.

For a current production pipeline, Fannie Mae's MBS process allows loans closed at any point in the month to be processed into MBS for settlement at any time. However, for trading efficiency, the market for MBS generally settles trades for a given pass-through rate and mortgage type on a single date each month. If loans cannot meet the conventional monthly settlement date, referred to as the Public Securities Association (PSA) settlement date, the Fannie Mae As Soon As Pooled® process allows those loans to be funded and removed from more expensive warehouse funding.

The Fannie Mae MBS program also offers remittance options for better management of monthly principal and interest cash flow. Fannie Mae will allow reductions in the negotiated guaranty fee when lenders agree to remit cash flows earlier than the standard monthly remittance date. The MBS program uses a Scheduled/Scheduled (S/S) remittance, requiring scheduled principal and interest, whether or not they have been received. Standard remittance requires all scheduled monthly payments for the current month and any unscheduled, or prepaid, principal for the prior month to be paid on the 18th of the month. One early remittance option, known as MBS Express®, requires any unscheduled principal from the prior month to be remitted on the 4th business day rather than the 18th calendar day. The other option, known as Rapid Payment Method (RPM®), requires the full monthly principal and interest payment to be remitted on the 10th calendar day rather than the 18th. These reductions in guaranty fee can be translated into higher upfront proceeds through use of the buy up and buy down feature.

One of the reasons why the MBS market offers such efficient and consistent pricing for a wide array of products and coupons is the development of derivative MBS structures that match mortgage characteristics to investor needs. Fannie Mae has pioneered and developed markets in Real Estate Mortgage Investment Conduits (REMICs) and Stripped MBS. Each of these securities involve putting MBS pass-through securities into a new trust which separates the cash flow into different combinations of principal and interest, and in the case of the REMIC, into different maturity dates. Many new production MBS end up backing a REMIC or Strip trust after the mortgage originator sells it to a dealer or the Fannie Mae CSTD. The flexibility of these structures has ensured an uninterrupted flow of investment dollars into the mortgage market in spite of the large swings in demand triggered by refinancing opportunities.

Fannie Mae's Affordable Housing Initiatives

In 1994, Fannie Mae made a far reaching commitment to provide $1 trillion in targeted housing finance by the end of the decade to help transform the housing finance system into one that works for every American. The company's commitment builds on the strong foundation of affordable housing products and initiatives the company had developed beginning in 1987. The company has pledged to help make the dream of home ownership come true for families who have been shut out of the housing finance system in the past. Fannie Mae has targeted low- and moderate-income families, minorities, immigrants, people with special housing needs and residents of central cities and distressed communities. The company will help them achieve home ownership by reaching out to them with the information they need to buy a home; by breaking down the arbitrary barriers in the housing finance system that deny mortgage credit to people who can afford to make a monthly payment; and by doing everything in its power to make the elimination of lending discrimination the number one priority of the housing finance system.

To carry out this commitment, Fannie Mae has developed a number of special mortgage products to meet the needs of families and communities that have been underserved in the past. Fannie Mae is continually refining its Community Home Buyer's Program, which builds key flexibilities into standard underwriting requirements to increase the family's buying power. The Community Home Buyer's Program allows buyers to qualify for fixed-rate mortgages up to 95% LTV with monthly payments equal to 33% of monthly gross income, and total monthly obligation-to-income ratio of 38 percent. These underwriting flexibilities were developed in concert with private mortgage insurance companies and involve home buyer education programs, offered by the lender, mortgage insurer or a nonprofit counseling group, to better prepare people for the responsibilities of home ownership. Another option under the Community Home Buyer's Program is the Fannie97, which allows buyers to provide a 3% down payment. Yet another option uses a subsidized second mortgage approach, with a local housing or non-profit corporation providing a second mortgage to help close the affordability gap.

Fannie Mae's affordable housing initiatives also include targeted flexibilities and accommodations in areas such as employer-assisted housing, rural housing and elderly housing. In the area of employer-assisted housing, Fannie Mae purchases the first mortgage, while the employer provides assistance with down payment, closing costs and ongoing monthly payments. In the area of rural home finance, Fannie Mae has developed special mortgage products to expand the secondary market. Similarly, Fannie Mae has worked with demonstration programs to expand the market for mortgage products that address the needs of older Americans. In December 1995, it announced an expansion of its reverse mortgage products, adding The Home Keeper, a conventional reverse mortgage product, to complement the existing purchases of the FHA Home Equity Conversion Mortgage loans. A reverse mortgage offers older homeowners the opportunity to receive a cash flow based upon the value of their home and their age.

Fannie Mae has committed itself to open 25 partnership offices in cities across the country, to expand its outreach into those communities and to better align its efforts with local needs and partners. By the end of 1995, it had opened or announced 21 of these partnership offices. In addition, Fannie Mae sponsors home-buying fairs and conducts consumer outreach advertising to reach potential home buyers and help them understand the steps on the path to home ownership.

Fannie Mae's Technology Initiatives

Fannie Mae has traditionally provided leadership to the mortgage industry in terms of underwriting standards, affordable housing outreach and secondary market processes and programs. In 1994, Fannie Mae initiated an expansion of its technology offerings to customers to enhance the integration of the secondary market processes with other points in the process, with the goal of cutting the cost of originating a mortgage by $1,000 by the end of the decade.

Fannie Mae's technology product line began with products to integrate secondary marketing with production, including applications such as Rate Sheet Express™ to fax rate sheets to multiple locations, Market Express™ to view current capital market conditions, Desktop Trader™ to automate Fannie Mae's cash commitment process, Desktop Originator™ to connect wholesalers with correspondents, and Guide Express™ to electronically view the selling and servicing guidelines.

The introduction of Desktop Underwriter™ in 1995 effected a big leap forward in the integration of processes. Desktop Underwriter™ represents an automated underwriting process that allows lenders to process and underwrite a loan for sale to Fannie Mae and get approval within minutes, bypassing traditional documentation steps, if the borrower's credit history and other loan factors support it. Automation provides consistent, objective underwriting decisions based on established criteria. If a loan requires further review, Desktop Underwriter™ will identify what aspects of the loan application need expansion or explanation. The process of ensuring that loans comply with the eligibility guidelines of Fannie Mae has become easier and faster, and the integration of the applications with other mortgage industry software streamlines the entire data management effort.

How To Do Business With Fannie Mae

Fannie Mae requires its approved lenders to meet certain minimum net worth, operational and staffing criteria. Once approved by Fannie Mae to sell loans, lenders seeking to conduct business with our Customer Service Trading Desk must also apply and receive such approval. Fannie Mae coordinates all of its lender relationships out of five regional offices, located in Philadelphia, Dallas, Chicago, Atlanta and Pasadena. Each regional office has assigned a team of marketing, lender administration and quality control staff to each lender. Fannie Mae is dedicated to meeting housing needs in all markets and is always looking for opportunities to apply its programs to specific needs.

This chapter provides an overview of the range of opportunities and structure of the programs offered by Fannie Mae, but is by no means complete. Fannie Mae continuously expands its program features and flexibilities, providing cost reductions, broader availability and speedier executions. Fannie Mae publishes an extensive series of customer education materials, in addition to the information formalized in its guides, and conducts regular customer training sessions. A catalog of training materials and seminar schedules designed for mortgage lenders is available by calling 1-800-471-5554. In addition, information about Fannie Mae is posted regularly on the Internet at http://www.fanniemae.com.

12

Freddie Mac: Programs for Mortgage Bankers

David Andrukonis, Senior Vice President,
General Manager, Seller Division
Freddie Mac

Freddie Mac was created to develop and maintain a stable and liquid national secondary market for conventional mortgage loans. This shareholder-owned company focuses on delivering new sources of capital by purchasing mortgages from primary lenders and combining them into securities that are then sold to investors. This process creates a continuous flow of funds to the primary mortgage market, making home financing more available and affordable.

Freddie Mac pioneered the securitization process for conventional mortgages, as well as many of the investment tools needed to attract large amounts of capital from global financial markets. Securitization has helped eliminate capital shortages in lending, bringing efficiencies and innovation to the housing finance industry and reducing the cost of mortgages to American consumers. The secondary market now finances about 55% of outstanding conventional residential mortgage debt, compared to only 7% when Freddie Mac was created in 1970. The company has purchased more than $1.2 trillion in loans from mortgage lender customers and has financed one in six American homes.

While Freddie Mac was originally formed to serve portfolio lenders, its customer base has broadened and changed. The restructuring of the primary market — which began in the 1970s and continued through the early 1990s — resulted in other lenders, such as mortgage bankers, relying more on the secondary market to keep mortgage capital flowing through interest rate fluctuations. Lenders began to embrace the practice of selling their mortgages to the secondary market to help them manage the risk that changing interest rates could pose to their holdings.

As a result, Freddie Mac's annual purchase volume skyrocketed from a few billion dollars in the 1970s to more than $90 billion in 1995. In the early 1980s, fewer than 1 in 10 Freddie Mac customers were mortgage bankers. Mortgage bankers now account for a majority of the company's customer base. Through these changes, Freddie Mac has structured its programs to make it easier and more profitable for mortgage bankers to conduct secondary market transactions with the company.

This chapter summarizes the types of single-family mortgage products Freddie Mac purchases and the programs and technologies that facilitate sales. It describes the major features and benefits of each program and the key elements of transactions, as of February 1996.

Special sections are devoted to descriptions of Freddie Mac's automated underwriting service, Loan Prospector , and GoldWorks®, an electronic network for the mortgage industry. The company's Expanding Markets program is also showcased, illustrating effective ways to balance lending to a greater number of underserved borrowers while maintaining credit standards.

Freddie Mac: Programs for Mortgage Bankers 279

For more detailed information, contact Freddie Mac's account managers or refer to the *Single-Family Seller/Servicer Guide* by calling the help line: 1-800-FREDDIE (or 1-800-373-3343).

Eligible Mortgages

Lenders can sell their mortgages for cash or swap them in exchange for Participation Certificates (PCs), Freddie Mac's MBSs. The following types of mortgages are eligible for sale to Freddie Mac:

- 15-, 20- and 30-year fixed-rate mortgages.
- 5- and 7-year balloon/reset mortgages.
- ARMs.
- 15-, 20- and 30-Year Fixed-Rate Mortgages.

Since most borrowers prefer the stable payments of the fixed-rate mortgage, this type of loan has long been a popular mortgage product. Those who can afford higher payments can obtain lower interest rates by borrowing for shorter terms (15 or 20 years, as opposed to 30 years), thereby reducing long-term interest expenses and building equity faster. For lenders, the fixed-rate mortgage is easy to service, features low and predictable costs and generally yields lower default rates. Under our swap programs, lenders can also sell FHA/VA fixed-rate loans with up to 30-year terms.

5- and 7-Year Balloon/Reset Mortgages
Freddie Mac buys fixed-rate mortgages with 5- or 7-year maturities and a 30-year amortization. These balloon/reset loans offer borrowers low, fixed start rates in the initial 5- or 7-year period, and, if the borrower meets certain conditions, the ability to reset the remaining 23- or 25-year loan balance. This type of

mortgage attracts borrowers who plan to remain in their homes for a short period of time, but want the security of being able to extend their mortgage after the initial period, if their plans change.

ARMs

Freddie Mac also buys rate-capped ARMs. These mortgages offer borrowers even lower start rates than balloon/resets, but usually adjust earlier. Freddie Mac buys ARMs that adjust after 1, 3, 5, 7 or 10 years. Annual rate adjustments on these mortgages are generally capped at 1% or 2% and are tied to the indices for U.S. T-notes, 11th District Cost of Funds or LIBOR. These mortgages also feature life-of-loan rate caps, and some ARMs include an option to convert to a fixed rate. Low start rates and the security of rate-change limits are the main attractions to borrowers seeking ARMs. For lenders, rate-capped ARMs minimize default risks and offer more flexibility in pipeline management through Freddie Mac's extended commitment and delivery schedules.

Cash Programs

Freddie Mac's Cash Programs offer lenders convenience, speed, and competitive prices. Under these Cash Programs, lenders can take out commitments to sell with a single phone call or computer link and receive funding within a few days. Lenders can sell Freddie Mac single loans or groups of loans and, under certain conditions, loans originated by third parties.

Freddie Mac offers three Cash Programs: Gold Cash®, Required Net Yield (RNY) Cash and ARM Cash. Gold Cash® and RNY Cash are outlets for 15-, 20- and 30-year fixed-rate mortgages and 5- and 7-year balloon/reset mortgages, while ARM Cash is the only outlet for Treasury-indexed ARMs.

Lenders can locate prices for the Cash Programs through major information networks such as Telerate, through their desktop personal computers, over Gold Connection® software or from Freddie Mac's commitment line at (703) 761-7170. Prices and required net yields may change at any time during the business day, depending on market conditions.

Gold Cash®
When selling fixed-rate and balloon/reset mortgages, lenders use Gold Cash® if the mortgage coupon is at or below Freddie Mac's posted maximum eligible note rate. The price Freddie Mac quotes to lenders is tied to the mortgage securities market.

RNY Cash
RNY Cash is a vehicle for two types of mortgage sales: participation interests (less than 100% of the mortgage balance being sold) of fully amortizing, fixed-rate mortgages and 15- and 30-year, fixed-rate and balloon/reset loans, with note rates above the maximum eligible Gold Cash® range. The RNY, posted for each eligible product, is the amount of interest that Freddie Mac must receive for each mortgage it purchases. Lenders can choose between two remittance cycles: They can either hold the payment and earn interest on the funds or choose Accelerated Remittance Cycle (ARC) for fixed-rate mortgages and trade float for a higher cash price up front.

ARM Cash
Lenders sell 1% and 2% annual rate-capped ARMs through ARM Cash. The interest rate is tied to the one-year Treasury index, is constrained by life-of-loan caps and can be converted to a fixed rate, subject to certain conditions. ARM Cash works well for new production ARMs that are originated to match Freddie Mac's program parameters. Freddie Mac usually posts 39 ARM

cash plans, giving lenders a wide range of start rates to offer borrowers.

Considerations in Cash Sales

There are several considerations in cash sales, including:

- Contract commitment requirements
- Delivery periods
- Remittance cycles
- Pricing

Contract Requirements

Through Freddie Mac's Cash Programs, lenders can sell whole loans with aggregate mortgage balances between $1,000 and $10 million for any one purchase contract. Lenders must use separate contracts for each mortgage type, keep servicing spreads of at least 25 bp for Gold Cash® and RNY Cash, and at least 37.5 bp for ARM Cash. They must also deliver the full contract commitment amount within certain tolerance levels and agreed-upon time periods.

Purchase Contracts and Commitments

Lenders sell their loans to Freddie Mac using either one-time purchase contracts or master commitments. One-time contracts cover one loan commitment and one mortgage product. Once a lender delivers mortgages sold under that commitment, the contract is fulfilled. The next time the lender wants to sell mortgages to Freddie Mac, it must enter into another contract.

Lenders who sell regularly to Freddie Mac or sell more than one type of mortgage product, often prefer master commitments. Master commitments give lenders flexibility in the dollar amount of each type of product they sell within a total contract commitment amount established over a fixed period of time, usually between six months and one year.

Master commitments help lenders efficiently manage their loan sales in a changing marketplace. For instance, lenders can use the same master commitment to sell various types of mortgages through the Cash, Guarantor or MultiLender Swap programs. They can apply certain negotiated underwriting waivers automatically to loans and lock in other vital contract features, such as the buy up ratio.

Freddie Mac allows a certain flexibility, known as a "purchase tolerance," between the aggregate dollar amount of mortgages a lender commits to sell and the aggregate dollar value of the loans actually purchased by Freddie Mac. In both one-time purchase contracts and master commitments, lenders have a $10,000 or 2.5% purchase tolerance level — whichever is greater — above or below the commitment/contract amount. Lenders who deliver mortgages falling below this level must "pair off" the amount of the shortfall. If lenders deliver mortgages worth more than the tolerance level and the contract price is no higher than the current price, Freddie Mac will pay lenders at the contract price; otherwise, Freddie Mac will re-price the excess amount.

Lenders selling through the Gold Cash® Program have a choice of two commitments: summary and detail. In *summary commitments*, lenders lock in prices for a specific 51 bp range within the eligible posted range for any given day, and then receive prices for each one-eighth percent coupon. In *detail commitments*, however, lenders select a specific note rate within the eligible range posted for the day, and they receive a price quote based on a single note rate. Lenders receive the same prices no matter which commitment path they choose. Summary commitments are best for covering a range of coupons in the pipeline, while detail commitments are designed for specific note-rate pricing on loans with note rates that are not set on an exact eighth percent.

Delivery Periods

Once lenders sell mortgages to Freddie Mac, they usually continue to service those loans. They will continue to receive monthly principal and interest (P&I) payments from borrowers, and forward them, less a *servicing spread* (the amount lenders keep to service mortgages), to Freddie Mac each month. The remittance cycle sets forth the timing of that monthly payment to Freddie Mac. An early remittance cycle brings lenders a higher price for their mortgages.

Under Gold Cash®, lenders have the option of two different cycles: Gold and First Tuesday. Under Gold remittance, which is Freddie Mac's standard remittance cycle, lenders forward P&I to Freddie Mac on the third business day after the 15th of the month. With First Tuesday remittance, lenders forward P&I on the first Tuesday of the month after they are due from the borrower. RNY Cash gives lenders the choice of First Tuesday or Accelerated Remittance Cycle (ARC), which is similar to Gold remittance. ARM Cash sales require First Tuesday remittance.

Pricing

Under Gold Cash®, Freddie Mac offers lenders competitive prices for premium (high-coupon), current rate (par) and discount mortgages. Freddie Mac posts a 100 bp to 150 bp range of mortgage coupons and the indication prices for each one-eighth coupon within that range. The company posts the coupon that is priced closest to par, and the coupons that are 50 bp to 75 bp above and below the par. Base prices are quoted using the Gold remittance cycle and a servicing spread of 25 bp.

Under RNY Cash, Freddie Mac pays lenders at par if their mortgage coupons are at least equal to the minimum gross yield (which is the RNY plus the servicing spread). While lenders will not receive premium prices for their premium mortgages, they retain the yield in excess of the minimum gross yield.

Under ARM Cash, Freddie Mac posts prices for both convertible and nonconvertible ARMs under each plan. Prices are quoted as a percentage of par. Freddie Mac pays premium, discount and par prices for ARMs. Unlike Gold Cash® prices, ARM Cash prices do not assume any specific servicing spread.

Cash indication prices and RNYs — based, where applicable, on mortgage product, note rate and delivery period — are posted daily between 10 a.m. and 4:30 p.m. Eastern time on the major market information services, including Freddie Mac's MIDANET, Telerate, Knight-Ridder and Bloomberg. Lenders also may call Freddie Mac's mortgage rate line at (703) 761-7170. For a firm price commitment, however, lenders must call Freddie Mac's commitment line; or, for Gold Cash® sales, they can access firm prices through their personal computers using Freddie Mac's Gold Connection® for Microsoft Windows™ software.

Sales Transaction

Lenders can make commitments to sell their loans by calling Freddie Mac's commitment line; or, if selling through the Gold Cash® program, they can input data into a personal computer using the Gold Connection for Windows™ software. Lenders provide the same information to Freddie Mac whether they use the commitment line or Gold Connection. Once lenders agree to the prices quoted to them, their next step is to complete the necessary documentation and submit it to Freddie Mac before the delivery date. Freddie Mac funds the lenders within a few days after it receives the documentation.

Swap Programs

Lenders may swap mortgages for Participation Certificates (PCs), Freddie Mac's MBSs. Once lenders obtain PCs, some immediately sell these securities through a dealer for cash. This is called "swapping and selling." Other lenders "swap and hold" the PCs in their portfolios. PCs are often used as collateral to obtain a variety of collateralized financing. Further, risk-based capital regulations encourage lenders to hold MBSs, since they require less capital to be held against them than mortgages held in portfolio.

PCs represent undivided interests in a group, or pool, of mortgages. The financial community regards these securities as sound investments. Using Freddie Mac's Swap Programs, lenders can enhance their liquidity and increase the flexibility of their pipeline and balance sheet management.

A PC generates an income stream that is used to pay investors. In a Cash or Swap transaction, the P&I on each loan in a pool is "passed through" to the investor. The borrower pays P&I to the lender who, as the servicer, takes out a servicing spread and passes through the principal and the remainder of the interest to Freddie Mac. Then, Freddie Mac takes out its guarantee fee (the company's compensation for guaranteeing payments to the investor) and passes through the principal and remaining interest to the PC holder.

Freddie Mac offers Gold PCs, ARM PCs, and 75-day PCs. Lenders receive Gold PCs by swapping their eligible fixed-rate and balloon/reset mortgages, ARM PCs by swapping eligible ARMs, and 75-day PCs by swapping their FHA/VA mortgages.

Gold PCs are Freddie Mac's premier security and the fastest-paying conventional mortgage pass-through security on the market. Investors receive funds from Freddie Mac just 15 days after borrowers' P&I payments are due to lenders. This quick pass-through feature makes Gold PCs attractive to investors and typically commands a higher price than other MBSs. Another reason for their popularity is that investors can use Gold PCs as collateral. And finally, because Freddie Mac guarantees the timely payment of monthly P&I, regardless of whether borrowers actually make their payments, investors view these MBSs as sound investments.

ARM PCs are also considered to be sound investments. They differ from other PCs in that Freddie Mac guarantees the timely payment of principal and interest. Securities backed by ARMs are typically purchased by investors looking for assets to match short-term liabilities and liabilities with floating rates. There are two types of Freddie Mac ARM PCs: Weighted-Average-Coupon (WAC) ARM PCs and Margin ARM PCs. A majority of Freddie Mac ARMs outstanding, particularly the newly issued, are WAC ARM PCs. Their popularity can be attributed to the greater flexibility concerning the mortgage delivery parameters.

Freddie Mac's original 75-day PC provides an alternative way for lenders to sell FHA production.

Guarantor and MultiLender

Freddie Mac offers two swap programs: Guarantor and MultiLender. The major difference between the two relates to the source of the mortgages. A Guarantor Swap gives lenders PCs that are backed exclusively by the lenders' own mortgages. A MultiLender Swap offers lenders a prorated share of a Gold PC that is backed by mortgages Freddie Mac purchases from several lenders.

Balloon/reset mortgages, as well as conventional and FHA/VA fixed-rate mortgages, can be swapped through the Guarantor Program. Lenders can swap only conventional fixed-rate and balloon/reset mortgages through the MultiLender program.

Eligible ARMs can be swapped through the ARM Guarantor Program. This program makes it easy for lenders to form large pools. PCs backed by larger pools trade particularly well because there are no specified ranges for mortgage coupons, margins, life caps, and adjustment rates. The PCs lenders receive from ARM swaps have coupons based on the calculated weighted average of the underlying mortgage coupons. The PC coupon is recalculated each month to reflect adjustments in the mortgage coupons, as well as in the total unpaid principal balances (UPBs) of the underlying loans.

Considerations When Swapping

Many of the same considerations affecting cash sales play a role in swaps, such as determining which mortgages are eligible for a particular program and choosing commitment types and remittance cycles. But swaps involve other considerations as well, including the formation of mortgage pools.

Whole Loan versus Participation Interests
Lenders may swap both whole loans and participation interests in the fixed-rate Guarantor and MultiLender Programs. But lenders may swap only whole loans through the ARM Guarantor Program. For whole loan deliveries, the swap amount is the UPB of the mortgages. For participation interests, the swap amount is the total UPB of the mortgages multiplied by Freddie Mac's participation percentage, which is generally 50% to 95% of the mortgage amount.

Minimum Swap Amounts and Servicing Spreads
For the Guarantor Program, lenders must swap at least $250,000 for 15-, 20- and 30-year fixed-rate mortgages, and $1 million for balloon/reset mortgages. The minimum swap amount in the ARM Guarantor Program is $500,000, while lenders may swap as little as $1,000 worth through the MultiLender Program. The MultiLender swap also allows lenders to select the Gold Rush option for overnight settlement of PCs. The servicing spread for eligible fixed-rate mortgage swaps, including balloon/resets, is

normally 25 bp, but ARMs can be swapped with spreads that range from 37.5 bp to 200 bp.

Purchase Contracts and Master Commitments
Loan commitments work almost the same way in Cash and Swap transactions. For instance, lenders can choose between one-time purchase contracts and master commitments. However, lenders swapping with Freddie Mac have an additional choice between mandatory master commitments and optional master commitments. Lenders using optional master commitments can choose to deliver a partial amount of a loan commitment, although they must "purchase" the option with an upfront fee.

As with the Cash Program, Freddie Mac allows a certain purchase tolerance for mortgages or lenders' deliveries against a commitment. In mandatory master commitments, lenders have a 10% tolerance level above or below the promised amount. Lenders using optional master commitments do not have a tolerance level for below the promised amount, but still must adhere to the "10% above" upper purchase tolerance. Lenders that deliver mortgages falling below these tolerance ranges are subject to a pair-off fee.

Lenders using one-time contracts may use optional or mandatory delivery. The purchase tolerance for each one-time contract under mandatory delivery is plus or minus 5% of the contract amount, or $100,000, whichever is greater. Optional deliveries are available only on a negotiated basis and are subject to the same purchase tolerances exceeding a loan delivery. Both deliveries are subject to the same pair-off fees as master commitments.

Pooling Mortgages
Under Freddie Mac's Swap Programs, lenders must form a pool of mortgages before they swap. Because PC investors take

a close look at the mortgages underlying the securities, the value of PCs is greatly influenced by how lenders pool, or "stratify," their mortgages. To obtain optimal securities pricing, lenders should keep the range of mortgage coupons and maturities within the mortgage pools they form as narrow as possible. The more lenders learn about the indicators investors use to predict cash flows and prepayment rates of PCs — the primary considerations in influencing an investor's rate of return — the easier it is to create more valuable securities.

One quick way investors gather basic PC information is through the use of Freddie Mac pool prefixes that identify specific mortgage and pool characteristics. The first two characters of the pool prefix provide traders and investors with an indication of what type of mortgages are in the pool. Separating loans by mortgage type according to pool prefixes is the first step in forming successful pools. Through Freddie Mac's software system, MIDANET, lenders can sort, analyze and organize their loans to create the pool that brings the best possible price or value for their PC.

In the Guarantor and MultiLender Programs, lenders may pool eligible 20-year mortgages separately or together with 30-year loans. However, pooling 20-year mortgages separately brings a higher PC value for lenders. In the ARM Program, lenders must pool their eligible ARMs by the same index, adjustment period, convertibility option and rate cap.

Buy Ups and Buy Downs

Lenders can adjust their guarantee fees through buy ups and buy downs. These options allow lenders to better manage their servicing income and thus receive the best possible PC coupon.

In the Guarantor and MultiLender Programs, mortgages in a pool with note rates above the minimum mortgage note rate bring lenders additional servicing income each month unless they use buy ups to sell Freddie Mac the additional yield. Servicing income above a 25 bp servicing spread for fixed-rate mortgages may be regarded as excess servicing by the IRS. If lenders retain excess servicing, the IRS may require them to allocate some portion of their mortgage investments to retained servicing, which in turn may influence lender tax gains or losses when they sell PCs.

With Freddie Mac's note-level buy ups and buy downs, which are offered through both the Guarantor and MultiLender Swap Programs, lenders can mix note rates within one pool and still minimize their retained excess servicing. Lenders can buy down their guarantee fee to zero. In exchange for paying a lower guarantee fee, the lender will owe cash to Freddie Mac. Lenders can also buy up their guarantee fee by as much as 12.5 bp and receive cash from Freddie Mac.

With note-level buy ups and buy downs, lenders do not need to buy up or buy down by the same amount for all of the note rates in the pool. Instead, lenders need only adjust their guarantee fee on each note rate to the extent necessary for it to support the PC coupon they request and leave them with the servicing spread they desire. The range of adjustment possibilities provides lenders with the greatest pooling flexibility.

Under the swap programs, lenders can also reduce their guarantee fee by negotiating swaps with recourse. This means that they agree to buy back loans which go into foreclosure and to pay foreclosure costs. Lenders who swap without recourse transfer the risk of loan default to Freddie Mac, but pay a higher guarantee fee.

Remittance Cycle

Under the Guarantor and MultiLender Programs, lenders have three remittance options: Gold, First Tuesday and Super ARC. Gold and First Tuesday work the same as they do in the Cash Programs. Super ARC is similar to the ARC option used in

Cash Programs, but it also allows lenders to convert much of their float income into a lower guarantee fee. Under Super ARC, lenders remit to Freddie Mac on any set date before the 16th of the month in which P&I is due them. Under Gold and First Tuesday, lenders do not have to advance scheduled principal payments that they have not yet received from borrowers; however, under Super ARC, they do.

Lenders swapping through the WAC ARM Program may choose from the original remittance cycle (which is the same as First Tuesday) and ARC. Lenders using ARC, which operates much like ARC under the Cash Programs, can reduce their guarantee fees by 4 bp to 6 bp.

Swap Transaction

Lenders conduct swaps with Freddie Mac by working through their Freddie Mac account manager. Through MIDANET, lenders provide essential information, including mortgage product, requested servicing spread, commitment amount, swap options, weighted average remaining maturity, remittance cycle and requested settlement date. Freddie Mac and lenders then electronically exchange contracts and forms. Lenders then receive the PCs by wire, in an amount equivalent to the mortgages they swap.

Once they receive the PCs, lenders have a number of choices. Lenders who have decided to "swap and hold" simply retain the pools; lenders who have decided to "swap and sell" can deliver the PCs to the buyers. Lenders who arrange to sell the PCs to Freddie Mac's Securities Sales and Trading Group (SS&TG) or other mortgage securities dealers before the PCs are issued can request that Freddie Mac send the PCs directly to the buyers, who then wire lenders the proceeds of the sale.

After a PC is Issued
Once lenders have swapped for a Gold PC or an ARM PC, they may choose to hold it in portfolio or to sell it. Those who choose to hold PCs in portfolio are usually institutions with the financial wherewithal to invest in mortgage pools. If they need liquidity later, these institutions can use their PCs as collateral for many low-cost forms of borrowing, such as reverse repurchase transactions (*repos*) and dollar reverse repurchase transactions (*dollar rolls*). When circumstances change or new investment opportunities warrant a subsequent sale, these lenders will readily find a liquid market for their PCs. Lenders should consult their own legal, financial and tax advisors before executing transactions using PCs held in portfolio.

Other lenders choose to sell their PCs. With more than $3 trillion in outstanding securities, the MBS market is quite liquid and dynamic. PCs are typically sold into the forward market — a trade agreed to on one day with settlement (delivery of the PCs in exchange for payment) occurring at a later date. Because of the large size of the MBS market, forward selling into the marketplace is relatively easy.

MBS prices are quoted in points and 32nds. A *point* is 1% of the unpaid principal balance of a pool. A price of 100 is called *par*; at par, investors pay $1 for every $1 in unpaid principal balance of the security. Below par (at a discount), investors pay less than $1 for every $1 of principal, which is generally the case for PCs backed by mortgages at below-market coupons. Above par (at a premium), investors pay more than $1 for every $1 in principal, which usually occurs when PCs are backed by pools of mortgages with above-market coupons.

SS&TG makes markets in all Freddie Mac securities and offers financing for Gold PCs and ARM PCs. SS&TG also provides lenders with up-to-the-minute market pricing on all PCs and assists lenders with pooling strategies for loans they plan to sell into the secondary market. Since SS&TG is part of Freddie

Mac, lenders are assured of a reputable and financially strong trading partner that can easily handle all lender trading and hedging activities.

Lenders usually forward sell their mortgages to hedge their pipelines and protect against a decline in value as interest rates rise. To forward-sell a PC, a lender informs the dealer of the trading characteristics of a PC pool, including the pool amount, mortgage type, PC coupon and requested settlement date. Dealers provide lenders with bids once the dealers have the critical information.

Another way to accelerate a lender's access to cash in a swap-and-sell situation is the Early Funding Program, offered exclusively by SS&TG. Under this program, lenders can forward sell PCs through SS&TG and receive payment before the PCs are even issued. Lenders receive 100% of the proceeds from the forward sales as early as five days before Freddie Mac forms the pool.

By taking advantage of the Early Funding program, lenders can use their proceeds to pay down lines of credit and to originate more loans. The program is especially beneficial when borrowers rush to refinance mortgages in a falling interest rate environment. By using the Early Funding program, lenders can continue to serve their borrowers without overextending their credit lines. Further, since an Early Funding trade is generally considered a sale of assets, it results in a smaller, cleaner balance sheet.

Whether lenders choose to hold or sell their PCs, they will find the financial community eager to invest in transactions supported by these MBSs. Freddie Mac is a key player in the conventional mortgage pass-through securities market with $1.2 trillion in MBSs issued as of Dec. 31, 1995. A 20-member group of securities dealers, including SS&TG and a variety of major national and regional firms, maintains an active market in Freddie Mac securities.

Lending to Underserved Borrowers: A Profitable and Expanding Business

Financing affordable housing has been a significant part of Freddie Mac's business since the company opened its doors over a quarter century ago. A large percentage of Freddie Mac's purchases are used to finance housing for low- and moderate-income families.

Freddie Mac believes affordable lending can best be done by integrating it into Freddie Mac's standard purchase programs. Indeed, the company's research shows that underserved borrowers share many characteristics with other borrowers. However, within the housing finance industry, several factors have combined to inhibit profitability and restrain the growth of lending to underserved communities — among them: higher costs to underwrite and service loans with higher balances.

Freddie Mac believes that there are sound, sustainable and profitable ways to extend lending to underserved borrowers while maintaining credit standards. The company is committed to doing so through its Expanding Markets program.

Expanding Markets

Freddie Mac's Expanding Markets program, which started in 1994, takes a three-pronged approach to creating products, programs, services, and tools to help lenders reach more creditworthy, yet underserved, borrowers:

Affordable Lending: Expanding the reach of affordable mortgage credit to all potential borrowers by making individual mortgages more attainable.

Fair Lending: Ensuring that all potential borrowers are treated fairly and equally in decisions to extend credit in an accessible mortgage system.

Community Development Lending: Supporting the revitalization of America's neighborhoods by partnering with public, private, philanthropic and community-based organizations.

Affordable lending is solid business for Freddie Mac. The company uses the same standards for Expanding Markets business — quality, investment, credit, pricing and profitability — that it uses for its standard purchase programs.

Freddie Mac believes the industry's success depends on quality lending that can be achieved by using Freddie Mac's Expanding Markets products, such as Affordable Gold®, Affordable Seconds® and Gold Measure®, as illustrated in the *Discover Gold Through Expanding Markets* booklet. The company's Community Development Lending strategies bring together the various players and their expertise in a community to leverage housing resources and expand access to home ownership. The company maintains that offering these programs, products, services, tools and technology expands opportunities for home ownership to underserved borrowers in target communities.

The following is a sampling of Freddie Mac's Expanding Markets initiatives, designed specifically to help lenders originate more affordable housing mortgages.

Affordable Lending

Affordable Gold. *Affordable Gold* lets lenders offer their borrowers three down payment options:

- Affordable Gold 5 — 95% LTV mortgages with 5% down payment from the borrower's personal cash.
- Affordable Gold 3/2 — 95% LTV mortgages with 3% of the down payment from the borrower's personal cash and the other 2% from other sources such as gifts or grants.

- Affordable Gold 97 — 97% LTV mortgage with 3% down payment from the borrower's personal cash.

Freddie Mac will purchase, on a negotiated basis, mortgages on two- to four-unit properties through the *Affordable Gold* program. The Two- to Four-Unit Affordable Lending Program allows higher LTV ratios and an alternate method of underwriting rental income. This pilot program, which also includes landlord counseling, improves the chances of a borrower having the income necessary to purchase rental income housing.

Affordable Seconds. Freddie Mac's *Affordable Seconds* program simplifies the process of originating first mortgages involving secondary financing. By using the automated or paper version of this checklist, lenders can find new ways to work with governments, agencies, nonprofits and employers to create secondary financing terms which can be coupled with Freddie Mac's Affordable Lending programs.

Gold Measure. *Gold Measure,* a reliable, easy-to-use worksheet available in hard copy and software versions, helps lenders review a borrower's total risk profile for qualifying under the Affordable Gold Program. Gold Measure helps identify and manage the layering of risk for loans with combinations of extenuating circumstances and compensating factors. It also helps lenders maintain consistency in their underwriting to ensure that all the quality loans that can be made are made.

Discover Gold through Expanding Markets. Freddie Mac's *Discover Gold Through Expanding Markets* booklet helps lenders qualify more borrowers without compromising credit quality. Using more than 100 actual case studies, this booklet illustrates how to make the company's products, programs, services, tools and policies work in real life situations. Many of these examples were developed through discussions in Freddie Mac's Underwriting Barriers Outreach Groups. This publication helps lenders meet their community and fair lending objectives by extending the reach of the housing finance system to more qualified borrowers.

Guaranteed Rural Housing Mortgages. *Guaranteed Rural Housing* (GRH) Mortgages give lenders another way to serve their communities' borrowers by using the U.S. Department of Agriculture's Rural Housing Service (RHS) program. GRH Section 502 mortgages meet the housing needs of low- and moderate-income borrowers in rural areas. Under this program and on a negotiated basis, Freddie Mac purchases 30-year fixed-rate mortgages allowing up to 100% LTV first-mortgage financing. Qualified rural borrowers have the necessary income and credit history, but not the down payment required for conventional mortgages.

Rural Leveraged Lending. The RHS offers *Section 502 Rural Leveraged Lending* as an alternative to direct GRH financing by providing a second mortgage of at least 50% LTV and giving borrowers lower financing costs since no mortgage insurance is required on the first mortgage. The interest rate for the second mortgage is based on the borrower's ability to pay. Freddie Mac will purchase the first mortgage, up to 50% LTV.

Native American Lending. To make more financing options available to Native American, Alaskan Native and New Mexican Pueblo borrowers, Freddie Mac buys mortgages originated under two programs — *FHA Section 248 Native American Program* for Properties Located on Indian Areas and Other Restricted Areas and the *HUD 184 Program*, which is also known as the Indian Housing Loan Guarantee Program.

Lease/Purchase Program. For low- and moderate-income renters who want to purchase homes but don't have sufficient savings for down payments and closing costs and little or no established credit histories, Freddie Mac has launched a *Lease/Purchase Program*. Through this pilot, the company purchases mortgages made to nonprofit organizations or public agencies for single-family, one-unit, non-owner-occupied dwellings.

The program permits tenants who have demonstrated the ability to make timely rental payments to assume the mortgage.

FHA 203(k). Through Freddie Mac's *FHA 203(k) Rehabilitation Mortgage Purchase Program*, the company will purchase, on a negotiated basis, fixed-rate FHA 203(k) mortgages that finance both the purchase and rehabilitation of a home in a single transaction. This pilot program gives families the money they need to improve the homes they want to buy, while providing lenders with an investment quality product.

Fair Lending

Freddie Mac's booklet, *Fair Lending: An Introduction to Self-Evaluation,* was developed in partnership with mortgage lending customers and the Mortgage Bankers Association (MBA). It helps lenders uncover any unintended bias in their lending processes through a self-evaluation program and offers advice on how to interpret and act on the results. The booklet presents matched pair testing, one of the best practices described in the agreement between the MBA and HUD.

Freddie Mac's booklet, *Discover Gold Through Homeownership Education,* helps lenders identify and evaluate suitable home ownership education programs for borrowers. When used effectively, this booklet gives lenders a means to mitigate losses and enhance the performance of the loans they originate and service. It helps lenders realize the benefits of partnering with housing-related organizations, especially home ownership education providers, and comply with home ownership education requirements for Affordable Gold. Included with the booklet is a copy of *A Consumer Home Inspection Kit* to help borrowers select and assess the long-term affordability of a suitable home.

Community Development Lending

Through its Community Development Lending effort, Freddie Mac reaches out to underserved communities and low- to moderate-income and minority residents in targeted communities to increase their access to mortgage money and to eliminate barriers to home ownership. By working in concert with national and local organizations with existing infrastructures to reach underserved communities, Freddie Mac helps to create a stronger infrastructure for Community Development Lending. To accomplish this, the company offers a host of products, programs, tools, services and technology.

Relationship building is the philosophy at the heart of Freddie Mac's Community Developing Lending. The company invests in targeted communities to encourage local housing industry-related institutions to build their capacity to produce greater results — each does what it does best.

Freddie Mac also joins forces with organizations that share Freddie Mac's commitment to improve housing opportunities. Together with these other organizations, Freddie Mac creates business alliances that leverage the resources of lenders and mortgage insurers, as well as housing service providers, nonprofit housing developers and religious organizations.

Through Community Development Lending alliances and initiatives, Freddie Mac provides a complete array of standard and negotiated mortgage products, programs and technical services, including those listed earlier as well as the company's Loan Prospector automated underwriting service. Freddie Mac then purchases investment-quality mortgages originated by Freddie Mac-approved lenders participating in these alliances and initiatives.

Other programs available through Freddie Mac's Community Development Lending include:

- *Partners in Participation* is a guide to help nontraditional lenders originating mortgages in underserved

areas — such as nonprofit organizations, lender consortiums, community development organizations and community banks — to gain access to Freddie Mac and the secondary mortgage market.
- *Mortgage Revenue Bonds* (MRBs), issued by local and state housing finance agencies (HFAs) combine the benefits of tax exempt borrowing rates with Freddie Mac's efficient securitization process. Lenders work with HFAs to originate mortgages under Freddie Mac's Affordable Gold Program or other approved terms, such as those negotiated through Freddie Mac's Community Development Lending. In many instances, Freddie Mac invests in the HFA-issued MRBs, giving HFAs the added flexibility of negotiating nontraditional MRB structures and program options.
- *NeighborWorks®* is a national program linking Freddie Mac and the Neighborhood Reinvestment Corporation, helping lenders participate productively in the revitalization of neighborhoods by providing home ownership financing that is supported by a "full-cycle" lending process.
- *HOME WORKS!* is an innovative program to leverage the use of HOME funds to increase home ownership opportunities and neighborhood redevelopment. Freddie Mac will work with lenders to adapt the HOME WORKS! model to match their community's housing needs and to support the revitalization of cities across the country.

Expanding Markets: Going Forward

Freddie Mac is committed to an effective and sustainable long-term approach to Expanding Markets. An *effective* approach means incorporating affordable lending into standard home financing programs. A *sustainable* approach means maintaining established credit and pricing disciplines so that all participants profit by doing what they do best.

The company believes Expanding Markets business should be:

- Quality business.
- Profitable for all participants.
- Achieved through broad-based, standard purchase programs.

Freddie Mac also believes that its one view of investment quality credit plays a major role in applying standards that have positive implications for borrowers and the long-term stability of neighborhoods. Where affordable loans meet its criteria, Freddie Mac will negotiate a win-win outcome for everyone involved. Where programs help borrowers become creditworthy by providing effective home ownership counseling, Freddie Mac will buy the loans. With its programs, such as Native American lending, Freddie Mac provides an outlet to encourage lenders to reach all the potential borrowers in the communities they serve and understand how certain programs, such as lease/purchase and 203(k), can be incorporated into standard programs.

Freddie Mac's Expanding Markets mission is to make home ownership possible for *all* creditworthy borrowers and to work with Freddie Mac lenders to expand the reach of home financing into underserved markets. The company will continue to drive down costs, making mortgages more affordable for all borrowers. Freddie Mac will continue to provide the efficient technologies, products, programs and services to help lenders make increasingly sound, profitable and fair lending decisions. Finally, Freddie Mac will continue to form alliances and create initiatives with organizations that can reach into communities across the country to connect borrowers with a full range of home financing professionals, including Freddie Mac-approved lenders.

A Freddie Mac Expanding Markets Case Study: Meeting a Community's Housing Needs

"Prince George's County has forged what will be a unique partnership with HUD, the state of Maryland, Freddie Mac, and the commitments of a number of major Washington-area lending institutions. We all have a common goal — to improve home ownership opportunities for low- and moderate-income residents and to stimulate the county's economic revitalization." — Henry Cisneros, Secretary of U.S. Department of Housing & Urban Development

The following case study illustrates how Freddie Mac's Expanding Markets Department works with a community to develop and implement a workable housing finance program to meet that community's specific housing needs. Working with housing leaders in these communities, together with federal, state and local governments, Freddie Mac helps forge an alliance of housing professionals who join forces to offer the best in Community Development Lending to low- and moderate-income and minority individuals and families.

Location
Prince George's County, Maryland, a suburb of Washington, D.C.

Participants
- Freddie Mac.
- Prince George's County Department of Housing and Community Development.
- The State of Maryland.
- U.S. Department of Housing and Urban Development (HUD).
- U.S. Department of the Treasury.

- 13 mortgage lenders led by a Freddie Mac-approved master servicer, Eastern Mortgage Services.

The Need

Prince George's County, a Washington, D.C. suburb, had two objectives:

1. To provide a wider range of home ownership opportunities, particularly for move-up buyers in the county.
2. To encourage construction and rehabilitation of homes in targeted neighborhoods near the Washington, D.C. beltway.

Home prices in the Washington area are among the highest in the nation and even modest homes are often beyond the reach of moderate-income buyers.

Typically, mortgage revenue bonds (MRBs) are limited to first-time home buyers who earn less than the area median income and purchase lower-priced homes. However, Congress permits state and local governments to set their own limits for the MRBs they issue. The Prince George's County Department of Housing and Community Development was therefore eligible to use MRBs for move-up buyers and home buyers purchasing higher-priced homes in economically distressed target areas. With the approval of the state of Maryland, HUD and the U.S. Treasury Department, Prince George's County was able to target a number of economically distressed communities and to provide financing in these communities for homes in the $180,000 to $220,000 price range, which is considered average for the area adjacent to the Washington, D.C., Beltway.

The Prince George's County Department of Housing and Community Development was able to issue MRBs and reach its objective to increase home ownership opportunities for move-up home buyers and help rehabilitate neighborhoods near Washington, D.C.

The Solution
Freddie Mac had been working for some time with state and local housing finance agencies (HFAs) throughout the country to make home ownership an affordable option for low- and moderate-income families through its own MRB program. This program combines the benefits of tax-exempt borrowing rates with the efficient securitization process Freddie Mac brings to the mortgage lending system.

With the proceeds from the issuance of the MRBs, participating lenders make below-market interest rate loans to eligible borrowers. The Freddie Mac PCs and Ginnie Mae MBSs serve as credit enhancements to the bond, thus allowing the bonds to command the very strong AAA rating.

In response to Prince George's County's unique need for its inner-beltway communities, Freddie Mac purchased $25 million of MRBs, issued by its Department of Housing and Community Development. By purchasing these bonds, Freddie Mac helped Prince George's County provide below-market-rate financing to eligible borrowers. In structuring this transaction, Freddie Mac was able to assist the county in meeting a diverse mix of housing needs.

Prince George's County selected 13 lenders to participate. The lenders were then trained by Freddie Mac, Prince George's County and Eastern Mortgage Services, the master servicer, so they could carry out the transaction effectively and successfully.

Background
Here's how the MRB program works. Lenders participating in the MRB programs designed by the HFAs originate loans under Freddie Mac's Affordable Gold Program or other approved terms. These loans, in many cases, meet Community Reinvestment Act (CRA) requirements for the lenders. Affordable Gold allows 3% of the down payment to come from a borrower's personal cash and allows 2% of the down payment to be a gift or loan from a nonprofit,

public agency or employer. Under this program, a borrower can also receive closing costs and prepayment assistance through a gift or loan, including a loan from a bank.

Freddie Mac then purchases the loans originated in exchange for its Participation Certificates (PCs). Lenders sell the PCs to the HFAs to back the MRBs.

The HFAs often back their bonds using both Freddie Mac PCs and Ginnie Mae MBSs. As a result, MRB programs can offer conventional and federally insured mortgages in a single bond issue. This provides flexibility in structuring bond issues and reduces transaction costs.

The Advantages of MRBs

Freddie Mac's Community Development Lending encourages all participants to work together to make decent, accessible housing a reality. Freddie Mac provides the benefits of the secondary mortgage market for a continuous flow of home financing into the community to all of the participants and the community at large.

With each participating organization doing what it does best, each target community is positively impacted. As a result of the Prince George's County transaction, tax-exempt financing was used to increase home ownership opportunities for low- and moderate-income borrowers and young move-up families in the county, while maintaining the county's economic diversity and preserving its tax base. Participating lenders originated investment quality loans by using Freddie Mac's programs and, in many cases, met their own CRA requirements.

This community development lending initiative demonstrates how Freddie Mac and other organizations in a community work together to make the most of their housing resources and to expand their ability to meet the housing needs of more families. It also demonstrates how alliances among private, government and community-based organizations can help meet housing needs community by community, state by state.

Loan Prospector

Loan Prospector is an automated underwriting service that uses loan application, credit and property information to evaluate a borrower's ability to meet a mortgage obligation. Loan Prospector now works for nearly any type of mortgage, even those that Freddie Mac does not buy. An innovative business solution designed to meet lenders' current and future mortgage origination challenges, Loan Prospector uses state-of-the-art technology to provide significant advantages across all divisions of a lender's mortgage origination business.

Lenders who use Loan Prospector report that its reengineered credit policy and collateral assessment techniques have enabled them to streamline and improve their mortgage origination processes, provide superior service to borrowers and create significant competitive advantages. These process efficiencies are unlike any others found in the industry today.

Freddie Mac pilot tested Loan Prospector with a number of lenders for more than a year to ensure that it would meet lender needs. As a result of this cooperative effort, Freddie Mac designed Loan Prospector so lenders can leverage their existing technology with the advanced technology of this new service. Loan Prospector's open-system design allows seamless access through a lender's existing loan origination system with minimal additional hardware and software expense.

Key Features
Loan Prospector offers lenders:

- A reengineered approach to credit and collateral assessment.
- Merged credit reports.

- An open-system design compatible with existing loan origination systems.
- Representation and warranty waivers for Accept and AcceptPlus purchase decisions.
- Feedback messages that provide guidance for resolving borrower creditworthiness and collateral issues.
- Mortgage insurance registration.
- Streamlined processing for low-risk refinances.
- Flood zone, census tract and HMDA information with collateral assessments.

How Loan Prospector Works

Credit Assessment. Loan Prospector reviews certain loan application data and compares the information both to Freddie Mac's eligibility requirements and to the lender's business agreement with Freddie Mac. Loan Prospector accesses information electronically from credit repositories, selects the information it needs to predict loan performance and then evaluates the credit quality of the loan. It incorporates statistical modeling and a rules-based assessment into a comprehensive analysis that weighs a variety of factors in determining risk. The result is a Freddie Mac purchase decision within four minutes.

Depending on the loan profile, Loan Prospector can eliminate the need for certain documentation required by traditional underwriting, such as business tax returns and borrower explanations. This is possible because Freddie Mac's credit policy has been reengineered to match documentation requirements more meaningfully to the credit risk of the application. For example, some applications may require only two documents and a phone call to make the loan.

Collateral Assessment. Loan Prospector's collateral assessment feature was designed to streamline the collateral assessment process and to reduce unnecessary costs. Lenders have two choices with Loan Prospector's collateral assessment feature — an expedited assessment and the standard Uniform Residential Appraisal Report (URAR). When lenders choose the expedited collateral assessment option, Loan Prospector selects one of a variety of assessment methods (ranging from statistical modeling to a URAR), depending on the risk profile of the loan. Every assessment receives, at a minimum, a fraud check and an exterior inspection. The second collateral assessment option, a standard URAR, is always available to lenders using Loan Prospector's collateral assessment service.

As a user of the optional collateral assessment feature, the lender is relieved of making all representations and warranties associated with managing and underwriting the appraisal for loans where the property adequately supports the transaction, provided the data furnished by the lender is accurate. This means the lender also would be relieved of most indirect costs associated with the appraisal process as a Loan Prospector collateral assessment user.

Freddie Mac's Purchase Decision. Once the lender submits the loan application data to Loan Prospector, a Freddie Mac purchase decision is provided as an Accept, Refer or Caution classification. Freddie Mac's purchase decision is available to the lender for credit evaluation within four minutes and for collateral assessment frequently within 72 hours.

Loan Prospector's Risk Classification Definitions
   Accept: The loan is approved for purchase by Freddie Mac. The highest quality Accept loans, called Accept Plus, require even less documentation and processing than any other category of loans.
   Refer: Either credit and/or collateral cannot be processed as an Accept loan by Loan Prospector. The application needs full

underwriting analysis to determine if the loan qualifies for purchase by Freddie Mac.

Caution: The application appears to involve serious issues. The application needs full underwriting analysis by an underwriter who can evaluate the loan carefully to determine if it qualifies for purchase by Freddie Mac.

Accept loans are eligible for purchase by Freddie Mac without additional review by an underwriter; they follow an expedited underwriting path. Refer and Caution loans are referred to underwriters to determine if they are of investment quality. For each loan, Loan Prospector provides feedback that helps underwriters in making credit decisions.

Electronic Access to Third-Party Service Providers

Loan Prospector helps lenders operate more efficiently because it automatically accesses information from third-party service providers. In the past, lenders typically requested information from credit bureaus, appraisal management firms, property database collateral assessment firms and mortgage insurance companies to complete a loan file. Now, Loan Prospector obtains this third-party information electronically and automatically assesses loan application data. For example, with Loan Prospector, lenders may request either in-file credit data or merged credit reports from a choice of independent credit reporting companies. Loan Prospector also allows lenders to select mortgage insurance registration from their choice of mortgage insurance providers. If Freddie Mac classifies a loan as Accept, then the mortgage insurer agrees to insure the loan, subject to specific additional eligibility requirements built into Loan Prospector.

Key Loan Prospector Advantages

Loan Prospector helps lenders compete in the marketplace because of the numerous competitive advantages it offers, including:

- A purchase decision in four minutes, including certain Affordable Gold loans.
- Superior customer service.
- Reduced repurchase risk and quality control costs.
- Reduced loan fallout.
- Expanded markets.
- Streamlined credit and collateral underwriting requirements.
- Improved risk management.
- Consistent and fair underwriting.
- Reduced production cycle time from 45 days to as few as three days.
- Lower origination costs.

Loan Prospector also provides the following benefits to home buyers:

- Reduces settlement time.
- Cuts closing costs, based on efficiencies obtained through technology.
- Reduces borrower anxiety by providing helpful, instantaneous feedback on the status of the loan application.
- Provides an easier, less intrusive way to secure a mortgage because it requires fewer documents and less information from the home buyer.
- Qualifies more borrowers who are deemed ineligible or discouraged by current underwriting practices.

Advantages for Loan Production and Delivery
According to lenders, Loan Prospector most significantly impacts their origination, processing and underwriting functions. In addition, lenders have seen dramatic improvements in their closing, shipping, quality control and secondary marketing areas. These improvements are based on the following advantages:

Reduction in production cycle time. On average lenders require 25 to 45 days of processing time to ready a loan for closing. Loan Prospector helps lenders shorten this cycle to as few as three days, thus positively impacting their closing, shipping and secondary marketing operations.

Early identification of investment-quality loans. Loan officers or processors who use Loan Prospector in the production process can quickly identify those loans that Freddie Mac will purchase without further underwriting. Secondary marketing, closing and shipping departments can process these loans rapidly.

Streamlined processing. Required documentation, standard representations and warranties associated with borrowers' credit data and property assessment are reduced dramatically with Loan Prospector.

GoldWorks: The Mortgage Industry's Electronic Marketplace

A Single-Link
Freddie Mac created GoldWorks®, a value-added network, so that mortgage industry companies could enjoy direct access to Freddie Mac and other industry participants through a single, electronic link. GoldWorks is an electronic marketplace, connecting participants who want to exchange business information and stay on top of industry news.

The GoldWorks "community" includes Freddie Mac, lenders, mortgage servicing companies and service providers such as credit bureaus, brokers, title companies and mortgage insurance companies. GoldWorks subscribers can communicate with other network members confidentially through this reliable private network. Services such as e-mail, enhanced fax, electronic data interchange (EDI) support, file transfer and home pages let subscribers communicate and deliver information right from their desktop or laptop computers. Subscribers can deliver information in a faster and more efficient way, eliminating much of the paperwork and telephone tag involved in traditional business transactions.

The Relationship with Advantis

Freddie Mac teamed with Advantis — one of the largest commercial Value-Added Network (VAN) providers and the U.S. arm of the IBM Global Network — to bring you GoldWorks. Advantis has long been acclaimed as a technology leader. The Freddie Mac-Advantis initiative ensures that the mortgage industry will have full and immediate access to the latest networking advances and features.

Electronic Commerce

Electronic commerce can be defined as the paperless exchange of information to conduct business. GoldWorks offers electronic commerce tools such as e-mail, an enhanced fax service, EDI support, file transfer and home pages, similar to those on the Internet.

E-mail. GoldWorks offers an electronic mail system that lets users send and receive messages, documents, database files and spreadsheets. This service is available 24 hours a day, 365 days a year. Users can exchange messages with GoldWorks e-mail customers or with other private mail system users connected to GoldWorks.

E-mail offers a much more efficient method of communication than other more traditional methods. For example, e-mail's speedy delivery eliminates the need to fax your documents or use costly overnight delivery services. In today's hurried and competitive business environment, e-mail has become an essential business tool, reducing time, cost and frustration.

Enhanced Fax Service. Enhanced Fax on GoldWorks offers an easy, convenient way to distribute information to clients and trading partners. Participants can initiate broadcast faxes directly from their desktop computer to multiple locations — across the street or around the world — within minutes. With GoldWorks Enhanced Fax, lenders can even distribute daily rate changes to all their clients at virtually the same time.

EDI. Electronic Data Interchange (EDI) is the computer-to-computer exchange of business transactions in a standard industry-accepted format. EDI replaces routine paper forms, letting businesses handle transactions faster, more efficiently and with fewer errors. GoldWorks EDI support offers mortgage industry players an open, advanced data communications network for conducting electronic transactions, including getting credit reports, processing loan applications, sharing appraisal information and securing loan delivery information.

GoldWorks EDI capabilities offer a variety of processing options. For example, participants can use the in-house EDI translation software, direct business-to-business connections or EDI translation services and mailboxes that link businesses using different communications protocols. Subscribers can choose the process that best suits their business needs.

File Transfer. GoldWorks® file transfer lets customers view files, send files to and receive files from partners across the street or across the continent. Either way, File Transfer makes it easy to exchange information quickly and efficiently. Any mortgage industry player linked to GoldWorks can send and receive information with an authorized file transfer host. The transfer is facilitated by GoldWorks through a dial-up or leased-line connection.

Navigator. GoldWorks Navigator is an online directory for companies, products and services listed on the GoldWorks® network. Users have access to *home pages*, documents with graphics and text that provide up-to-date information on what's available to the mortgage industry. Participants can browse the network, locating information on different organizations, product descriptions, services, common questions, news and other industry-related information.

Lenders and other mortgage industry participants also can post their own home page to advertise their company's background, products and services. Home pages are a popular selling tool that reaches mortgage industry participants without the expenses of traditional advertising.

GoldWorks and the Mortgage Industry

GoldWorks is continually changing to address the needs of its participants and to take advantage of advances in technology. Freddie Mac is adding new programs and services such as Dow Jones Telerate, MERS and Dun & Bradstreet to the network so lenders will have even more choices in the way they do business. By offering mortgage industry members new, more efficient ways to communicate, participants can conduct their business with more speed and less paperwork, ultimately improving the quality of service for the borrower.

Conclusion: Meeting Lender Needs

Freddie Mac works to provide mortgage originators with the right mix of programs and flexible product features to meet borrowers' needs, regardless of the interest rate environment. Securitization, market liquidity and loan standardization have been the company's hallmarks. Freddie Mac remains responsive to lender needs by purchasing a variety of loans and by continually refining programs to meet the changing nature of the lending business.

For more than a quarter century, Freddie Mac's mission has been a driving force of sound business principles and credit management leadership that have built on the strengths of the housing finance system. Through recent initiatives like Expanding Markets and Loan Prospector, the company is reaching out to more borrowers and revolutionizing the way Americans finance homes.

Working hand in hand with lenders, Freddie Mac will help shape the future of housing finance by continuing to:

- Provide a less costly, more accommodating system to simplify the mortgage lending process.
- Develop innovative products, programs, services and technology to help lenders compete more effectively in serving borrowers.
- Promote lending practices that accommodate the neighborhoods of a diverse America.

It is a process that will benefit the primary and secondary mortgage markets while making the dream of decent, accessible housing a reality for more Americans.

13

The Role of Conduits in the Nonconforming Mortgage Market

Bruce J. Paradis, President and CEO
General Motors Acceptance Corporation/Residential Funding Corporation (GMAC RFC)

A conduit is a company formed to purchase mortgages before repackaging and selling them as securities to investors. The process is accomplished by acquiring the loans individually or in bulk, underwriting the loans, aggregating them into pools, and selling securities collateralized by the loans. Between the time whole loans are delivered and the time they depart transformed into MBSs, they undergo a series of evaluations to ensure that they meet various compliance and quality control requirements.

Freddie Mac, the government-sponsored corporation whose products are covered in Chapter 12, was the first conduit. It provided private sector participants with the necessary conceptual framework to build conduits.

The Nonconforming Mortgage Market

The combined agency and nonconforming (jumbo) market has grown at an average annualized rate of approximately 20%, having peaked in 1993 along with the three-year refinancing boom. Since 1993, it has leveled off to pre-refinance boom levels. As shown in Figure 13-1, single family originations in 1996 are estimated at $720 billion dollars; jumbo production contributes approximately 20% of this volume, equating to an estimated $144 billion dollar market in 1996.

Conduits were designed to bring the same efficiencies to the nonconforming sector of the mortgage market that Freddie Mac and Fannie Mae bring to the conforming sector. Given the agencies' dominant positions in the conforming market, conduits had to uncover niches to create profitable opportunities in areas where the agencies were not operating, whether by choice or preclusion by law. The single largest category of residential loans the agencies could not purchase were those with unpaid principal balances exceeding their statutory limits. In 1972, when the agencies began purchasing conventional loans, the limit was $55,000; today, the ceiling changes annually. At the time of this writing, in 1996, the limit is $207,000.

Loans with amounts above this limit are referred to as nonconforming or *jumbos*. The jumbo market lacks the uniformity and liquidity of the conforming market, which is centralized and has access to subsidized funds.

Despite these inefficiencies, the conduits' market was at approximately $132 billion in 1995. In certain regions of the United States — such as along the east and west coast, for example — jumbos account for a majority of new originations. While a large percentage of these originations remain in portfolio as whole loans, a significant percentage are financed through private-label issuance, as Figure 13-2 shows.

FIGURE 13-1

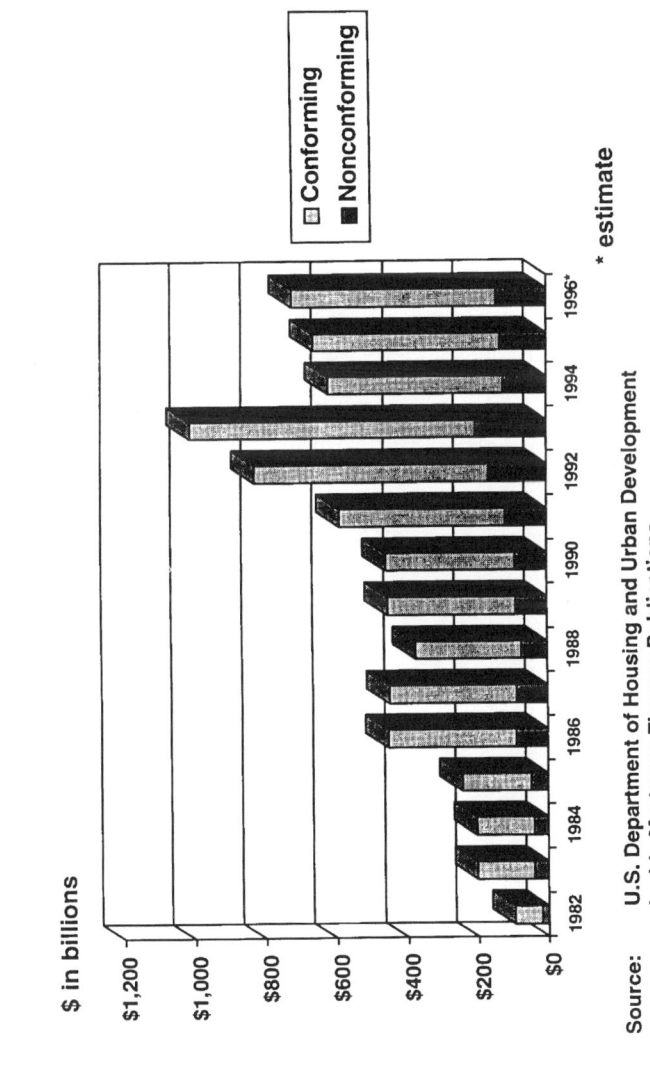

FIGURE 13-2

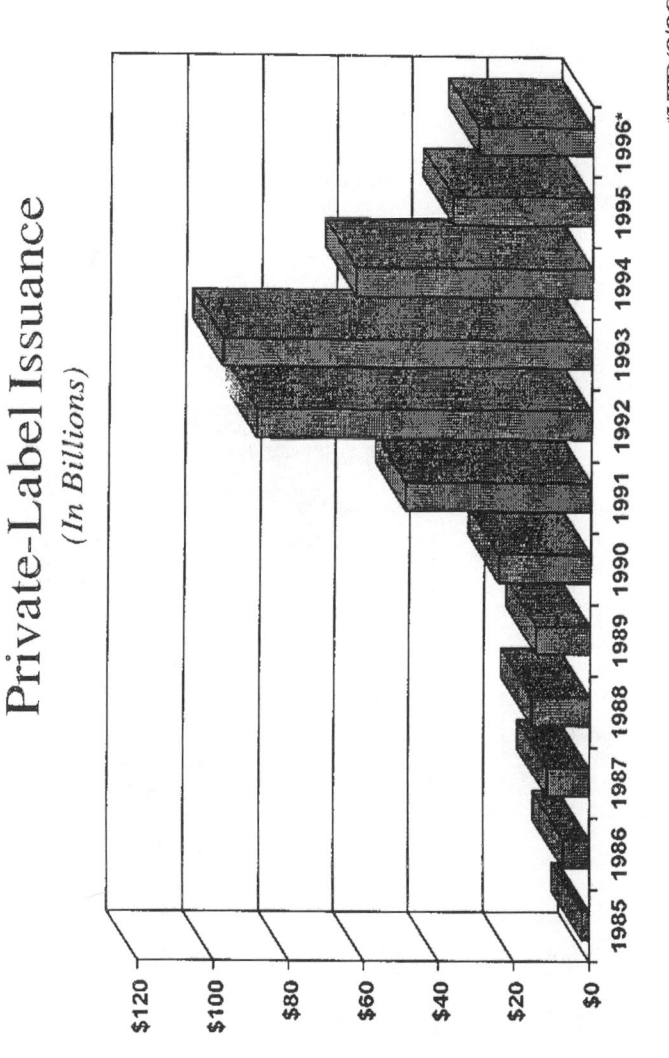

The public securities issued by whole loan issuers are generally rated in the highest rating categories by one or more of the following rating agencies:

- Standard and Poor's Ratings Service.
- Moody's Investors Service.
- Fitch Investors Service, L.P.
- Duff & Phelps Credit Rating Co.

Structures have included single class and multiclass, with credit enhancements provided by mortgage pool insurance, letters of credit, mortgage certificate (or bond) insurance and senior/subordinate structuring.

The Benefits of Conduits

Until conduits were established, mortgage bankers relied on private investors, mainly thrifts, to purchase jumbos. However, these buyers were notorious for tightening underwriting standards if interest rates exceeded the returns available in the immediate-delivery market. One of the causes of this was the lack of any standard underwriting. The conduits' appeal initially was based on their perceived impartiality and demonstrated consistency in underwriting, purchasing or funding.

Conduits offer benefits to home buyers, investors and lenders. For home buyers, the benefits may include lower interest rates, lower fees and greater choice among lenders. Several studies have shown that spreads between conforming and nonconforming mortgages narrowed considerably during the 1980s. Much of this improvement was due to the efficiencies the conduits brought to the market. Essentially, all of these benefits are due to the conduits' ability to attract capital from nontraditional investors, such as pension funds and insurance companies, who historically did not invest in one- to four-family residential mortgages.

Investors benefit from higher yields, maturity matching capabilities, safety and liquidity. Yields on AAA-rated pass-throughs generally trade from 25 bp to 50 bp above comparable Fannie Mae securities. Safety stems from solid legal structures, the nature of the collateral pool and the credit-support structure. Liquidity, which is reflected in narrow bid-to-ask spreads, is substantial in a market with a depth of over $190 billion, though it pales when compared to the liquidity found in the conforming sector.

For lenders, the rewards are larger origination and servicing fees and an opportunity to diversify product menus to generate more loans.

Early Conduits

Formation of the conduits in the late 1970s followed closely on the heels of the first mortgage securities issuances. *Securitization* — the process of converting whole loans into securities — merged the mortgage instrument into the capital markets. In essence, investors who would never have considered investing in whole loans were now potential buyers. The private mortgage insurance companies (MICs) were the conduit pioneers, especially Mortgage Guaranty Insurance Corporation (MGIC). In 1978, MGIC created Maggie Mae, the first private sector conduit. Maggie Mae was a "ready to go" company complete with documents, the requisite products, pool and special hazard insurance and custodial arrangements designed to link buyers and sellers. Within a year, several of MGIC's competitors, including PMI (Pennie Mae) and Verex (Verex MBS, Inc.), started conduits which were vehicles for the MICs to sell insurance.

Several developments affected the current market in the closing years of the 1970s. One was the recognition of a widening mortgage credit gap; demand was growing faster than supply. If lenders were going to meet the housing demands of the merging baby-boom generation, they had to find new sources of capital. Low delinquency and foreclosure rates painted a picture of the home mortgage as an AA credit. More geographically diverse, the default risks from well-underwritten pools of mortgages were minimal, especially in the inflationary environment that existed at that time.

By the 1980 recession, about a dozen conduits were operational. The MICs had been joined by trade association and state-sponsored conduits.

Second Generation Conduits

During the recession years, the conduits, like the mortgage market itself, coasted in low gear, as high interest rates kept consumer demand at bay. As the recession lifted in late 1982, Residential Funding Corporation (RFC) was born out of the existing conduits' inability to do two things:

1. Take or hedge the risks which existed between commitment issuance and final delivery of the security to the investor — typically 10 to 75 days.
2. Maintain a consistent market presence.

MIC conduits were neither risk averse, nor risk takers. Moreover, experience had demonstrated that a consistent market presence was necessary: A conduit needed to be in the market everyday, not monthly, quarterly or several times a year.

With Wall Street's financial expertise in place, the second generation of conduits stepped forth. RFC married the talents of Minneapolis-based Northwest Bancorp's mortgage subsidiary, Banco Mortgage, MGIC and Salomon Brothers. Each brought something to the table: Banco provided packaging, pooling, warehousing and servicing; MGIC brought insurance, third-party underwriting and marketing; Salomon underwrote and distributed the securities. RFC's introduction was received with fanfare by lenders seeking a consistent market for nonconforming mortgages.

Within one year, Sears Mortgage Securities Corporation (SMSC) was formed. Like RFC, SMSC combined the three elements necessary for a post-1982 conduit — insurance, back office and distribution. Within two years, Citicorp (CitiMae), General Electric (GEMSCO), Bear Stearns (BSMCC) and Shearson Lehman (SLMC) established conduits. Each followed a general formula and personalized it by staking claim to a specific market niche. For instance, SMSC initiated an expanded choice of products and commitment options; CitiMae pioneered the use of new credit enhancements; GEMSCO promoted the EQUAL, a 15-year graduated-payment mortgage; Bear Stearns marketed the use of negotiated transactions; Shearson Lehman moved to Newport Beach, California, and focused on developing intrastate business.

After 1983 — when the number of conduits increased annually — and before 1988 — when the number of conduits peaked, RFC was sold to Salomon Brothers. FCA Mortgage Securities were concurrently purchased and merged to create RFC.

During this five-year period, many conduits turned in fair to poor financial results. One reason for this was that thrift investors frequently undercut the market prices the conduits needed to sell securities. Another factor was the yield curve: Its steepness periodically made ARM pricing much more attractive to mortgagors. Thrifts, already laying the foundation for their later collapse, simply had too much money to invest.

New Credit Enhancements Evolve

Before the advent of conduit issued securities, credit-support systems were superfluous. Agency securities carried federal guarantees, while whole loan buyers, who understood credit risk and were comfortable managing mortgage credit risk, assumed it rather than sacrifice yield to offset the risk. However, investors in privately issued securities were unwilling to assume credit risk, so the protection of credit-enhancement structures was needed to add a layer of loss protection between themselves and the pool payments. If the payments proved insufficient to cover the pass-through, a third party stood ready to pay the security holder.

There are many ways to protect a mortgage pool from credit losses: pool insurance, subordination, letters of credit, corporate guarantees, surety bonds and hybrid combinations of these arrangements. Between 1983 and 1988, the conduits developed these new forms of credit enhancement. Alternatives to pool and special hazard insurance were needed because capital constraints in the mortgage insurance industry raised prices.

Pool Insurance

Pool insurance, which allows for regulatory and Generally Accepted Accounting Principles (GAAP) asset sales treatment for 100% of the pool, was the first form of credit enhancement used. Pool insurance covers credit losses other than those due to fraud, special hazard or borrower bankruptcy. A fixed percentage of the pool is insured, based on a rating agency's requirement, which is derived from a series of default simulations. The insurer covers losses up to the amount of the policy.

Pool insurance had four weaknesses: cost, underwriting stringency, excluded risks and exposure to third-party event risk. Because of these weaknesses, new, less costly forms of credit support were sought.

Subordination

The senior/subordinate structure continues to be the most popular form of credit enhancement. In this structure, a percentage of the pool is subordinated to a senior class. Any losses from the pool are generally taken by the holders of the subordinated position; holders of the senior securities are generally unaffected by losses unless the subordinated portion is exhausted. The senior/subordinate structure has two inherent advantages:

1. It can be used to cover all types of credit losses.
2. It is not subject to third-party event risk.

Subordination's main shortcoming is that regulated financial institutions, because of the risk-based capital rules, find it difficult to hold subordinate securities; unfortunately, these so-called "B pieces" are highly illiquid and very capital consumptive.

The previous were true of the late 80s to early 90s. Today, various credit grades of subordinate bonds are actively traded to pension funds and insurance companies. Many of these investors view these subordinate securities as cheap alternatives to corporate debt issues.

Letter of Credit

A third credit-enhancing structure is the letter of credit. Introduced by CitiMae, letters of credit require a highly-rated financial intermediary to provide a credit line that can be drawn upon to cover losses up to a specified maximum amount. Writers of letters of credit establish reimbursement agreements that are bonded by the issuer based on monthly allocations of excess servicing cash flows. Losses are reimbursed to the writer from the set-aside funds.

Letters of credit have four drawbacks:

1. They may create a lien on the issuer's excess servicing rights so they may not be capitalized for accounting purposes.
2. Excess servicing cash flows cannot be taken into income until the reimbursement account is fully pledged.
3. AA and AAA rated banks are increasingly difficult to find in the United States or abroad.
4. A credit downgrading of the bank subjects the investor to event risk.

Corporate Guarantees

Corporate guarantees, which may or may not be provided by the issuer, guarantee a fixed portion of the pool and losses to that amount are covered. Like letters of credit, these guarantees are subject to event risk and therefore have balance sheet implications.

Surety Bonds

Surety bonds provide a form of insurance on a portion of the pool. The issuer apprises the surety of the amount to be insured and the cost is incurred immediately.

The Middle Years — A Transition

To understand the factors affecting conduits during this period, the economic environment and changes in the thrift industry must be reviewed. Following 50 months of economic expansion, from January 1983 through March 1987, mortgage lenders produced the largest origination volumes in U.S. history. When interest rates began climbing in April 1987, origination activity slowed, and the market shifted from fixed-rate mortgages to ARMs.

Though to a lesser extent than several years earlier, ARM pricing undercut the conduits.

Another setback occurred several months later when the stock market crashed, setting off a prolonged period of declining revenue and income and sharp cutbacks throughout the investment banking business. Many mortgage finance departments were pared back, and several Wall Street-owned conduits were closed or sold. RFC was put up for sale by Salomon Brothers and subsequently sold to Anchor Savings Bank.

For the conduits, 1987 was a watershed year; thereafter, a consolidation phase began as the number of new conduits stopped growing and the number of existing ones declined. The consolidation began for several reasons:

1. Mortgage banking stopped being profitable.
2. Wall Street suffered a bond market plunge and a stock market crash.
3. Interest rates for fixed-rate jumbos rose to 11% or more, and the yield curve steepened.
4. Thrifts, especially those offering low introductory rate ARMs, briefly recaptured their dominant positions in the primary market.

In response to such changes, the conduits shifted gears. New programs, such as streamlined documentation, and new products, such as ARMs debuted. Limited documentation programs, in particular, generated ample additional volume.

Many conduits also shifted to targeted customer bases in the late 1980s. Since experience indicated that 80% of a conduit's volume came from 20% of its customers, the emphasis was directed toward developing a manageable list, usually 500 or less, and working closely with these customers. Pursuing too many correspondents was inefficient. Regional offices were established by RFC and others during this period, and account managers were hired to solidify relationships with customers.

Led by GEMSCO, a small number of conduits, including Ryland Acceptance Corporation (RAC), American Southwest and SE-CURNET redirected their activities to specialized mortgage securities transactions rather than offer purchase programs priced on a daily basis. These "execution conduits" offered sellers the option of either pledging mortgages as collateral for a securities issue or selling the loans. In this arrangement, the commitment amount became the mandatory delivery obligation of the seller on the day of the pricing. "Execution conduits" never caught on with sellers because the marketing and repackaging risks remained with the seller as they had with the early conduits.

Clearly the second-generation conduits proved superior to their predecessors in terms of structure and volume. However, only a few proved to be profitable enough to survive the competitive environment of the late 1980s. Lackluster profitability, reduced origination volume and cyclical markets explain the shrinkage.

The 1990s — Expansion, Consolidation, Differentiation

The cycle continues. As Figure 13-1 clearly illustrated, the residential mortgage originations market experienced unprecedented volume and growth in the early 1990s. As the plight of the savings and loan industry continued from the late 1980s, savings and loan institutions (S&Ls) lost significant market share. Mortgage bankers were in good position to take advantage of the S&Ls collapse, and their market share grew accordingly.

Demand for private-label MBSs kept pace with origination volume. In addition to the already existing conduits, such as Prudential and RFC, G.E. and Countrywide surfaced during the expansion phase, becoming prominent players in the jumbo market. Volumes peaked in 1993 when private label issuance exceeded $100 billion. Figure 13-3 shows the leading whole issuers in 1996.

In addition to increased volume, securities structures grew in complexity. Simple sequential-pay structures gave way to more complex securities structures. Cash flows were structured to include Planned Amortization Classes (PACs) and Targeted Amortization Classes (TACs). The subordinate bond in senior/subordinate structures gave way to more complex subordinate structures. The single subordinate "B" class transformed into a more complex structure including public mezzanine and private "B" classes.

As with all maturing markets, the jumbo market became increasingly efficient. In the 1990s, margins began to shrink. New entrants, in their quest for market share, put an additional squeeze on margins. Rational pricing, at times, disappeared. Competition and the drive for market share directed some participants toward strategies of playing capitalization games with servicing valuation. For these strategies to be successful, bets had to be made on prepayment speeds.

As was clearly demonstrated by the events in 1994, this strategy did not work for all participants. Due to high prepayment levels in 1993 and the subsequent major down turn in origination volume, many participants were consolidated or liquidated as a result of mounting losses. With plummeting origination volume, the market was once again burdened with overcapacity. Many firms that sprouted in the midst of the expansion cycle were victims of the contraction and consolidation phase.

While many originators and conduits have either been consolidated or closed, the market leaders have survived. Survivors have had to be innovative. While the overall primary origination market has rebounded, it has not returned to 1993 levels. The market has, however, expanded into several new markets and products.

The Role of Conduits in the Nonconforming Mortgage Market 331

FIGURE 13-3

Top Private Label MBS/CMO Issuers In 1996
(For 9 Months - Dollars in Millions)

Rank	Issuer	Volume
1	Residential Funding Corp.	$8,755.12
2	GE Capital Mortgage Srvc.	$4,335.37
3	Independent National Mortgage	$2,496.47
4	Merit Securities	$2,095.12
5	Norwest Asset Securities Corp.	$2,067.70
6	Prudential Home Mortgage	$1,950.52
7	Merrill Lynch Credit Corp.	$1,222.75
8	Donaldson Lufkin & Jenrette	$ 953.28
9	Salomon Brothers	$ 913.00
10	Bear Stearns Mtg. Sec. Corp.	$ 833.05
11	Countrywide (CWMBS)	$ 714.93
12	Structured Asset Securities Corp.	$ 642.71
13	PNC Mortgage Securities	$ 416.43
14	MorServ	$ 391.12
15	Capstead Capital Corp.	$ 322.62

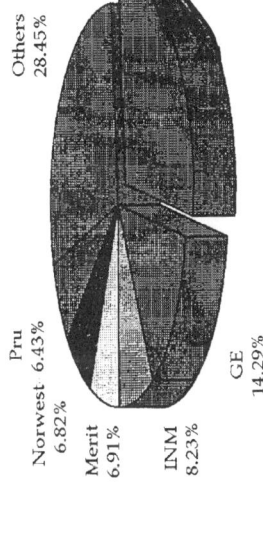

Third Quarter Market Share - 1996

Others 28.45%
Pru 6.43%
Norwest 6.82%
Merit 6.91%
INM 8.23%
GE 14.29%

Source: *Inside Mortgage Securities*; October 4, 1996

Product Differentiation

The secondary mortgage market was initially designed to satisfy the need for an efficient means of sourcing money. This led to the development of an intermediary process for investment quality loans, often referred to as "A" paper, considered to be backed by strong mortgage collateral and borrower quality.

In the last few years, demand for, and subsequently the supply of, consumer mortgage products has grown to include loans that span the credit curve and expand traditional property criteria. In most instances, these products are considered to hold more inherent risk than "A" paper or "conforming standards" mortgage products. Higher inherent risk results in higher required yields, and accordingly, borrowers pay a higher rate of interest to attract the interest of the investment community. Whole loan conduits who historically served primarily "A" paper have increased their focus on these markets. As an example, RFC — in addition to its long standing and primary "A" paper shelf, RFMSI, Inc. — recently registered the following complimentary shelves with the Securities & Exchange Commission (SEC):

- Residential Funding Mortgage Securities II, Inc. (RFMSII).
- Residential Accredit Loans, Inc. (RALI).
- Residential Asset Securities Corporation (RASC).

By creating shelves that parallel these product groups, RFC provides the investment community with the ability to differentiate and more accurately price the associated risk.

The Home Equity Sector

Just as investors have grown to understand and accept the secondary mortgage market through MBSs, the asset-backed securities

(ABS) market has also shown tremendous growth and acceptance by investors, as Figure 13-4 demonstrates. Home equity lines — residential mortgages by definition — are nonetheless grouped by the industry in the ABS category. The combined success of both markets in the past 10 years is illustrated in Figure 13-5, which shows combined issuances in excess of $100 Billion annually since 1991.

Figure 13-6 illustrates the steady and consistent growth of the home equity sector of the ABS market from $2.61 billion in 1989 to an estimated $25.02 billion in 1996. In 1994, RFC developed its Goal Line home equity line of credit program with the intent of tapping into this growing marketplace.

RFC, as an example, has developed home equity programs designed to leverage the loan purchase expertise and aggregation capability of RFC and to complement its traditional first mortgage product offerings. Through these programs, RFC purchases open-end revolving lines of credit (HELOCs) and closed-end, fixed rate loans (both fully amortizing and balloons). Any home equity loan is secured by a lien on the mortgaged premises that is subordinate to the lien securing the first mortgage loan.

RFC filed a $2 Billion shelf registration for RFMSII to serve as issuer for securities backed by home equity loans and lines of credit. The RFMSII shelf allows for both a REMIC structure and an owner's trust structure.

The "B and C" Mortgage Sector

The A/B/C mortgage market, commonly referred to as the "B and C" mortgage market, has emerged to facilitate the intermediation of residential mortgage paper that has characteristics which are not consistent with this historically defined A paper.

As an example, RFC has developed a program to purchase "B and C" paper. The program provides a vehicle for the purchase of

FIGURE 13-4

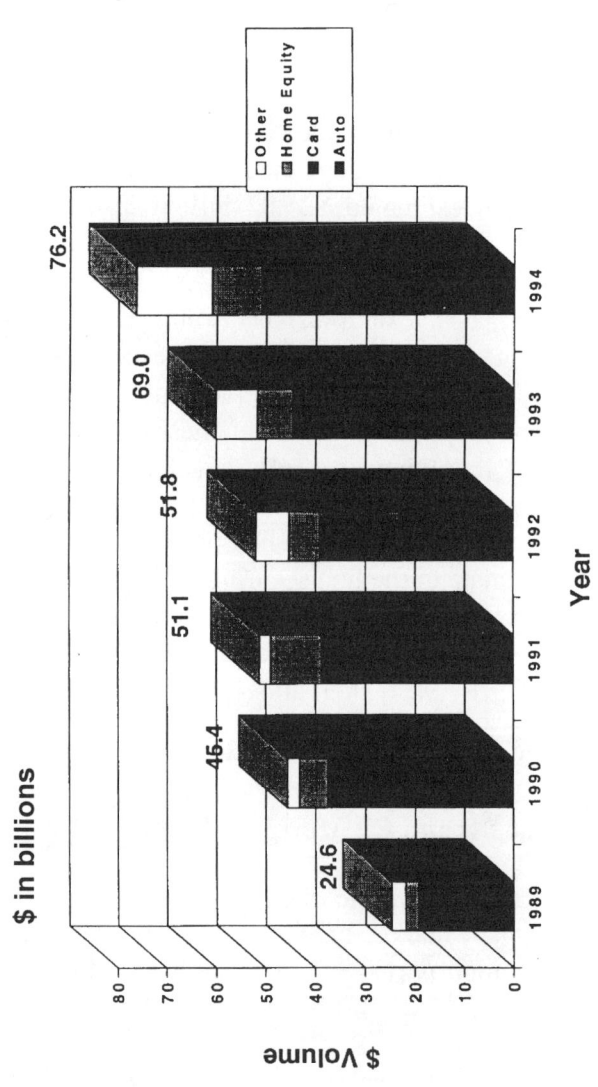

The Role of Conduits in the Nonconforming Mortgage Market 335

FIGURE 13-5

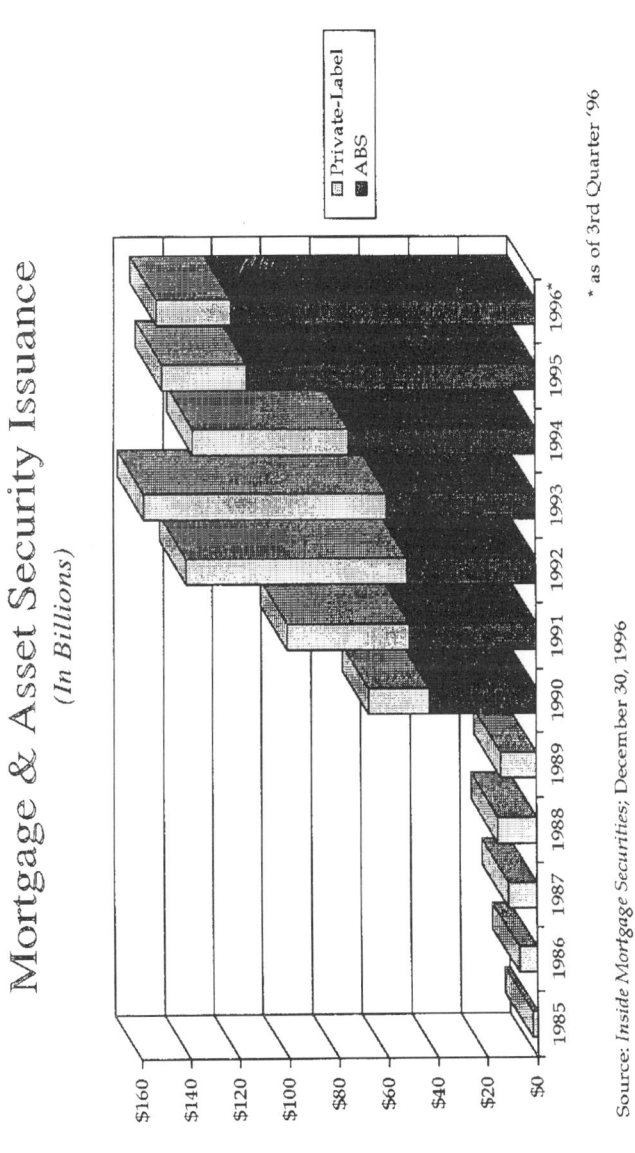

FIGURE 13-6

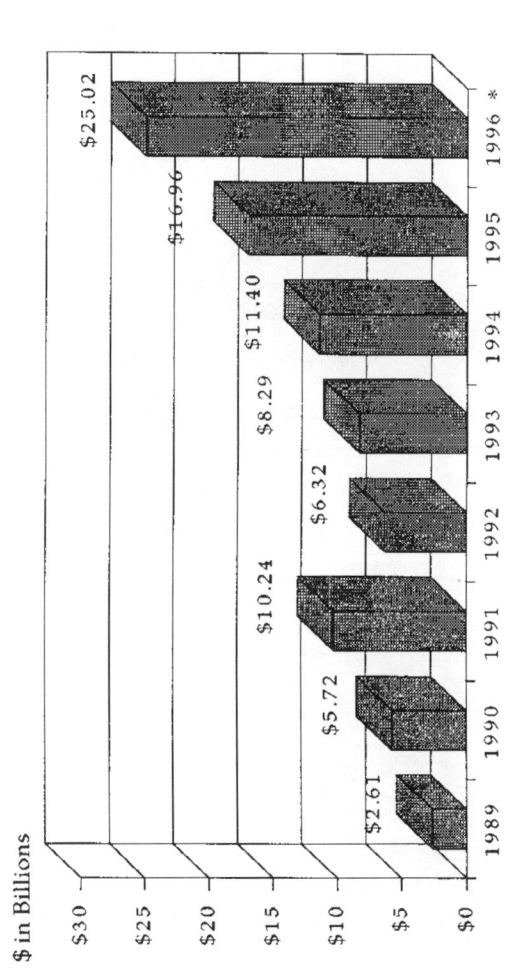

Home Equity Issuance

Source: *Inside Mortgage Securities;* October 11, 1996

a wide range of products, features and characteristics that expand and complement the realm of traditional conduit collateral. The program is designed to fully maximize the mortgage expertise and aggregation capacity of RFC. Products are distributed using an independent shelf, RASC, or through private placements.

"B and C" paper implies a credit standard oriented to the less-than-"A"-credit-quality borrower who has demonstrated a recovery in financial position. This may apply to first and second mortgages, as well as home equity loans. Specific credit and loan criteria detail the parameters for purchasing these loans, generally allowing for a poorer recent payment pattern on consumer, installment and mortgage debt, as well as higher income and debt ratios. This leniency is extended in exchange for a lower loan-to-value ratio.

The broad range of differences in acceptable program criteria published by competing aggregator/conduits, to a much greater degree than with historic agency-aligned product, requires the allowance for variances to published criteria. Rather than evolving to program standardization across all "B and C" conduits, this business will lead to a continued refinement of a "by feature" loan valuation method. This trend is evident from the extensive variation across the industry in prices for features such as LTV, loan size and occupancy type. A "by feature" evaluation method implies that the price for an individual loan would be constructed from a price matrix reflecting cash-flow attributes (fixed or adjustable, term, rate and margin where applicable) as well as the extensive variations of features such as LTV, occupancy, property type and loan size. This is in contrast to a bucketing method used for agency loans where an established price assumes a reasonably consistent mix of standardized credit and property type.

RFC has already begun building such a feature list of prices. It measures each loan's specific cash flow attributes against a matrix of credit enhancement cost factors derived from rating agency risk models, FICO scores and experiential models generated over time.

The "Expanded Feature" Mortgage Sector

An additional market — expanded feature — bridges the "A" paper and "B and C" paper markets. As discussed earlier, the "A" paper market encompasses "A" quality borrowers and mainstream mortgage product, and the "B and C" market supports the sub-credit market. In comparison, the "expanded feature" market supports paper that, from a credit perspective, parallels or surpasses "A" paper, but as a result of expanded collateral criteria does not conform to the traditional notion of "A" paper standards. This category of borrower is solid from a credit standpoint, yet the loan characteristics are different from prevailing secondary market standards. The need of these borrowers for financing creates an additional market.

As an example, RFC has developed a program to purchase "expanded feature" paper. The program provides a vehicle for the purchase of a wide range of products, features and characteristics that expand and compliment the realm of traditional conduit collateral. It is designed to fully maximize the mortgage expertise and aggregation capacity of RFC. This product is not considered for inclusion in securities issued through RFC's "A" paper shelf, RFMSI. Products are distributed using an independent shelf, RALI, or through private distributions.

The program balances a collateral standard incorporating expanded features with strict credit guidelines and additional underwriting considerations. This program expands on the features of the Core A Conduit program in such ways as:

- Non-Owner Occupied.
- Higher loan balances.

- Cash-out refinances on higher balance loans.
- Cash-out refinances on second homes and investor properties.
- Higher LTVs for a given loan balance.
- Alternative documentation instead of full documentation.

The Accredit Program offers both 30- and 15-year fixed-rate products, as well as 6-month LIBOR, 1-year CMT and hybrid ARMs.

Product Sources

Conduits have established networks of approved originators across the United States, made up primarily of mortgage bankers, S&Ls and other banking institutions. Usually, these originators are required to meet established approval criteria, including loan performance and servicing requirements. In many cases, originators are required to make certain representations and warranties. If a breach occurs, the seller may be required to repurchase the loan.

Product is generally purchased on a flow or bulk basis. If loans are sold on a flow basis, they generally meet the purchase guidelines set forth in predetermined guidelines. Conduits also purchase bulk packages that may have been originated based on other guidelines, however, because of compensating factors such as seasoning or strong net worth seller, are deemed acceptable.

RFC introduced its home equity line of credit products, "B and C" products and "expanded feature" products through its existing network of approved first mortgage originators. Many of these originators have established divisions to actively pursue this expansion of the nonconforming market.

An additional source for "B and C" paper are customers who are already established as originators of this product. Many are second mortgage and consumer finance providers that have expanded into the first mortgage business in response to market demand for refinancing precipitated by the decline in interest rates.

Evaluating a Conduit

To determine which conduit fits a seller's needs, seven areas must be evaluated:

- Product menu.
- Pricing.
- Back-office customer services (including underwriting, funding and servicing).
- Financial strength.
- Quality of management.
- Experience.
- Availability of complementary products and services.

A conduit that is utilitarian offers flexible programs and commitments to maximize the customer's competitiveness throughout the interest rate cycle. It is essential that the products offered, loan limits, LTVs, mortgage insurance requirements, property type, occupancy status, commitment options and so on are reviewed carefully. Numerous questions should be asked.

A comprehensive analysis of pricing should consider flexibility, consistency and aggressiveness. Flexibility is determined based on the range of rates purchased, whether loans are purchased at a premium and whether special pricing is available for nonstandard deals. Consistency means that pricing against a benchmark indicates a high correlation coefficient over many months. Aggressiveness is measured by comparing net yields on different products to ascertain if all — not just one or two — are attractively priced.

Evaluations of customer services, including underwriting and funding and servicing should consider consistency, flexibility and responsiveness. Consistency is evident if the same underwriting standards are applied over time. Flexibility demands a case-by-case approach to underwriting, since jumbos often involve self-employed borrowers and affluent individuals who prefer high payment-to-income ratios. Responsiveness is determined by the turnaround time required for underwriting and funding. Servicing considerations include such things as knowing the requirements for reporting and remittances, custodial accounts, prepayments and advances.

Financial strength, quality of management, experience, and the availability of complimentary products and services must also be examined when choosing a conduit. Sellers should evaluate each, considering what it indicates about the conduit. Financial strength implies staying power; management quality is reflected in knowledge of the business, accessibility, responsiveness and corporate financial results; experience provides a track record that can be used as a proxy for customer service; complimentary products and services, such as warehouse lending and contract underwriting, point to a desire to assist sellers and enhance their ability to generate business.

Evaluating a conduit takes time, skill and initiative, but the reward is a profitable, long-lasting relationship.

14

Selling Nonstandard Whole Loan Packages

Stephen Z. Hoff, Chairman & CEO
Brokers Commitment Corporation

Background

The growth in the market for nonstandard whole loan packages is a function of the success of the asset-backed securities market. Nonstandard whole loans, for the purpose of this chapter, will be defined as 1st and 2nd mortgage liens on property owned by borrowers with subprime credit. These loans are also referred to as B and C paper or equity-based loans.

It is estimated that securitization of this type of paper totaled over $13 Billion in 1995, an increase of about 34% over 1994. In the first half of 1996, over $40 Billion of B and C paper was originated, most of it being securities. Finance companies have been large issuers of this type of product, and as more of it comes to market, and as prepayment expectations accelerate because of falling interest rates, their spreads over treasuries widen. In this respect, they trade in a similar fashion to agency securities. The pools are credit enhanced to carry a triple A rating through the use of monoline insurance or senior/subordinated structures. B and C paper issuance continues to increase as deal sizes increase and new issuers enter the market. For example, one finance company brought a $1 billion dollar deal to market in late 1995. Although pools of nonconforming mortgage loans have been issued since the 1980s, the market for nonconforming credits did not take off until the early 1990s.

Because buyers of nonstandard whole loan packages have access to a broad and deep universe of securities investors, activity in this segment of the mortgage lending arena has been accelerating rapidly. Its rapid growth in the 1990s is also attributable to growing investor sophistication, technology and increased supply, some of which was caused by the activities of the Resolution Trust Corporation (RTC). Investors seeking higher spreads over treasuries have become familiar with nonconforming issuances. Because of technological innovations and the development and enhancement of data collection and retrieval services, investors better understand how these assets will perform over time. The great bond rally of the early 1990s resulted in an explosion of refinances in all segments of the market. The supply of MBSs had never been greater. The RTC's private-label securitizations increased investors' awareness and interest in the nonagency segment of the market.

Sellers of bulk packages of subprime loans are usually correspondents of commercial banks, mortgage conduits, insurance companies, Wall Street investment banks and consumer finance companies. Favorable accounting rules seem to give the latter a competitive advantage in the market place. Table 14-1 illustrates in simplified fashion how the accounting treatment works. Finance companies are able to manage their growth in earnings by the amount of paper they purchase and securitize in any given accounting period. The companies, upon issuance of the securities, can book most of the excess spread (which they

TABLE 14-1

Price Paid for Bulk	(108.00%)
Securities Price	106.00%
Net Loss	(2.00%)
Excess Yield Over Pass Through	2.50%
Cost to Service	0.50%
Net Excess Servicing	2.00%
Capitalized at 3x Multiple	6.00%
Net P&L Impact to Firm	4.00%*
	*6.00%
	- 2.00%
	4.00%

anticipate receiving over the life of the loan) as upfront income. In our example, what appears to be an overly generous dollar price of 108 generates accounting gains of four percent. To the extent that the loans pay off as anticipated, the accounting treatment makes sense. The appetite for B and C paper continues to grow, making more funds available to the credit impaired.

Consequently, the interest by lenders in this segment of the market has also grown. Many firms that were traditionally conforming lenders have entered the nonconforming market. They originate packages of nonstandard product, bid the packages out and deliver them to the highest payer.

Product Descriptions

Nonstandard loans come in many shapes and sizes. Programs exist for borrowers who have generally good credit but higher debt-to-income ratios than are acceptable to the agencies. There are also programs designed for people in bankruptcy and/or foreclosure. As one moves down the alphabet, the more important the appraisal becomes in connection with making a determination if the loan will be made. Table 14-2 gives a brief description of credit grades and some of the key underwriting variables.

It is important to focus on the underwriting parameters of the different credit grades. The B and C market can be divided into three segments and it is important to understand the types of loans and to what credits they are being made in order to maximize value when the bulk package is sold. The market is divided

TABLE 14-2
Selected Underwriting Parameters for Different Credit Grades

Credit Grade	Max LTV	Max DTI	Mortgage Lates Last 12 Mos.	Consumerr Credit Last 12 Mos.
A+	100%	42%	0x30	0x30
A	95%	42%	1x30	1x30
A-	90%	50%	2x30	0x60
B	85%	50%	6x30	5x30, 2x60, 1x90
B-	80%	50%	0x60	0x90
C	80%	55%	1x60	1 Continual 60 per account
C-	70%	60%	Not more than 120 days delinquent	Less than 60% of credit accounts derogatory
D	65%	60%	Current Action Allowable	Not a factor

generally along the lines of minimal credit impairment, severe impairment, and everything in between.

In addition to full-documentation programs, No Income Verification (NIV) programs, also called stated-income programs, are also available. These programs allow borrowers to qualify for a loan based on the income they state on the 1003. This is a popular product, especially for the self-employed. Available loan programs include 6-month LIBOR and 1-year Treasury ARMs, 2- and 3-year fixed-rate programs, as well as the usual 15- and 30-year fixed-rate products. The 2- and 3-year fixed-rate programs are particularly attractive because most borrowers believe that given that amount of time, they can put their credit problems behind them and refinance into a conforming program at a lower rate. These loans also offer an ARM feature after the initial fixed period.

Pricing and Delivery

Someone once said that mortgage lending, like baseball, is a simple activity: "You originate the loan; you sell the loan; you service the loan." In the segment of the market that deals with nonconforming credits, it's even simpler because most, if not all, of the bulk transactions are sold servicing released. This is a function of the unique character of the borrowers and the importance of rapid intervention when a payment is missed. The buyers of the loans feel that this specialized servicing expertise is critical to the ongoing well being of their investment. Investment bankers, rating agencies and monoline insurance companies also view servicing as a key element in ensuring the integrity of the securities.

Finance companies and mortgage specialists firms developed the market for providing credit-impaired borrowers with a source of financing. Before the advent of securitization, the loans were underwritten to the specifications of specialist portfolio lenders whose interest was investing in high-yield whole loans. Most of these institutions serviced their own portfolios.

The conduits, spurred by the declining A paper market, have built on the success of the pioneers and capitalized on the development of structured product grading by the rating agencies. Most of these conduits use contract subservicers. The servicer's performance is heavily considered by the rating agencies in assigning the bond's rating and credit enhancement levels. As originators are able to generate large volumes of production, become more comfortable with nonconforming credit profiles, and begin to recognize the long term revenue potential, more will retain ownership of the servicing.

The typical size of a bulk transaction is between $2,000,000 and $10,000,000. After the lenders have originated the loans, the question becomes: How do they maximize their market value? First, it is important to determine at which end of the credit spectrum the loans belong. As mentioned in the previous section, it is difficult to compare apples to apples unless the focus is on the credit criteria and not on whether a loan falls into a particular buyer's B program, for example. The credit grading parameters generally fall into three segments:

- Credits that just miss conforming guidelines.
- Credits that are severely damaged (that is, are in bankruptcy or foreclosure).
- Credits that are somewhere in between.

Most of the borrowers fall into the third category. It is essential to package the loans in a way that the buying firm is motivated to pay its best price. Usually this results from creating a group of loans with similar characteristics, targeting the buyers' particular appetite. For example, buyers interested in loans to severely damaged credits are few and far between. It would be counterproductive to put these loans in the same package with loans to borrowers that just missed agency guidelines. The buyer

Selling Nonstandard Whole Loan Packages

of agency turndown product usually won't even price the D credits. A firm specializing in D credits, on the other hand, would probably be delighted to bid on the "just missed" product, but probably at a price that would not maximize value to the seller. It is important to keep in mind that buyers of loan packages usually specialize, with most buyers focusing toward the A minus end of the spectrum.

Homogeneity is the key to a good execution. The closer the individual loan characteristics are clustered around the portfolio averages, the more desirable the package, all other things being equal.

Once the loans have been packaged by credit type, the loan information is put on a floppy disk and distributed to potential bidders. There is a minimum set of information that the buyers need to price the loans. Besides the credit grade, loan term and type, amortization and so on, the buyer will also want information that is unique to the nonconforming credit market. These additional pieces of information might include such things as how much equity remains in the property or whether the loan is a "Section 32." Section 32 disclosures have been required since October 1995. The disclosure, mandated by the Federal Reserve Board as an amendment to Regulation Z, provides the borrower with an additional cooling-off period prior to closing, places restrictions on prepayment penalties, and removes holder-in-due-course protections from assignees. A Section 32 mortgage is a high-priced, closed-end consumer credit instrument which is secured by the borrowers principal dwelling and for which the APR will exceed the yield on a comparable maturity Treasury by more than 10% or for which the total points and fees paid by the consumer at or before loan closing exceeds the greater of 8% of the loan amount or $400. Financing connected with the purchase of the borrower's principal residence is excluded from Section 32.

Needless to say, these and other pertinent characteristics need to be included in "the spread" to avoid a reprice during due diligence. The minimum set of characteristics is outlined in Table 14-3.

TABLE 14-3
Spreadsheet Data Files

MATURITY DATE	LOAN PURPOSE
TERM	SECTION 32
AMORTIZATION	LOAN NUMBER
DOCUMENTATION (FULL, LIMITED, OR STATED)	1ST PAYMENT DATE
FUNDING DATE	1ST ADJUSTMENT DATE
LIEN POSITION	NAME
PREPAYMENT PENALTY	LOAN AMOUNT
DEBT RATIO	LOAN TYPE
PROPERTY TYPE	STATE
START DATE	OCCUPANCY
CURRENT RATE	CREDIT GRADE
MARGIN	LTV
ESTIMATED MAX. RATE	ESTIMATED VALUE
COMBINED LTV	ADJUSTMENT CAPS

Based on the information provided on the spreadsheet, potential bidders will price the loans either on a loan-level basis or a weighted-average-coupon (WAC) basis. Loan-by-loan pricing is self explanatory.

WAC pricing is based on certain characteristics of the portfolio being within stated parameters and in many cases, can yield a better price overall. In other words, the package of loans will be priced on the weighted average characteristics of the portfolio rather than pricing each individual loan and coming up with an aggregate price. WAC pricing should result in a better execution in most instances. Figure 14-1 shows a sample letter of intent using WAC pricing.

The general methodology for pricing the loans is beyond the scope of this chapter but essentially it follows the methodology used for pricing assets with uncertain cash flows, while taking into account anticipated losses, prepayment exceptions, call protection, geographic and other diversification characteristics and uniformity of documentation standards and underwriting. It is worth repeating that the less dispersion of the characteristics of the individual loans around the mean characteristics of the overall portfolio, the better the price will be.

Subsequent to accepting a bid, the seller will either send the files to the purchaser, or the purchaser's due diligence team will visit the seller and perform the loan review on site. The due diligence team will be interested in ensuring that the files contain the required documentation as well as how the loans conform to the purchaser's definitions of the different credit grades. Underwriting nonconforming credits is more of an art than underwriting conforming credits. A conforming underwriter's job is to make sure no substandard credits make it to the agencies. A nonconforming underwriter, on the other hand, is interested in trying to fit a particular borrower into a credit grade and loan program to which the credit-impaired borrower "conforms." In the extreme case, where the borrower is in bankruptcy or foreclosure, the underwriter is really depending on the collateral, its market value, and the accuracy of the appraisal in making his or her underwriting decision. Additionally, the due diligence team will make sure that all necessary documents are in the loan file, all underwriting

FIGURE 14-1
Sample Letter of Intent

LETTER OF INTENT

In response to the Offer by _____, a _____ corporation ("Seller"), dated _____, to sell the Offered Loans described in the Loan Documents, XYZ Company (":Buyer"), hereby proposes to purchase the Loans in the Offered Loan Schedule other than the Excluded Loans listed on *Schedule A* attached hereto.

If this Response is accepted by Seller, the Bid Percentage for the Loans described in *Schedule 1* shall be ____ percent. The Purchase Price for the Loans will be calculated according to the formula set forth in the definition of that term.

This Response is being executed and delivered pursuant to the terms of the Loan Purchase Agreement dated as of _____ which is hereby incorporated herein by reference. Please indicate your acceptance of this Response and your agreement to execute the Bill of Sale with respect to the Loans on the Settlement Date by signing in the space provided and returning an executed copy of the Response to me.

1. COMMITMENT AMOUNT: $ _____

2. LOAN PRODUCT TYPE:
          FIXED
   A. LIEN POSITION: ____% 1ST
                            ____% 2ND
                            ____% OTHER
   B. CREDIT GRADE: ____% A
                            ____% B
                            ____% C
                            ____% D
   C. TERM: ____% 30 year
                            ____% 15 year
                            ____% 3 year
                            ____% adjustable

3. NOTE RATE/YIELD: Not greater than ____% or less than ____%.
The minimum gross WAC shall be no less the ____ percent. If the gross WAC of the finalized pool is less than ____%, an adjustment in price will be made utilizing the difference between the final gross WAC.

4. Buyer reserves the right to delete loans from this transaction in order to achieve the gross WAC stated herein. Seller may substitute loans pursuant to Section 16 of the commitment.

5.   OCCUPANCY: ____% Owner-Occupied Residences
                                ____% Secondary Residences
                                ____% Non-Owner Residences

6.   LOAN PURPOSES: ____% Purchase
                                ____% Rate/Term Refinance
                                ____% Cash-Out Refinance

7.   GEOGRAPHIC LOCATION:_____

XYZ Company
By: _____
Name: _____
Title: _____

Agreed and Accepted. Attached hereto as Schedule 1 is the Loan Schedule.

By: _____
Name: _____
Title: _____

conditions have been met and all collateral and legal documents have been properly executed.

Upon completion of due diligence, the shippers will prepare the bulk package for delivery. Any quality control issues required by the purchaser will be done prior to assembling the loan files in the manner requested by the buyer. Figure 14-2 shows a typical stacking order. Upon receipt of the loans, the purchaser will re-verify that all necessary documents are included in the file before consummating the transaction pursuant to the terms of the purchase and sale agreement. Usually the loans will be funded within 48 hours of receipt by purchaser.

Market Dynamics and Future Outlook

We expect to see the number of bulk sales of nonstandard loan packages increase over time. There are several reasons for this. For one, the securitization process brings ever increasing funds to a sector of the market that has traditionally looked to portfolio lenders for funding. Capital costs should decrease as the market becomes more efficient through greater economies of scale and the utilization of better methods of assessing risk. In theory, fewer bad loans will be made because securitization supplements the credit analysis of the originator with multiple "up stream" collateral reviews from conduits, rating agencies and providers of credit enhancement.

The future looks bright in terms of attaining greater operational efficiencies as well. More firms will specialize in the origination of nonstandard product and will probably leave the servicing and securitization to those having specialized expertise. As sellers of bulk packages of B and C paper become more adept at underwriting and originating for firms whose best skills are loan servicing and securities placement, we should see a displacement of

FIGURE 14-2
Documents in Funding File

LEFT SIDE OF THE FILE	RIGHT SIDE OF THE FILE
NOTE & SECURITY INSTRUMENT	Wire Instructions
Original Note & Applicable Riders	**APPLICATIONS**
Allonge*	Typed Fannie Mae Form 1008
1 Certified copy of the Security Instrument (Deed of Trust or Mortgage, including all riders & legal)	Typed, signed Final Fannie Mae Form 1003 Application or original, signed, handwritten Fannie Mae Form 1003 Application
Affidavit of Recording	**CREDIT**
Intervening Assignment(s)*	Credit Report(s)
TITLE	Verification(s) of Mortgage/Rent or Canceled Checks for 12 months of Payments
Preliminary Title Report/Title Commitment	Credit Explanation Letter*
Final Title Policy	Copy of Senior Lien Note(s)*
Escrow/Closing Instructions	Complete Divorce Decree/Separation Papers*
Purchase Contract (if purchase money loan)	Complete Bankruptcy Documentation*
INSURANCE	**INCOME**
Hazard Insurance Documents	Verification(s) of Employment
Flood Determination Certificate	Most Recent Paycheck Stubs
Flood Hazard Disclosure Notice	W-2(s)
Flood Insurance Policy or Binder/Application	1040(s)
Proof of Payment of Premium of Binder/Application	Verbal Verification of Employment (by Seller, prior to funding
Tax Service Contract	Profit & Loss Statements*
Loan Sales Letter (Loss Payee Letter	Rental Agreement(s)*
DISCLOSURES & NOTICES	Personal Bank Statements
Final HUD-1 Settlement Statement	**ASSETS**
Final Good Faith Estimate (Regulation Z)	Verification(s) of Deposit*
Truth in Lending Act Disclosures	Gift Letter/Source Letter*
Mortgage Servicing Disclosure	Appraisal Review
Variable Rate Loan Disclosure*	Appraisal Review Rebuttals*
Equal Credit Opportunity Act Notice	**PROPERTY**
Fair Lending Notice	Original Appraisal, with All Attachments
Compliance Agreement	(Photo Page, etc.)
State & Local Disclosures*	Property Certifications/Reports (Pest,
Notice of Right to Cancel (Recession Notice)	Clearance, Well, Septic, Roof *)
Signature Certifications (Name Affidavits)	Miscellaneous Documents
W-9 Form(s)	
4506 Form	
Transfer of Servicing Letter (Good-Bye Letter)	
Non-Impound/Escrow Notice	
Borrower's Certificate of Authorization	
Notice of Transfer	
Lender's Instructions	
Section 32 Disclosure	

originators with less expertise and a reduction in unit operating costs by those firms who do it best.

The traditional lenders to the credit impaired will be subject to increased competition from conforming lenders eager to exploit the opportunity to replace revenue lost from the slowdown in refinancing activity. More conforming lenders are entering the market as more outlets for subprime paper are developed by Wall Street. Some traditional home equity lenders are reigning in their operations as they find it difficult to compete with the new wholesale-based firms who depend on brokers — and not brick and mortar — for their loan volume. As prospects for the wholesale firms improve, we expect to see larger sums of money being made available to those who traditionally have been excluded from access to mortgage credit.

15

The Secondary Market for Mortgage Servicing Rights

Stephen Z. Hoff, Chairman and CEO
Brokers Committment Corporation

Historical Overview

The secondary market for mortgage servicing has changed dramatically since its inception in the early 1980s. The servicing process involves the collections, record keeping, remittances, late fee payments, foreclosure procedures and other functions necessary to maintain the integrity of the loan until it is fully paid. When spoken of as an asset, *mortgage servicing* refers to the contractual right to perform these functions, collect servicing fees and derive other benefits for doing so. Loan servicing is created when a loan is sold and is recognized as the primary component of value for most mortgage lenders. Once servicing is separated from a loan, it is treated like any other financial asset and may be sold individually or as a part of a portfolio of servicing rights.

The principal balance of all single-family mortgages in the United States exceeds $3.8 trillion, and for every mortgage loan, servicing exists or has the potential to be created. The gross amount of new mortgage debt added each year is over $600 billion. The net addition after accounting for prepayment of existing mortgages is $200 to $300 billion. Table 15-1 shows the servicing volume for each year from 1990 to 1995.

The government agencies — Fannie Mae, Freddie Mac and Ginnie Mae — dominate the secondary mortgage market and have established standards that most participants in the mortgage market must meet. By doing so, these agencies have fostered a servicing marketplace that is dependent upon the interchangeability of servicing portfolios among mortgagees.

The price of servicing has continued to rise since the early 1980s because of a number of changes in the way loans are serviced and because of structural changes in the marketplace itself. Inflation, for example, has caused a tremendous increase in average loan balances and a corresponding increase in servicing

TABLE 15-1
One- to Four-Family Mortgage Servicing Volume Outstanding (in Millions)

Year	Ginnie Mae	Fannie Mae	Freddie Mac	Total
1990	$401,278	$385,517	$308,369	$1,095,164
1991	$425,241	$463,054	$351,906	$1,240,201
1992	$419,516	$559,995	$432,557	$1,412,068
1993	$414,066	$638,114	$487,423	$1,539,603
1994	$450,934	$682,923	$527,187	$1,661,044
1995	$475,000	$737,846	$559,804	$1,772,650

fee income. This, coupled with more sophisticated valuation techniques, resulted in a bull market for servicing rights which lasted until 1989, the year the Financial Institutions Reform and Recovery Act (FIRREA) was introduced. FIRREA slowed the market because it restricted the amount of purchased mortgage servicing rights that could be counted toward regulatory capital requirements.

Mortgage servicing rights can be acquired through bulk purchases, on a loan-by-loan basis (sometimes called concurrent transfer), through the purchase of another company's stock or through the normal course of the origination process when loans are sold but servicing is retained. Servicing sales have supported a variety of purposes, such as portfolio restructuring, income recognition and cash generation for operations. No matter what the acquisition technique or purpose of the sale, the valuation methodology is the same. The evaluator will present-value any incremental benefit over the cost to service the portfolio during its expected life. Until 1992, there had been a trend toward more bulk purchases and less originations, although the heavy refinance activity in 1993 reversed the trend temporarily.

Market growth has tracked the increase in origination volume over the last 10 years. For example, in 1982, origination volume was about $100 billion; by 1993, it had increased to about $1 trillion. Over this same time period, the volume of servicing transactions increased to around $250 billion per annum from about $20 billion in 1982. The market for mortgage servicing rights grew as more mortgage bankers and other participants in the mortgage lending arena developed the need to be able to liquify one of their principal assets — their servicing portfolio.

The value of servicing rights depends upon how much servicing fee income exceeds the servicer's projected loan administration costs. As servicing costs decreased due to automation, attainment of scale economies in data processing applications and improvements in cash management techniques, servicers were able to capture more value from their portfolios. As value increased, the number of transactions increased. At the same time, more participants began to realize the advantages of scale economies associated with larger and larger servicing operations. Buyers were willing to pay more, and sellers were willing to sell more at a higher price. In 1984, for example, an estimated $80 billion in mortgage servicing rights changed hands. At that time, the price for Ginnie Mae servicing exceeded 250 bp of the unpaid principal balance (UPB). By 1986, sales volume had increased to around $100 billion and more firms were beginning to view both the purchase and sale of servicing rights as a standard part of their operations.

Early on in its evolution, the market was dominated by financial institutions such as banks and thrifts or their mortgage subsidiaries. In the early 1980s, a large mortgage servicer was considered to be one that serviced between $600 million and $1.5 billion worth of loans. The megaservicers in those days, by contrast, were those that had portfolios of between $2 billion and $8.5 billion of unpaid principal balance. Today, the megaservicers are considered to be those who service $100 billion or more.

In 1986, we saw the advent of smaller blocks of servicing being traded — those in the range of $20 to $30 million. At the time, the market experienced increased liquidity and increased pricing, especially given current production. The 1980s also saw the production of computerized servicing valuation models which tended to standardize the pricing process. Toward the end of the decade, more firms became comfortable with not only valuing servicing, but also buying and selling it. At the end of the decade, the trading in servicing portfolios reached about $250 billion. In 1995, about $220 billion worth of servicing rights changed hands.

The 1980s also saw a rapid growth in the market share of thrifts holding servicing portfolios. Thrift involvement started to decline at the end of the decade because of the savings and loan crisis and its concomitant regulatory changes. The S&Ls were

The Secondary Market For Mortgage Servicing Rights 361

effectively taken out of the market as buyers of servicing rights in 1989, when FIRREA was introduced. The market share for thrifts peaked in 1987 at about 30% of all loans serviced and declined to about 20% by 1989. As of early 1996, the latest round of regulations regarding restrictions on purchased mortgage servicing were embodied in the Federal Reserve rule issued late in 1992. The Fed allows the inclusion of purchased servicing if the amount does not exceed 50% of tier 1 capital.

After the passage of FIRREA, many insolvent institutions were taken over by the RTC, and as a consequence, the RTC was responsible for servicing upwards of $200 billion worth of mortgages. Because of these and other regulations affecting depository institutions, fewer thrifts are pursuing the strategic option of growing their servicing portfolios. Many commercial banks, on the other hand, increased their presence in the mortgage industry by stepping up the pace of mortgage originations and/or building large servicing portfolios through acquisition. One consequence of FIRREA and RTC sales activities with respect to loan servicing rights was the entry into the market of outside investors seeking to capture the generous yields associated with owning servicing. During 1990, which was one of the worst years for sellers of servicing, yields on high quality servicing portfolios approached 20 percent. Prices for Ginnie Mae portfolios, which two years prior had been sold for 250 bp, had dropped to 150 bp. High quality, conventional, conforming product, which had commanded prices as high as six times servicing fee, had dropped to four times servicing fee during 1990. Outside investors took advantage of this and ended up buying mortgage entities, mostly from the RTC. For sale at the time were servicing platforms with portfolios ranging in size from $500 million to $10 billion in unpaid principal balance.

By 1991, prices had started to recover, and during January of 1992, the market saw a 20% increase over the previous year's pricing. Supply and demand had a lot to do with the increase in the value of servicing portfolios. Later in 1992 and in 1993, the focus of the industry changed to loan originations and the secondary market for servicing rights languished as buyers became reluctant to pay high premiums for existing portfolios that were rapidly prepaying as interest rates fell. The refinance boom was in full swing and mortgage bankers replenished their portfolios through their retail, wholesale and correspondent origination activities.

As of this writing (early 1996), the market had almost totally recovered, with the exception of Ginnie Mae servicing and recourse servicing. For example, conventional, conforming, nonrecourse, 30-year fixed-rate product is selling for close to six times service fee, while Ginnie Mae portfolios are selling for around 200 bp. The fact that Ginnie Mae portfolios have not recovered as much as conventional product is a function of the recourse risk associated with the VA's No-Bid policy. This was not evident in the early 1980s when servicing was trading at 250 bp.

Servicing prices for newly minted loans are meeting or exceeding historic highs as industry consolidation continues and large efficient servicers are building their scale economies into flow transaction prices. For the first time in industry history, a single entity has been able to break the 5% market share barrier. The top 30 firms in the industry service almost $1.5 trillion — about 42% of all residential loans serviced. The end to the consolidation is nowhere in sight.

Why has the secondary market for mortgage servicing grown so much since the early 1980s? On a cash basis, the origination business is marginally profitable, but on a value-created basis, it is quite profitable. Origination creates servicing that is valuable either as an asset which produces income over the life of the loan or as a financial asset which be can sold for the present value of its expected cash flows. As stated earlier, to the extent that servicing revenues exceed costs, companies will want to own servicing. As average loan size grows and technological advances make the servicing process less costly, prices will increase.

The real question is: Does it make more sense to produce servicing or to buy it? Depending on the level of origination activity, it may be possible to purchase servicing for approximately the same cost as its origination. During periods of heavy origination activity, acquiring servicing through production of loans is a more cost-effective alternative. Those who entered the industry by buying servicing platforms and operated solely as servicers are reevaluating their strategies. Market participants have come to realize that servicing can no longer be put into portfolios and ignored. Like other assets, servicing must be managed, especially during periods of rapidly declining interest rates.

FASB Statement 65 has been amended, changing accounting standards for servicing. FASB Statement 122 allows, among other things, the capitalization of originated, as well as purchased, servicing rights. FASB Statement 122 states: "When a mortgage banking enterprise purchases or originates mortgage loans, the cost of acquiring those loans includes the cost of the related servicing rights."

If the originator retains the servicing, it can allocate to the servicing rights that portion of the total which represents the relative fair value of those rights. In terms of measuring impairment, the new FASB statement calls for a disaggregated method "based on one or more predominant risk characteristics of the underlying loans." Essentially, the firm is required to adjust the value of the rights to the lower of cost or market.

Valuation

Valuing servicing is part art and part science, since servicing has no explicit principal repayment, no coupon and no precise term.

It is up to the analyst to decide on the appropriate assumptions to use in modeling the cash flows.

In simplest terms, the value of a loan servicing portfolio is equal to the present discounted value of the after-tax cash flows generated by a portfolio over its expected life, less operating expenses and adjusted for prepayments. While this may appear to be a scientific methodology, the valuation process can evolve into a somewhat subjective process as a result of the assumptions and expectations that a firm has for a particular portfolio. Unlike some fixed-income securities, servicing is a dynamic asset with many fluctuating variables. As a result, the ultimate determination of the value of a loan servicing portfolio often rests on assumptions made about future economic conditions.

While there are several types of values that can be assigned to a portfolio (for instance, economic value or market value), the fair market value is the most widely used method. FASB Statement 122 defines it as the "amount at which the asset could be bought or sold in a current transaction between willing parties, that is other than a forced sale or liquidation." Additionally, the types of representations and warranties that a seller is willing and able to offer has a significant effect on the value of a portfolio. If a seller is unable to provide representations and warranties that reflect industry standards or close approximations thereof, the market value of the portfolio will probably decrease.

The value of servicing rights is a function of the actual characteristics of a particular portfolio (such as UPB, WAC or weighted average service fee), certain forecasted variables (such as payoff rate, future delinquency and foreclosure figures) and the impact that these components have on one another over time. To a large degree, the value depends on a firm's ability to maximize income through the best use of its resources and accurately project it's operating costs. In other words, beauty is in the eyes of the beholder, and the market value of a portfolio is the highest price that any particular buyer is willing to pay at any given time.

Valuation Methodology
The first step in the assessment of a portfolio's value is the stratification of a portfolio into homogeneous segments based on predominant characteristics such as loan type, term and note rate. This exercise provides the groundwork needed to proceed with the remainder of the valuation process. Once a portfolio is segmented into homogeneous groups, it is easy to see its effect on value. For example, a portfolio of 10,000 loans with a WAC of 8.25% is valued on the basis of a single calculation using the averages of the different segments. The result is a price of 1.11% using a 10% pretax discount rate, a unit servicing cost of $50 per loan and payoff assumption based on the aggregate note rate. The same portfolio, when segmented by note rate, has a value of 1.16% or a difference of about 4.5 percent.

Industry standards do not exist for portfolio stratification but some of the more typical subsets are investor, coupon, loan type, geographic location and original term. Additionally, segmenting loans by remittance cycle is necessary in order to obtain meaningful results. For example, if Freddie Mac ARC were not separated and valued differently from Freddie Mac regular remittance, the float on principal and interest would be overestimated, as would the overall value of the portfolio.

A carefully stratified portfolio is the basis from which to assess the effect of other components on value. The essential components of a valuation include projecting income, expenses, and prepayments; then, the after-tax cash flows are discounted to arrive at the net present value.

Components of Income

The most important elements of income in a servicing valuation are service fee, principal and interest float, escrow earnings and ancillary or other income. The relative importance of these elements changes over time due to the changing characteristics of the portfolio.

Service Fee

The service fee is usually the major contributor to a portfolio's value. It represents the difference between the coupon and the investor yield less any guarantee fee. Single family service fees typically range from 0.25% to 0.44% depending on the investor and the loan type. Early in a portfolio's life, the service fees contribute greatly to value because they are directly related to the unpaid principal balance. As the principal balances decline, so does the service fee income. Additionally, change occurs through the prepayment of higher coupon loans which often carry higher service fees. Accurately reflecting the runoff and the loss of income associated with these loans is essential to a valuation. When portfolios are traded, the bids are often expressed as a multiple of the service fee. This clearly illustrates the importance of the service fee on the value of a portfolio. The multiple is loosely interpreted by market participants as the number of years that the buyer needs to derive income from the portfolio before her purchase price is recouped.

P&I Interest Float and Interest Earnings on Escrow

The float earned on principal and interest (P&I) received each month depends, to a great extent, on the size of the balances and the number of days that the servicer has those funds available for investment purposes. The number of float days may range from 1 to 20 days. Although the number of float days appears to be static, the actual float can be reduced as a result of slow payments or delinquent payments. A servicer can be further penalized by late payments or prepayments if the servicer is obligated to advance the uncollected principal and/or interest to the investor. Factoring in the loss of interest income is important to the servicing valuation.

Along with the principal and interest portion of the payment, a mortgagor is more often than not required to contribute to an account established for taxes and insurance (T&I). The value of the funds held by the servicer will vary depending on the frequency of tax payments, the average balance of the account and the expected annual return on balances. While T&I balances often are assumed to have a longer float period, and since escrow balances usually grow as a portfolio ages because of tax increases, T&I balances can continue to contribute to portfolio value as all other income components appear to be declining.

A loss of value occurs when interest on escrows must be paid to the mortgagor. As of early 1996, interest on escrow is regulated by the individual states (See Table 15-2). However, federal legislation has been proposed that would require the payment of a fixed amount of interest to all mortgagors. If the legislation is passed, the value of the T&I interest component will decrease. To the extent that a servicer derives a great deal of value from escrows, the passage of a national interest-on-escrow law would have a materially adverse impact on the value of servicing. For example, Table 15-3 shows the impact on a hypothetical portfolio; there is a 25% deterioration in value.

Ancillary and Other Income

This category of income refers to late fees, assumption fees, optional insurance fees and prepayment penalties. Of these, late charges are the most significant. They contribute approximately 5% of the income on an average Ginnie Mae portfolio, for

TABLE 15-2
States Requiring Interest on Escrow

State	Interest Rate (%)
California	2.00
Connecticut	5.25
Iowa	5.50
Maine	3.00
Maryland	5.50
Massachusetts	2.00
Minnesota	5.00
New Hampshire	5.00
New York	2.00
Oregon	4.50
Rhode Island	4.00
Utah	5.25
Vermont	5.00
Wisconsin	5.25

example. This category can contribute significantly to value if pursued. It is important to keep in mind, however, that income earned through late fees does not replace the income lost as a result of lost float on P&I or T&I advances. Also, the benefit of late fee income can be partially offset by the increased cost to service delinquent accounts.

In other words, late fees, assumption fees, optional insurance and prepayment penalties can add value if the servicer makes an effort to either collect what is due or cross-sell other financial products to mortgagors. Lately, this component of value, which one market observer has called the "consumer relationship portion of servicing," has been driving market values to new highs. This perceived incremental value is based on the perception that the holder of the servicing rights has the ability to engage the mortgagor in additional, non-mortgage-related relationships,

TABLE 15-3
Hypothetical Portfolio (Base Case)

Balance	$1 Billion
Number of Loans	10,000
Mortgage Type	Conventional
Average Loan	$100,000
Note Rate	8.25%
Original Term	360
Remaining Term	336
Service Fee	0.25%
Service Cost/Loan	$50/year
Average Escrow	1.00%
No Interest on Escrow	
Delinquencies	3.00%
Foreclosures	0.75%
Amortization	12 Year Sum-of-the-Year's-Digits

such as checking accounts, consumer loans, credit cards and investment accounts.

Certainly, commercial banks and other depository institutions have the product mix to execute this strategy. The question becomes: Do they have the marketing savvy to pull it off? They obviously believe they do. Commercial banks have been aggressive accumulators of servicing rights. The value of this ability to cross-sell the mortgagor can be worth as much as $250 per loan.

Components of Expense

The elements of income will not be realized to their fullest extent if expenses are not kept in check. That is to say, the income earned from service fees and float and ancillary fees can be quickly eroded if the costs related to servicing the portfolio are not controlled. As a portfolio ages, service fee income is reduced. Therefore, if the expenses are not reduced proportionately or if economies of scale are not achieved, the market value of a portfolio could well exceed its economic value to the holder. This means that the unit cost used by a potential acquirer of a portfolio would be less than the actual cost of the present owner. Therefore, all other things being equal, the portfolio would be of greater value to the potential buyer.

Servicing Costs

Servicing cost essentially reflects the direct unit cost associated with servicing a loan excluding amortization and foreclosure expense. Historic servicing costs have been made available and appear to be relatively good indicators of what it costs to service a loan. Currently, the figures range from $50 to $70 per loan per year for a conventional fixed-rate loan and $65 to $85 for an ARM, although some servicers report that it costs them no more to service an ARM than it does a fixed-rate loan. Bidders on servicing may use unit costs less than these numbers to reflect their perception of scale economics attainable through acquisition, with the concomitant reduction in excess capacity that may exist at the time of the acquisition. Commercial and multifamily loan servicing costs range from $750 to $1,000 per loan and, depending on the investors servicing requirements, could even be in excess of $1,000 per loan. The unit cost used in the valuation should be adjusted for the impact of inflation. The aggregate single-family unit cost is distributed across the functional areas as follows:

- Customer service: 25%.
- Collections and foreclosures (excluding REO losses): 25%.

- Payment processing and billing: 20%.
- Administration: 15%.
- Data processing: 12%.
- Document filing and record retention: 3%.

To the extent that a purchaser's overall portfolio changes with respect to loan type, increased delinquencies or geographic diversification as a result of an acquisition, the purchaser will likely experience an increase in costs related to servicing. For example, it costs about 10 times as much to service a loan that is 90 days delinquent than it does to service a current loan. These sometimes not so subtle changes, if ignored, can add to a servicer's expenses. The ability to recognize the factors that lead to increased expenses is the key to maintaining costs and effectively forecasting expenses over the long term. The prospect of increased servicing costs over time looms large as the national and state governments pass legislation that will not only increase actual costs associated with servicing loans, but also will impose additional costs associated with compliance.

Foreclosure Costs

Foreclosure costs are driven by foreclosure rates, which in turn are driven by defaults. Default activity is closely related to the amount of equity borrowers have in their homes. If the equity in the house drops below its market value, there is a strong incentive to mail in the keys to the investor. As a rule, default rates are tied to the age of the loan. For example, default rates on conventional loans reach their peak in years three and four.

Foreclosure expenses are directly proportional to the foreclosure percentage and directly related to who bears the exposure in the event of default. For instance, loans sold "with recourse" require that the servicer retain the collateral risk, while loans sold on a nonrecourse basis transfer all credit risk to the investor.

These two types of portfolios should be valued separately, utilizing an arbitrage pricing methodology for the recourse segment or a substantial increase in the foreclosure cost estimate for the recourse loans.

Another reason for foreclosure cost variance occurs with loans that have a higher frequency of default. FHA and VA loans, largely as a result of less equity contributed by the borrower, often default at a higher rate than conventional loans. This higher frequency and the servicer's exposure to VA No-Bids puts these two product types in a higher foreclosure cost category. The cost assumption also increases as a result of higher administrative expenses associated with FHA and VA loan defaults.

Foreclosure costs are part and parcel of servicing and are not likely to be avoided. Most servicers have the ability to forecast foreclosures to a certain extent, and if foreclosure efforts are well managed, foreclosure losses can be kept to a minimum.

Amortization

The more accelerated the amortization, all other things being equal, the higher the net present value of the portfolio. FASB Technical Bulletin 87-3 provides, among other things, guidance on accounting for mortgage servicing rights. While amortization is a noncash expense, it does have an effect on the economic value of the portfolio. The amortization expense is a function of the length of the amortization period and the amortization method (sum-of-the-year's-digits or straight-line, for example) that is used.

The straight-line amortization method required for tax purposes has no relation to the economic life of most servicing assets. For tax purposes, servicing is usually amortized over nine years using a straight-line method. If the acquirer purchases substantially all of the assets of a business for book purposes, the servicing may be amortized over 15 years, using the straight-line method. Mortgage servicing rights are amortized in proportion to, and over the period of, estimated net servicing income.

Other Costs
Loan set-up costs and interest on escrows are examples of some of the other expenses incurred by a servicer. If economies of scale are achieved, these expenses can be absorbed with little effect on the servicer's bottom line. They, too, require oversight and management in order to keep them in check.

Computing the Net Present Value

Once the income and expense elements have been forecasted, the after-tax cash flows are computed by adding the amortization expense to the net after-tax income. The after-tax cash flows are then discounted at a desired yield to arrive at the net present value or purchase price. The purchase price for servicing is usually quoted as percentage of the UPB.

Discount Rate
Any discussion of discount rates needs to begin by saying that servicing yields are, to a large degree, a function of supply and demand. For example, the number of portfolios on the market is at a much more manageable level than at the height of RTC activity in 1990 and 1991. As a result, yields have declined and prices have increased. The appropriate discount rate to use for the present value calculation is subjective, but it is effectively the yield that must be obtained from the investment. The discount rate can be a function of a firm's hurdle rate or marginal cost of capital plus a spread, or it can be based on a risk-adjusted spread over the Treasury yield curve. Often, a number of discount rates are used in order to model multiple future scenarios.

Presumably, the more simple a portfolio is, the lower the risk associated with the loans and the lower the desired yield. As a portfolio becomes more complex, the required rate of return will increase to reflect the added amount of perceived risk associated with the underlying loans. Keep in mind that yields are market driven and should be changed to reflect what the market requires at a given point in time.

Participants in the secondary servicing market have a strong preference for portfolios with low service fees and manifest this preference in their choice of discount rate. Note that loans with higher servicing fees usually have a higher discount rate applied to their cash flows than those with lower servicing fees. For loans with identical characteristics except for the service fee, there is no rational explanation why the risk of the higher-service-fee loan is greater, and therefore requires a higher discount rate, than the loan with a lower service fee. The tendency of the market to value higher-service-fee portfolios at lower price multiples is called compression.

Prepayments

Mortgage loan prepayment estimates are fundamental to servicing portfolio analysis. The rate of prepayment has a profound effect on the value of servicing rights as evidenced by the refinance wave of 1993. Lower interest rates create an incentive to refinance. Research by Freddie Mac indicates that if interest rates decline by 100 bp five years after a pool of conventional fixed-rate mortgages is originated, prepayments on those mortgages with a least 15% equity will increase from the normal rate of about 12% to a rate of 19 percent. An additional 100 bp decline causes prepayment rates to go over 30 percent. Other research indicates that there is a strong relationship between prepayments and equity in the property. Notwithstanding periods of falling interest rates, there is a direct relationship between equity build-up and prepayments: As one increases, so does the other.

There are many other variables available for the explanation and prediction of prepayment rates. Demographics, loan type, geographic location of the loan, economic conditions and the age of the loan are all factors that affect prepayments. Even attributes specific to the borrower — financial condition, mobility and interest rate sensitivity — have important implications for prepayment rates. While many borrowers are likely to refinance in a period of falling interest rates, differing degrees of interest rate sensitivity among individuals will cause other borrowers to choose not to prepay or, at least, to be slow in prepaying. The estimation of prepayment rate is not an exact science and may never be; however, for valuing servicing rights, this estimate is key to the process.

Today, the Public Securities Association (PSA) Standard Prepayment Model is probably the most widely used. It assumes 6% of a given portfolio per year will prepay after the third year. Expressed as a multiple, 100% PSA equates to 6% payoff on seasoned loans, 200% PSA equates to 12%, and so on. The estimated prepayment is based on a loan's interest rate relative to the expected level of interest rates over the life of the loan. Prepayments can be modeled using scenario analysis or an OAS model. Obviously, the greater the number of interest rate paths that can be incorporated into the analysis, the more useful the output of the model will be.

Valuation of ARM-Servicing Portfolios

The valuation of ARM portfolios often results in cash flow values of 50% to 70% of the value of a comparable fixed-rate package. The reason for this lies in the fact that three of the four primary determinants of a portfolio's cash flow stream are significantly inferior for ARMs relative to fixed-rate product. ARMs are typically subject to higher prepayment rates, are more costly to service and suffer higher delinquency/foreclosure rates. These disadvantages are not offset by any concessions in the fourth major factor, servicing fees.

There are many theories that explain the rapid payoff characteristics of ARMs:

1. A flat or inverted yield curve would cause fully-indexed ARM rates to approach or exceed long-term rates. Since mortgagors seem to have a strong preference for fixed-rate financing, this would cause borrowers to refinance into fixed-rate mortgages.
2. ARM indices, because they are averages, tend to lag rate movements when the yield curve shifts downward. When long term rates fall quickly, ARM borrowers find it possible to refinance into fixed-rate mortgages at a lower rate than they would experience at the current fully-indexed rate.
3. ARM borrowers are often more mobile. Many home purchasers who do not expect to remain in a house for more than two or three years find it more cost effective to borrow at an adjustable rate.
4. Under certain circumstances, borrowers may find it advantageous to pay off fully-indexed ARMs and refinance into other adjustable-rate loans with attractive teaser rates even if they have no plans to move.

Higher unit servicing costs are associated with ARMs, especially those with negative amortization and short adjustment intervals and those few that have adjustable servicing fees. Today, some servicers estimate that ARMs are no more costly to service than fixed-rate products, due to the enhancement of their systems to accommodate ARM requirements. The majority of servicers, however, still feel that unit servicing costs are higher for ARMs than for comparable fixed-rate loans. Many secondary servicing market participants estimate the difference to be on the order of $15 per loan. Since many ARMs are newer and have high average balances, the added cost has had a relatively minimal impact on the present value of the servicing.

Additional factors that affect the valuation of ARM servicing are adjustable servicing fees and convertibility. If the servicing fee fluctuates over time, this must be taken into account when modeling the cash flows. It is possible to overcompensate for this added uncertainty, resulting in lower values for portfolios with adjustable servicing fees. Also, if an ARM has a convertibility option, and a servicer deems the probability of conversion to be high, the servicer would presumably modify the payoff assumptions to reflect those currently being used for fixed-rate mortgages.

Prices for ARM servicing are considerably more volatile than those for fixed-rate products. ARM prices are extremely sensitive to anticipated prepayment rates, which in turn are greatly affected by the interest rate environment. The ARM market is thinner than the fixed-rate market, which also adds to its price volatility. As with fixed-rate loans, ARM prices tend to strengthen when buyers anticipate relatively little run-off and when the yield curve is expected to remain positively (normally) sloped. On the other hand, an abrupt interest rate decline or an inverted yield curve would bring higher short-term rates (upon which the ARM rates are indexed) than long-term rates (which are closely related to fixed-rate mortgage interest rates) and lead to a high level of ARM refinancing. Buyers then adjust by increasing their prepayment rate expectations, often to three or four times PSA or more. The result is a drop in the value they place on ARM portfolios.

Multifamily Servicing Valuation

Multifamily servicing valuation follows the same methodology as fixed and ARM servicing, but there are a few differences. Because multifamily portfolios are made up of fewer, larger loans, it is customary to value each loan separately. Unlike a single-family portfolio, a multifamily portfolio will feel the effects of the behavior of one loan — one loan can significantly alter the multifamily portfolio's performance. For instance, while multifamily loans prepay for the same reasons that single-family loans prepay, the rate at which they prepay can vary significantly from project to project depending on the type of loan. For example, a loan that carries a five-year lock-out period, during which the mortgagor cannot prepay, provides assurance that the loan will be in existence for at least that long.

A large number of multifamily loans originate with government assistance under certain sections of the National Housing Act. The section of the Act, therefore, is a determining factor in estimating the life of the portfolio. For example, loans made under Section 232 may carry an interest rate subsidy, depending on the state where the property is located. Since the mortgagor is indifferent to fluctuations in interest rates, this type of loan will have unique payoff characteristics. The loan will probably be refinanced when it comes time to rehabilitate the building, however. The advent of Wall Street's interest in commercial and multifamily loan securitization has made modeling prepayments even more difficult. Multitranche, LIBOR-based structures have materially changed traditional notions about the prepayment behavior of multifamily loans.

Service fees are often lower on multifamily loans. This means there is relatively more benefit from other income, most notably interest on escrows and reserves for replacement. More experienced multifamily servicers gain from other ancillary income sources as well.

Costs to service multifamily loans are considerably higher than the costs associated with single-family loans. This is largely a result of the number of activities involved in multifamily servicing and the labor-intensive nature of the activities, such as the review of financial statements and annual property inspections. In recent years, costs have increased even more as investors have further expanded their servicing requirements. With the increase in expenses as a result of the new requirements, the valuation process is further complicated based on the uncertainty of future increases in costs. To exacerbate the already increased costs to service multifamily loans, lenders who had entered the coinsurance program have experienced losses that have threatened their servicing portfolios, and in some cases their entire businesses.

OAS Analysis

OAS analysis can be a valuable complement to static and scenario analyses since servicing cash flows are strongly affected by changes in interest rates. OAS analysis can be used to assess the cost to the investor of variations in servicing cash flows caused by changes in interest rates. The OAS calculation involves valuing the portfolio over a large number of randomly generated interest rate paths. The effects of interest-rate variation on cash flows are then factored into the analysis. OAS provides a measure of how much impact interest rate variation and resulting changes in prepayments are likely to have on the value of the portfolio.

Another way to think of OAS is as the expected spread over the Treasury yield curve after adjusting for the prepayment risk inherent in the asset. An OAS model simulates a set of future interest rate paths. Usually, 200-500 paths are used to obtain good convergence in the model. Each interest rate path will have its associated cash flow path. The entire set of cash flow paths represents the current expected cash flows to be received from the portfolio. These cash flows are then valued using a standard discounting method. Unfortunately, most OAS models do not allow users to measure the impact of varying interest-rates on default and reinvestment risk. The OAS model, in essence, values the servicing, determines the expected price sensitivity of the current servicing asset and indicates the amount of imbedded prepayment risk and the expected rate of return over a range of interest and prepayment rate scenarios.

As a practical matter, when the output from a static cash flow model and an OAS model are compared, the OAS model usually results in a higher price. This is because OAS is unbiased in its measurement of the impact of prepayment risk on expected investment returns. In other words, it assigns equal probability that interest rates will rise and that interest rates will fall. In the static scenario case, there is always a predisposition on the part of the valuer to overestimate the likelihood that interest rates will fall and underestimate the likelihood that interest rates will rise. An easy way to interpret the output of an OAS model is to think of it as the amount by which the internal rate of return should be reduced to obtain a yield that has been adjusted for the adverse impact of interest rate variation.

Price Sensitivity

The principal variables that affect the value of a servicing portfolio are payoff speed, discount rate, and cost to service a loan. Foreclosure cost, foreclosure rate and rate of earnings on escrow are also key variables. Compounding the issue of trying to figure out the servicing portfolio's sensitivity to changes in payoff speeds is that servicing rights have large negative convexities — that is, they lose more when interest rates fall than they gain when interest rates rise. Table 15-4

TABLE 15-4
The Impact Changes in Key Valuation Variables Have on Pricing

Scenario	Price (% of UPB)
Base Case	1.11
14-Year Straight-Line Amortization	1.05
1% Decline in Intereset Rates	0.84
1% Increase in Interest Rates	1.30
$250 per Loan Decrease in Foreclosure Cost	1.12
$250 per Loan Increase in Foreclosure Cost	1.10
$5 per Loan Increse in ncillary Income	1.13
1% Decrease Interest on Earnings	1.05
1% Increase Interest on Earnings	1.17
50% Reduction in Average T&I	0.99
50% Increase in Average T&I	1.22
$5 per Loan Decrease in Unit Cost	1.14
$5 per Loan Increase in Unit Cost	1.08
1% Decrease in Discount Rate	1.15
!% Increase in Discount Rate	1.07

illustrates this asymmetry, as well as price differences based on changes in other variables.

While the value of servicing rights may be largely driven by supply and demand, their intrinsic value is derived from the actual portfolio characteristics and the forecast of future economic events. For example, if analysts foresee interest rates rising in the future, they will use slower prepayment assumptions which, if all other things remain the same, will result in a higher value for the portfolio. A forecast of higher interest rates will also affect the relative amount of income derived from interest on escrow and impound accounts. The higher the expected level of interest rates, the greater the benefit of float will be. During periods of extremely high rates, the cash management function becomes critical to the manager of servicing assets. To the extent that servicers can accelerate remittances and lag outflows, they can maximize the benefit of float. Linear programming models are often used to optimize both the "remoteness" of the disbursement facility and the "nearness" of the centralized lockbox. An increase of 1% in the interest rate paid on escrows increases the value of the hypothetical portfolio by about 5 percent.

Since most of the relationships among the variables are nonlinear, it is extremely important to be cognizant of the effect that each has on the other. Keeping abreast of current market assumptions and using your own experience is fundamental to portfolio valuation. In other words, the results from a valuation model must be tempered by common sense and interpreted in light of past experience.

Taking into consideration that more than 33% of the typical portfolio's cash flows are realized in the first three years of its life, it is evident that an understanding of the impact of changes in certain key variables on price is essential to the successful valuation of servicing. The factors that influence value range from whether or not a portfolio is recourse or nonrecourse to whether you are discounting cash flows on a monthly or a yearly basis. Since the relationship among the variables is nonlinear, some of the results obtained when valuing a portfolio may be counterintuitive. For example, very old portfolios, those with 15 or more years of seasoning, produce a higher present value when the discount rate is increased. Normally, increasing the discount rate decreases the present value, but since older portfolios have a larger number of periods of negative cash flow, increasing the discount rate decreases the impact of the later years' negative cash flows on the present value. Consequently, the higher the discount rate used to determine the portfolio's present value, the higher the value will be.

As stated earlier, the prepayment forecast is extremely important in valuing servicing because the major servicing income components are tied to either the balances outstanding or the number of loans remaining in the portfolio. Since no one can predict the course of future interest rates, it is important to use a valuation methodology that incorporates as many interest rate scenarios as possible.

Other factors influencing price are the amount of ancillary income, how the portfolio is amortized, the loan quality of the underlying collateral, economic conditions in the geographic area where the loans are located, the type of loan product, the purpose of the loan when it is originated (owner-occupied, investor-owned or refinance), the property type, the LTV ratio and the treatment of late fees and foreclosure costs. As the number of delinquent loans increases, ancillary income increases (assuming that the mortgagors who are late are paying their late charge), and as ancillary income increases, portfolio value increases. Keep in mind, however, that late-fee income is offset partially by lost float income and interest expense on any P&I advances that may be required. Additionally, a higher delinquency rate usually leads to higher foreclosures, which increases costs because a default subjects the servicer to lost interest and substantial administrative expense.

A factor that is often overlooked by investors in servicing is reinvestment risk. As much as one third of a portfolio's value is returned to the investor in the first few years of its life. Users of static cash flow models usually assume that monies are reinvested at the discount rate used in the valuation. However, you must consider the possibility of reinvesting at a yield lower than the original discount rate. Under this scenario, the effective return on investment will be lower than the expected return. Yields on servicing are still at a substantial spread above other investments of similar risk. If you are unable to redeploy assets into other servicing investments at a comparable yield, then your expected rate of return may be materially overstated.

The Market in 1996

As of this writing, we are in an environment of declining interest rates, which has accelerated payoffs on fixed-rate mortgages. At the same time, an increasingly steep, positively-sloped yield curve has decelerated payoffs on ARMs.

Faced with a falling interest rate environment, the question is: Are servicing prices going higher or are they going lower? The answer is that prices are going both ways. Since the key element in determining value is the prepayment assumption, many buyers of portfolios during periods of declining interest rates either are reluctant to bid at all or factor higher prepayment assumptions into their price. This is especially true for portfolios with above-market interest rates. Current coupon servicing, especially that which is being valued and purchased on a flow basis, is commanding record pricing when viewed as a multiple of service fee.

There has been a trend over the last 10 years for manufacturers of servicing rights, whether they be banks, thrifts or mortgage banks, to focus more intently on their most valuable asset. Previously, management did not have the accounting systems to consider servicing value in their production programs. Today, originators are focusing their efforts on loan products that will command the highest servicing premiums. Clearly, the market provides a strong incentive to concentrate on higher premium products, especially since the cost to originate a loan is the same no matter what the value of the servicing.

The Impact of FASB Statement 122 on Hedging

To a large degree, the accounting changes expressed in FASB Statement 122 have increased interest in hedging servicing portfolios. Before originated mortgage servicing became a financial asset on the balance sheet, the economic risk of loss of value through premature repayment of the loan existed. Many firms, however, failed to adequately manage the risk because the loss of originated servicing had no impact on the financial statements of the firm. The common view was that production provided a "macro hedge" because the firm could originate new loans and retain the servicing as the existing portfolio paid off. This rational is analogous to a home builder not worrying about his uninsured inventory burning down because he has the ability to build new houses to replace the burning ones.

When unhedged servicing pays off prematurely, there is a real economic loss whether or not the asset is carried on the balance sheet. The mortgage lender will incur new expenses to replace the old portfolio. The arrival of FASB Statement 122 has forced the firms to implement, or at least understand, the mechanics of hedging because having the asset on the balance sheet creates financial risk to the firm.

The early- to mid-1990s has seen the development of better and, in many instances, more cost-effective hedge vehicles. The late 1980s were dominated by hedges that relied primarily on principal-only strips or a derivative thereof. Today, there are many other types of hedges available. They generally fall into two categories: on-balance-sheet hedges, such as inverse floaters, and off-balance-sheet hedges, such as prepayment caps.

Indexed principal swaps have emerged as a popular hedging vehicle because they are relatively inexpensive and can be tailored to the risk profile of the user. No matter what type of hedge is utilized the goal is the same: to recoup all or a portion of the economic loss incurred through prepayments in excess of the prepayment expectation to book the asset.

Today, it is common for mortgage lenders to assess the risk profile of the entire firm to determine what the best hedging strategy is. A mortgage bank, for example, has two primary assets, the servicing portfolio and the mortgage loans being produced. When interest rates fall, servicing loses value while the loans become more valuable. To understand the overall impact on the firm for a given move in interest rates, it is first necessary to quantify the gain or loss for servicing and production. To a degree, loss in one will be offset by a gain in the other. Once this relationship is known, the firm is in a position to hedge whatever residual risk remains. This is not a static exercise because for any given level of interest rates, the ratio of production to prepayment will change. Needless to say, whatever method of hedging is chosen, the hedge must be monitored periodically and adjusted for changes in market conditions.

Future Outlook

We anticipate that the trend toward a higher awareness of the value of the industry's primary asset will continue. As the market continues to mature, it will become more efficient. Plans are already in the works to deliver portfolios, provide for their valuation and auction them on an interactive basis. There is also talk of someday securitizing loan servicing portfolios. Market practitioners will continue to explore and develop vehicles that will allow the investment in the interest-only component of the servicing stream, thus opening the market to an even larger audience of investors. Valuation methods will continue to improve, and we will see more market participants using OAS technology as they grow in their sophistication.

Advances in technology in connection with the actual servicing of the loans augers well for increases in servicing prices. For example, it is estimated that the utilization of electronic imaging can cut approximately $15 per loan per year from the unit cost of loan servicing. For a large servicer whose unit cost is $60 per loan, this represents a reduction in cost of 25 percent. All other things being equal, a reduction in servicing costs of this

TABLE 15-5
Top 10 Mortgage Servicers in Combined Servicing

Rank	Aggregate Portfolio Size for 1989, 1992 and 1995 (in Millions)		
	1989	1992	1995
1	$54,800	$64,600	$132,140
2	$34,346	$60,590	$109,500
3	$26,999	$42,484	$107,410
4	$26,376	$40,033	$103,610
5	$21,380	$34,118	$81,800
6	$17,466	$32,659	$81,430
7	$16,248	$32,273	$73,750
8	$13,857	$31,352	$65,220
9	$13,852	$30,027	$63,120
10	$13,723	$29,959	$54,610
Total	**$239,097**	**$398,095**	**$872,590**

Source: *American Banker* and *Inside Mortgage Finance*

magnitude will have a significant positive impact on value, especially for seasoned product.

The consolidation of servicing into fewer and fewer institutions will continue (See Table 15-5). The megaservicers today are servicing portfolios of $100 billion or more. It is difficult at this time to assess the impact of such vast scale on unit costs, but it will almost certainly be positive.

As discussed earlier, FASB Statement 122 has changed the way the industry looks at originated mortgage servicing rights. It has resulted in a 25% decrease in the number of servicing portfolios coming to market, which has caused prices for servicing to increase. We also have seen a more acute focus on the management of the servicing portfolio from a financial perspective.

Additionally, FASB 125, which became effective on January 1, 1997, modifies FASB 122 in a number of ways. First, it requires all capitalized servicing rights to be stratified for impairment measurement based on the predominant risk characteristics of the underlying assets; this includes assets that FASB 122 exempted because they were capitalized according to an existing stratification policy in use prior to the application of FASB 122. The new approach will require write downs on segments that have lost value, but doesn't allow recognition of gains on segments that have increased in value. Second, "assumed" servicing rights that are assumed, usually in connection with a commercial or multifamily transaction, are recognized as an asset at fair market value. Third, the new rule requires that bulk acquisitions of servicing be amortized as a unit rather than by disaggregated segments. At the very least, these changes will complicate hedge accounting and obfuscate the impact of market changes to these balance sheet assets.

The secondary market for mortgage servicing rights falls somewhere between that of MBSs and mortgage derivative products. If servicing could be traded as a commodity (even though it clearly is not a commodity), the bid/ask spread would be relatively large. Absent any unforeseen legislative developments, participants will be afforded an even more efficient market in which to unlock the value created through the loan origination process. The American consumer has been the biggest beneficiary of what is the most vibrant market for housing finance in the world. The U.S. mortgage market is the child of an enlightened legislative and regulatory environment. We hope it remains that way.